Easy knitting designs - Unconventional patterns

Author: Eyla Gray.

Artist. Knitter. Author.

ISBN: 978-1-989844-04-5

Publisher: Natalie Grignon 202

About this book.

I never learned how to read a real pattern. I learned how to knit at a young age, but nothing more. When I got pregnant with my first child, the idea of squares, quilt-like, but knitted came to mind.

Little feet, a tree, a rainbow, a dog, an umbrella. The ideas came quickly. I grabbed a graphic paper and started drawing. For me, it was simple, a square equals a knit. At that time, the internet was new to me, and instead of searching if it already exists, I drew the patterns myself.

The patterns inside this book have been tried once. A lot of them are my favorites, the monsters, the dogs, the turtle. Some of them I have done a couple of times in different colors. In blue, for my grumpy old cat. A little knitted cover with 4 squares for the front and 4 for the back. I have also done in pink for my female cat, who is delicate and a little silly.

About the patterns:

Created **by hand** by an artist, not computer-generated. Design creation started in 1998.

Each pattern has been tried at least once

It is a perfect square of 40 by 40, if you need to modify its size, apply the same ratio of 1:1. Design might look different if it is not used as is. Bigger looks fine, but for some it will not look good.

Tips on using these patterns

Do not use needles that are too big

Use chunky wool

Designs look better when it is a tight knit

Looks better with 2 or 3 colors max

Marking the pattern with a pencil as you go along, so you can erase after for another use.

Tips on creating your own patterns.

Picture cannot be too small or have intricate details

Use graphic paper, one square is for one knit

Just draw on the graphic paper using a pencil, and then use the lines of the graphic paper to create the final design.

It might not always look good on paper, or you might feel that the look is too square and not smooth enough, but once knitted, the shape comes through.

Monsters

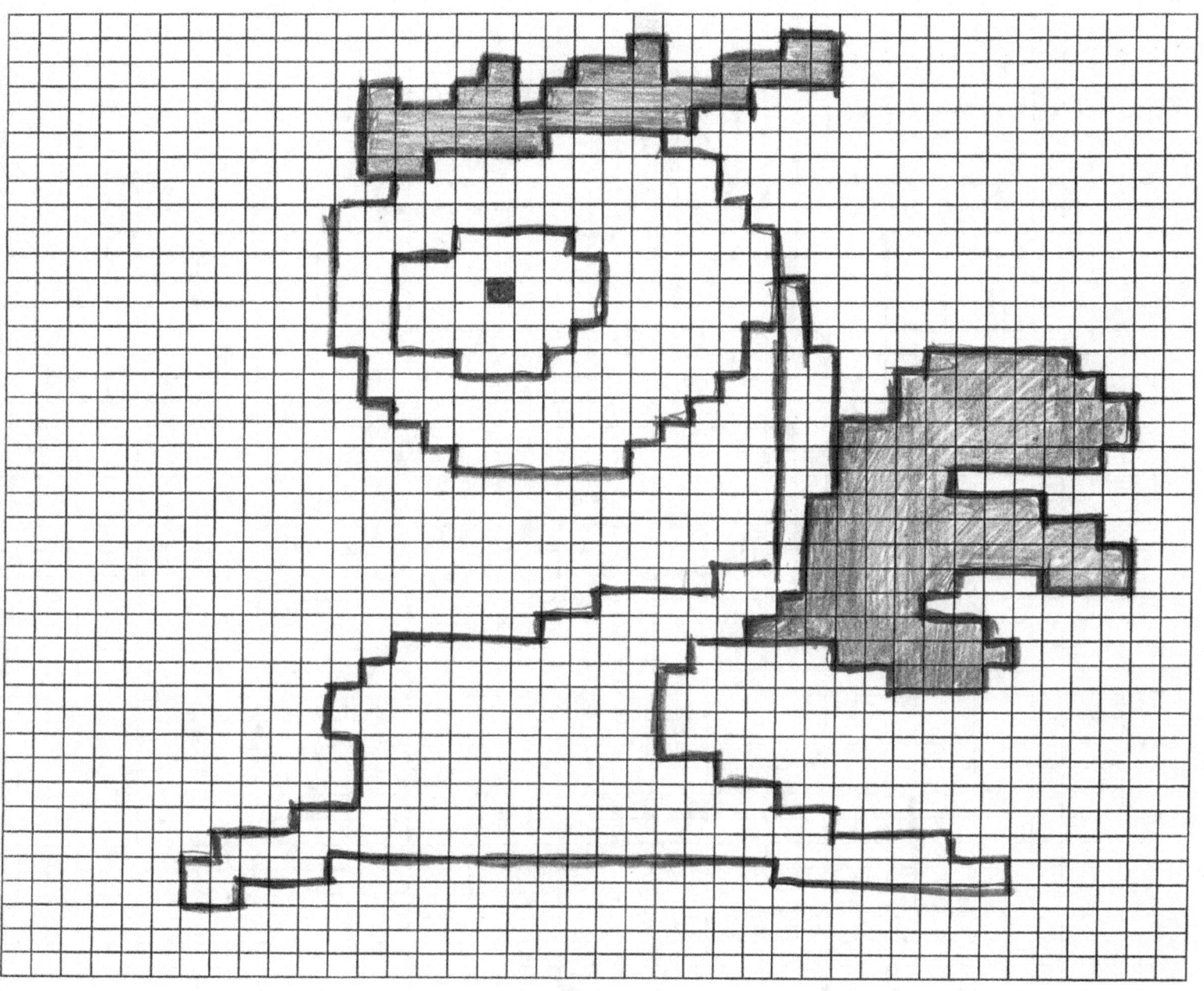

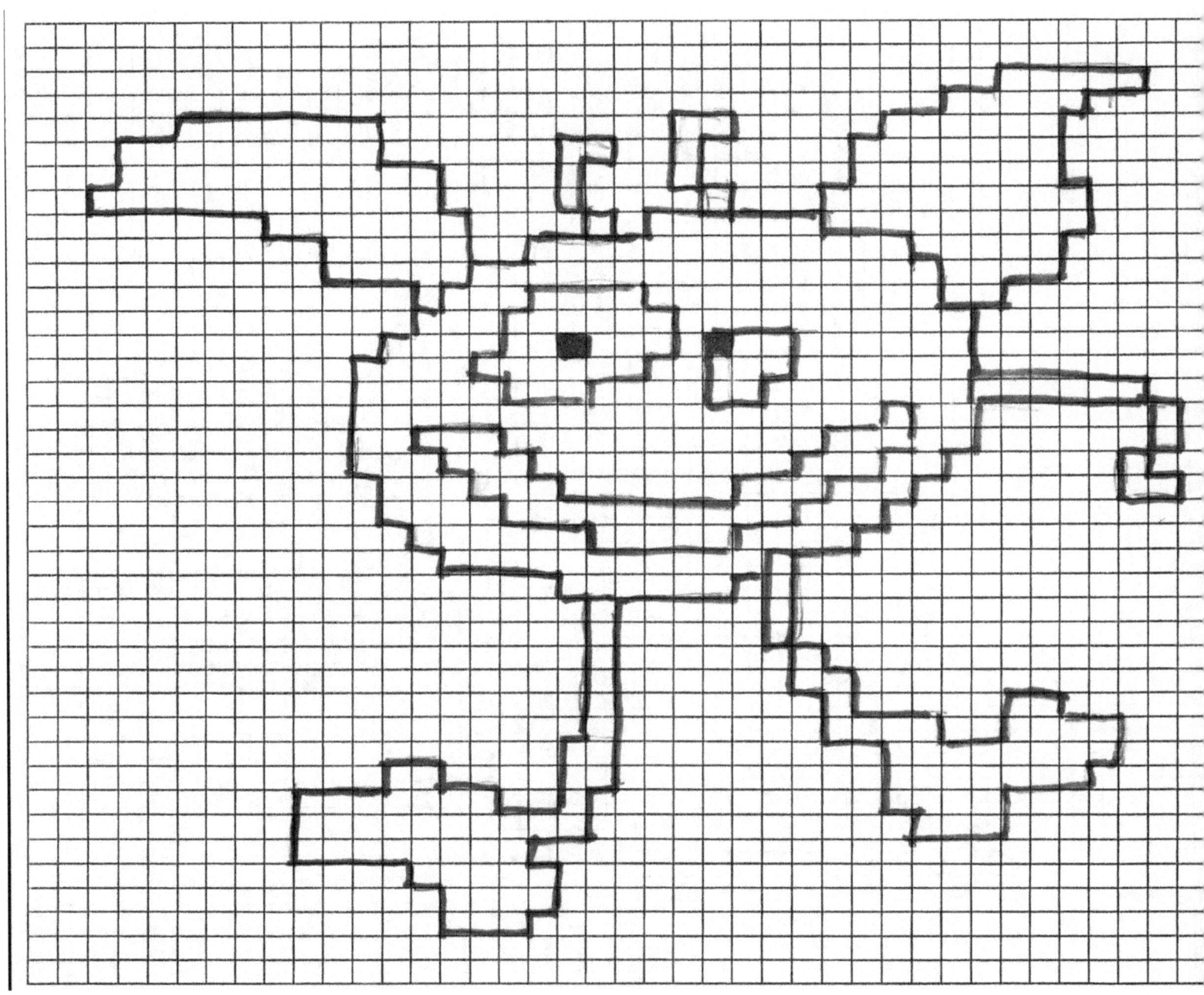

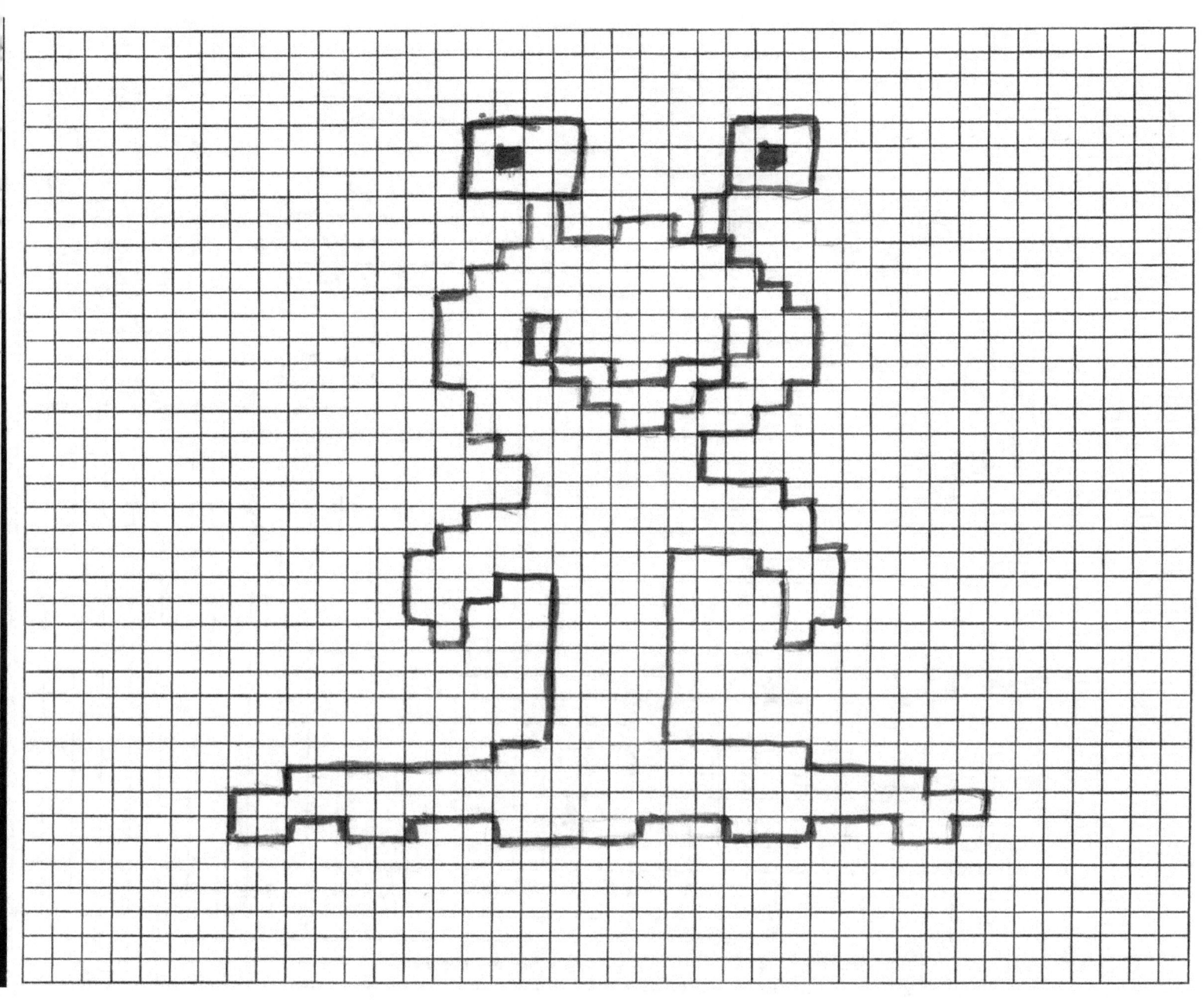

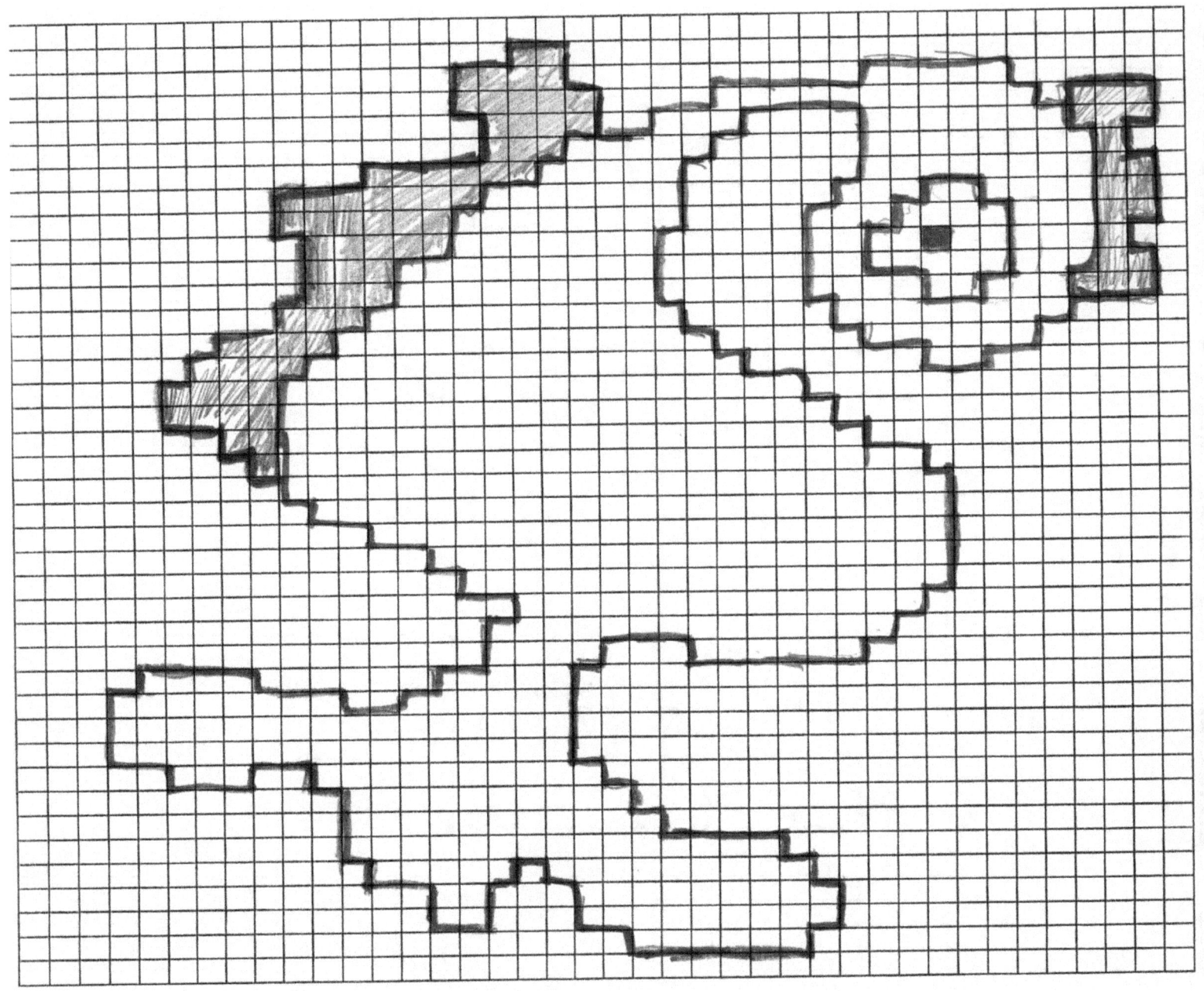

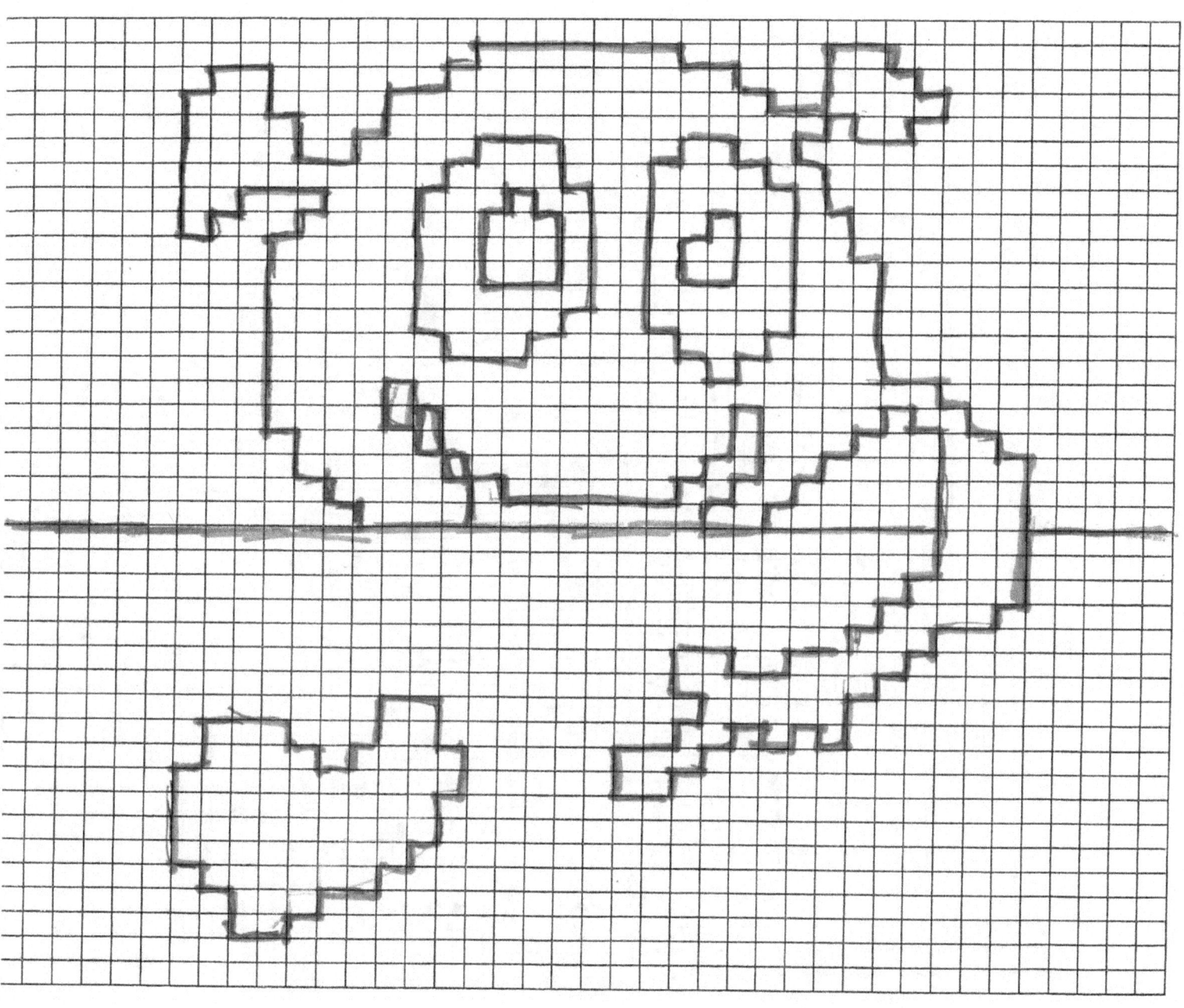

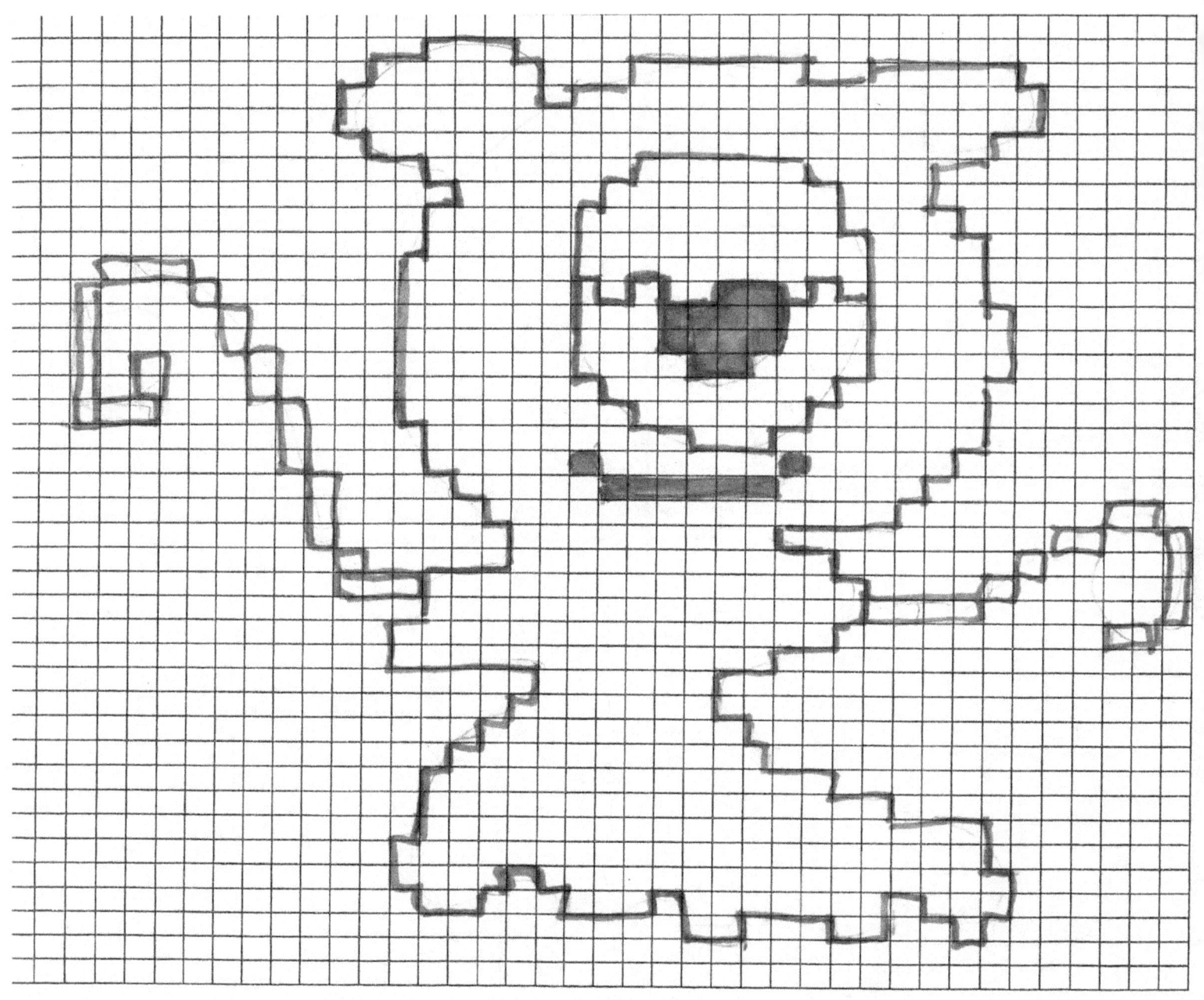

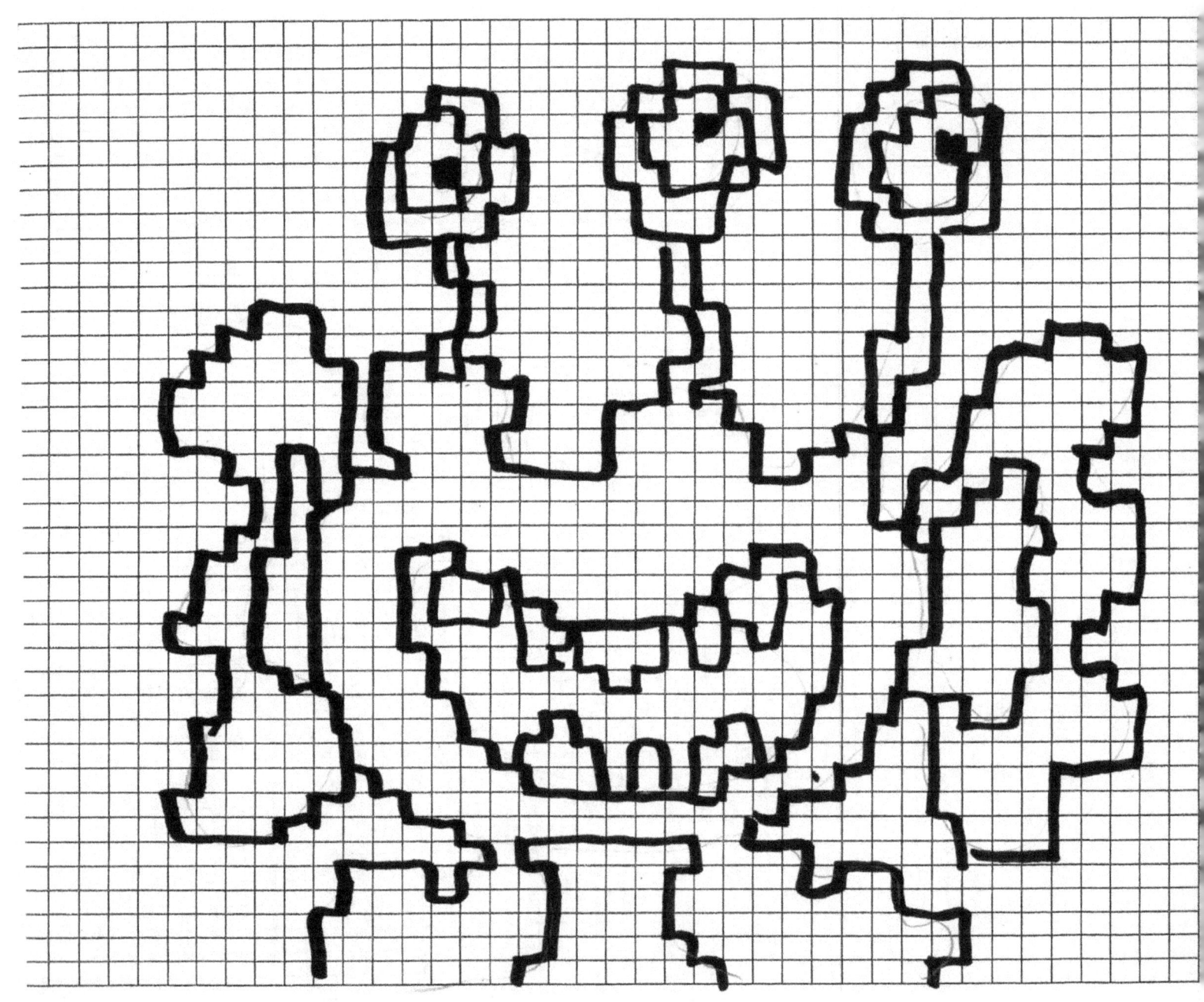

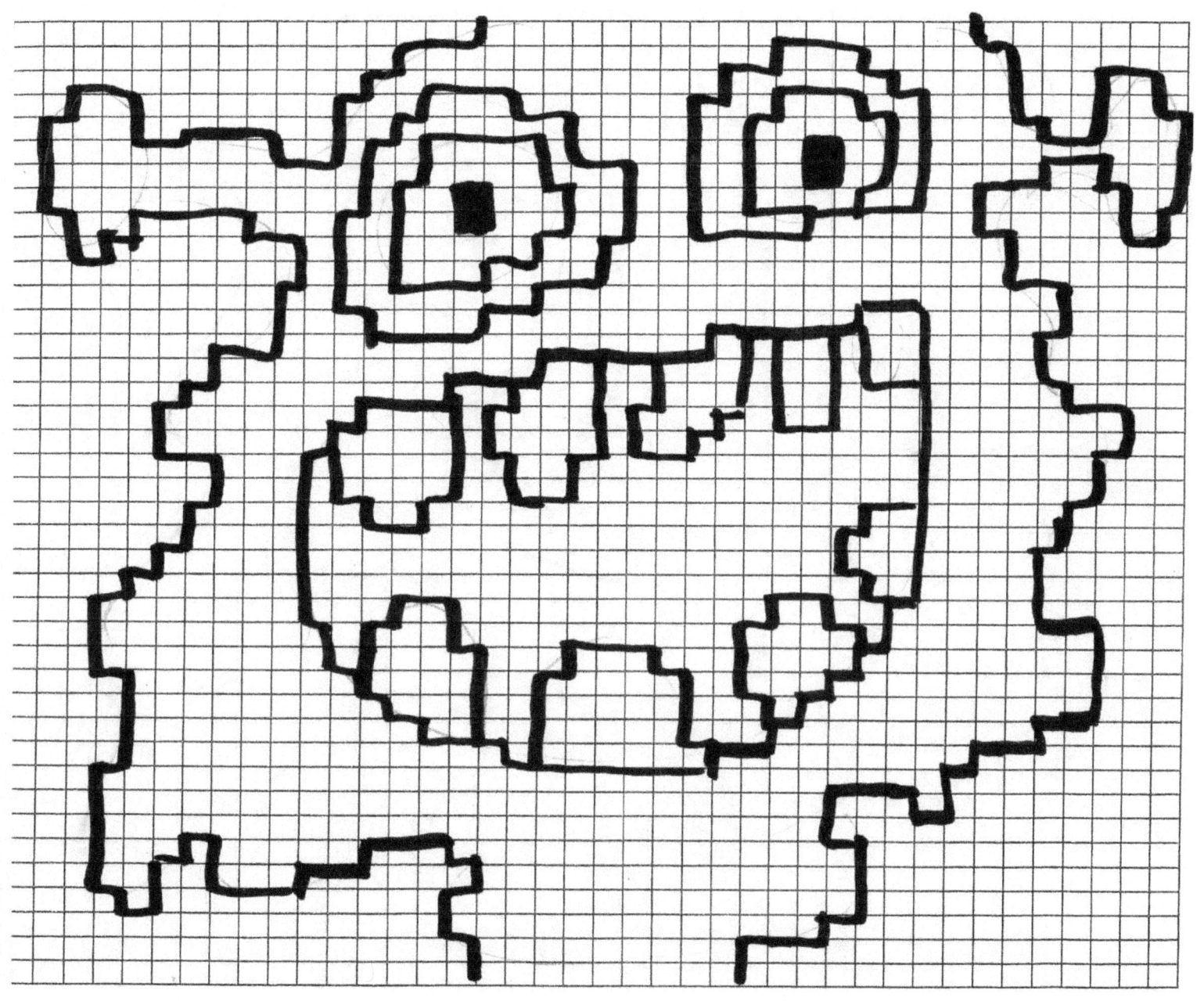

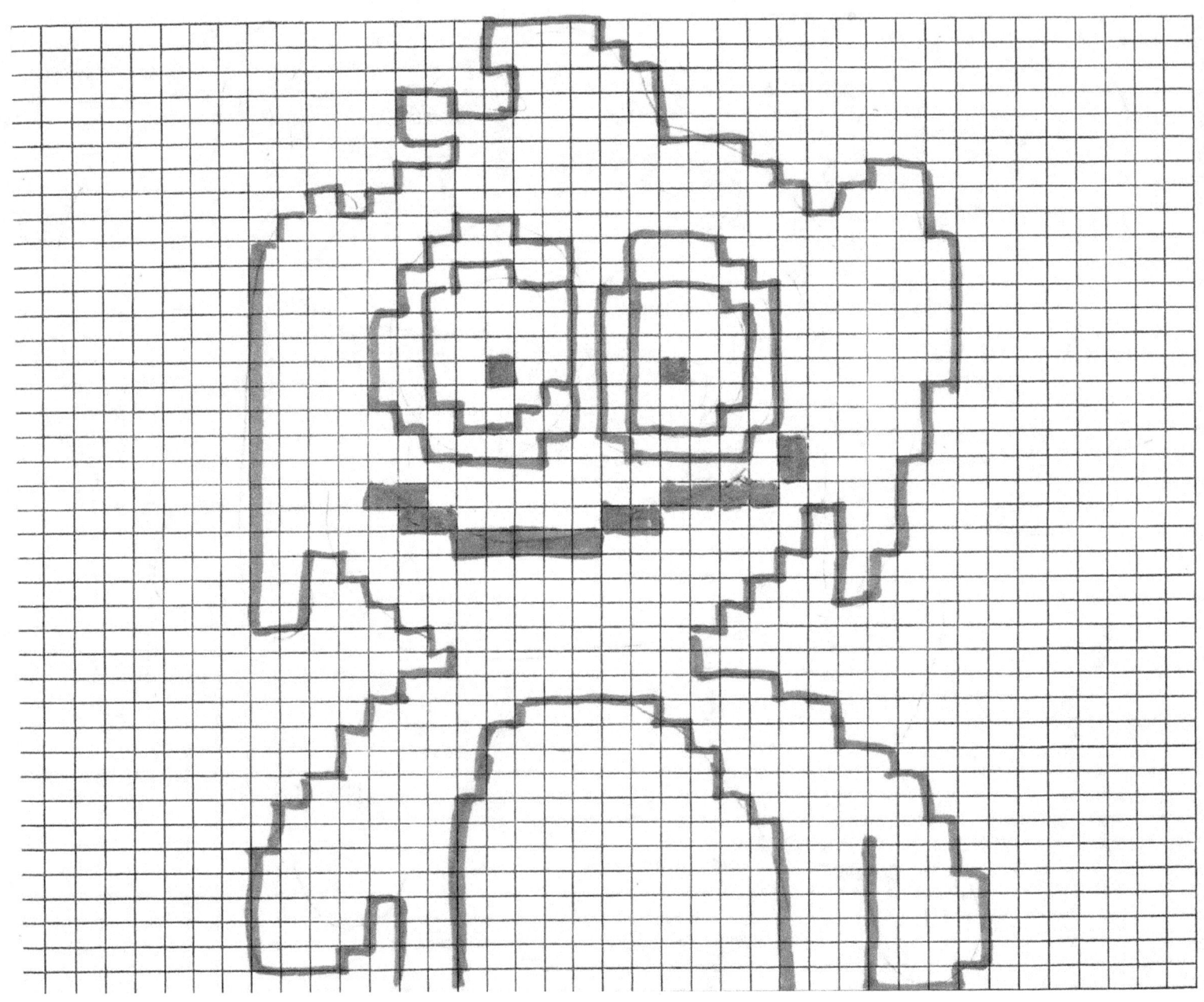

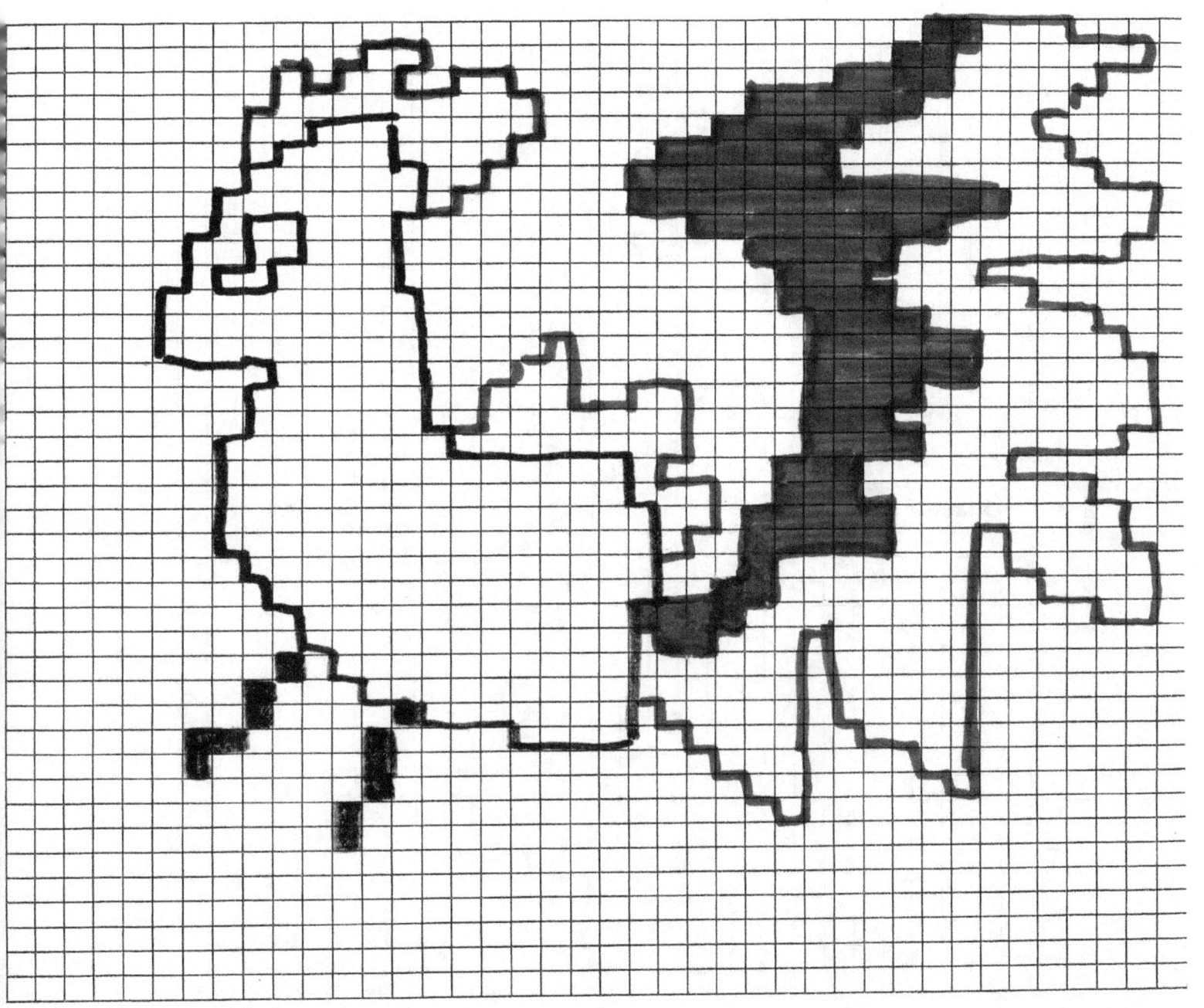

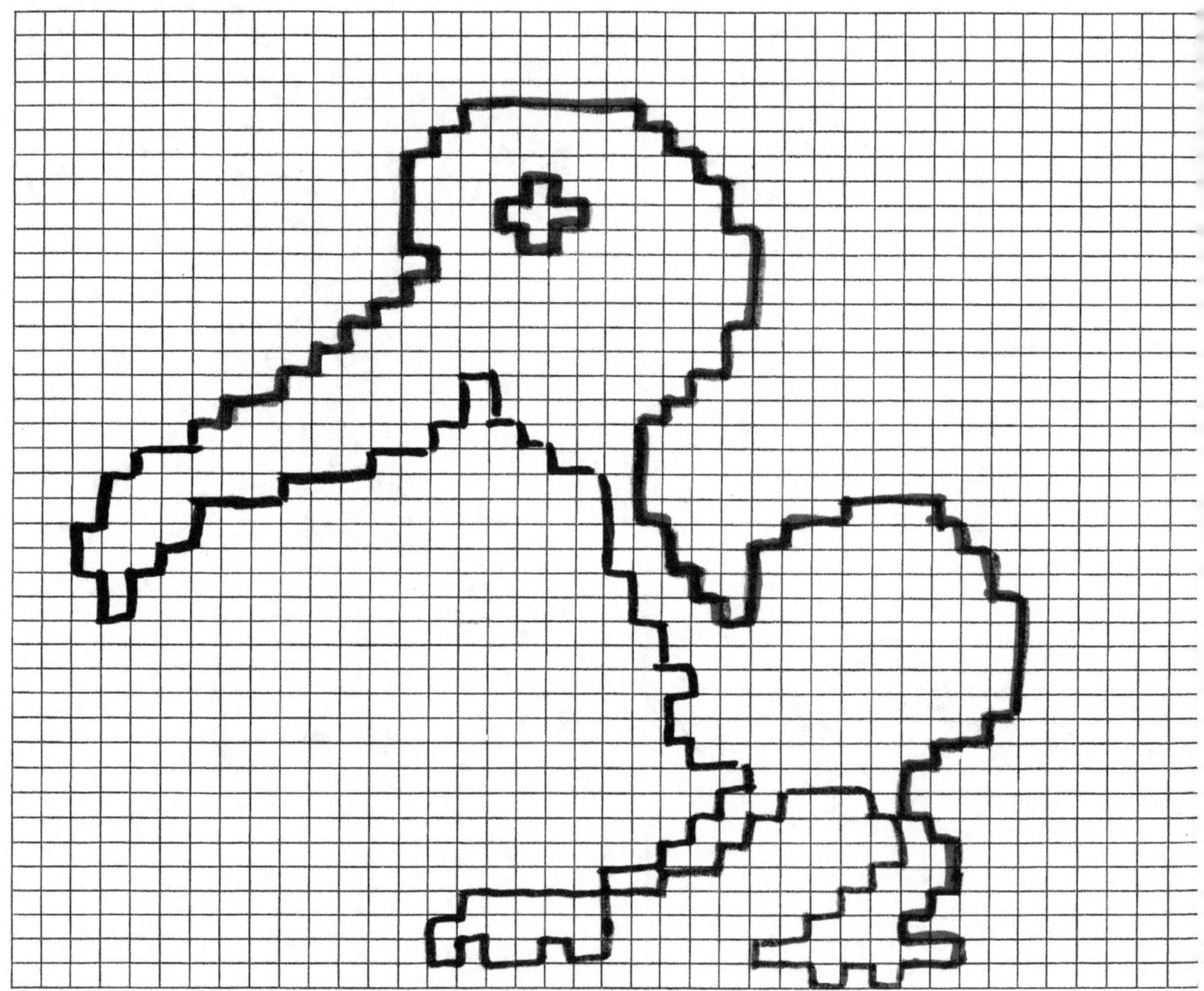

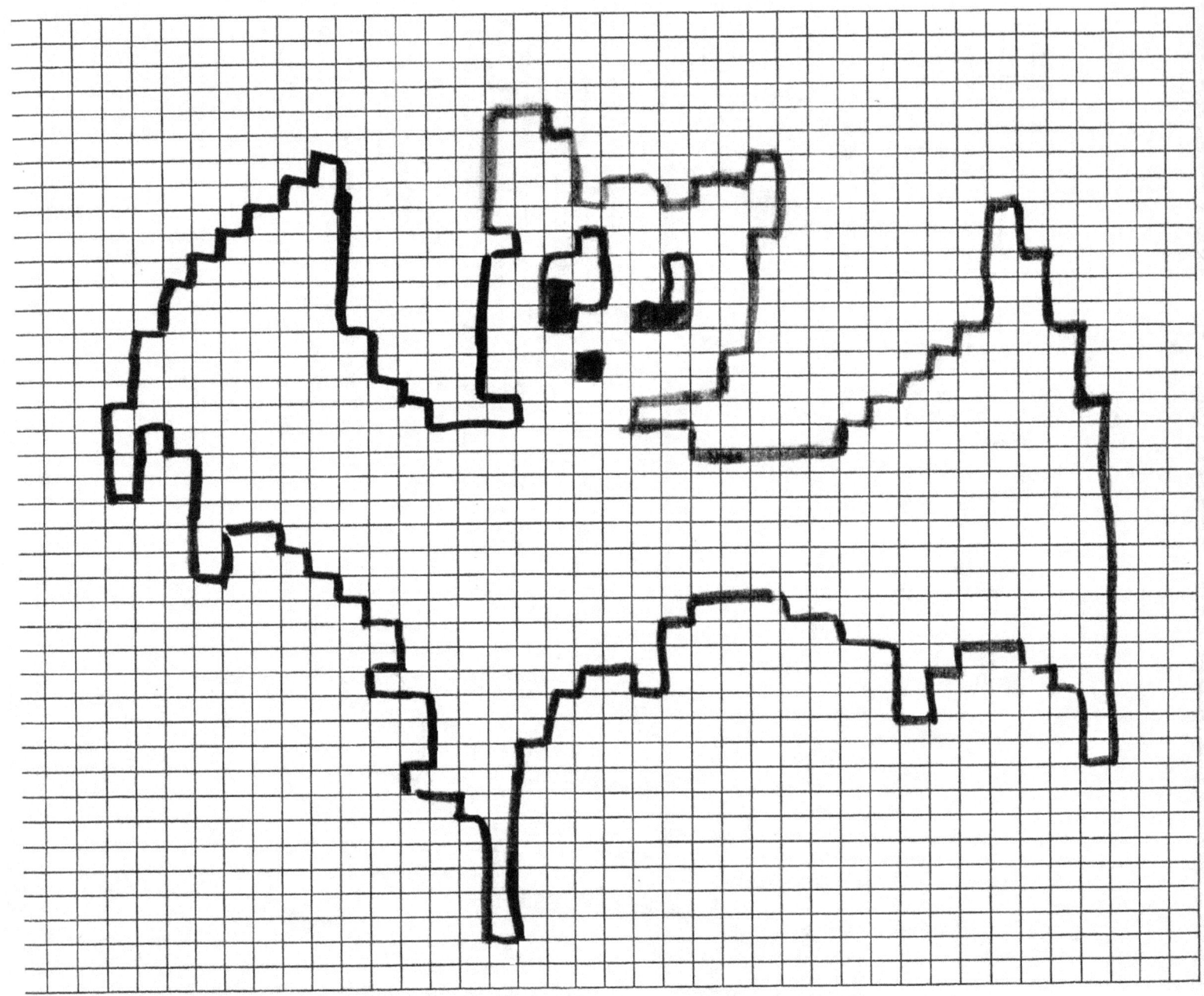

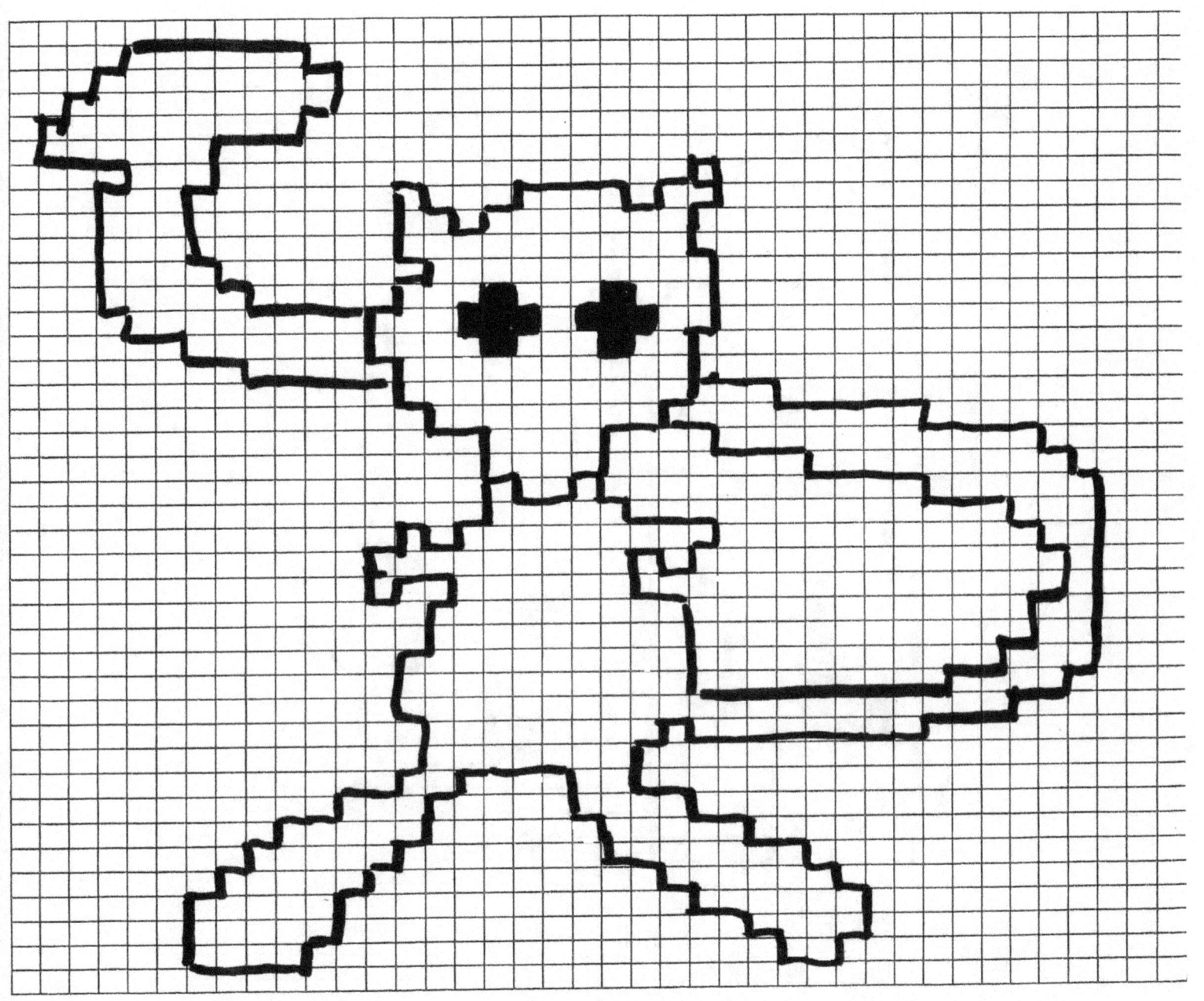

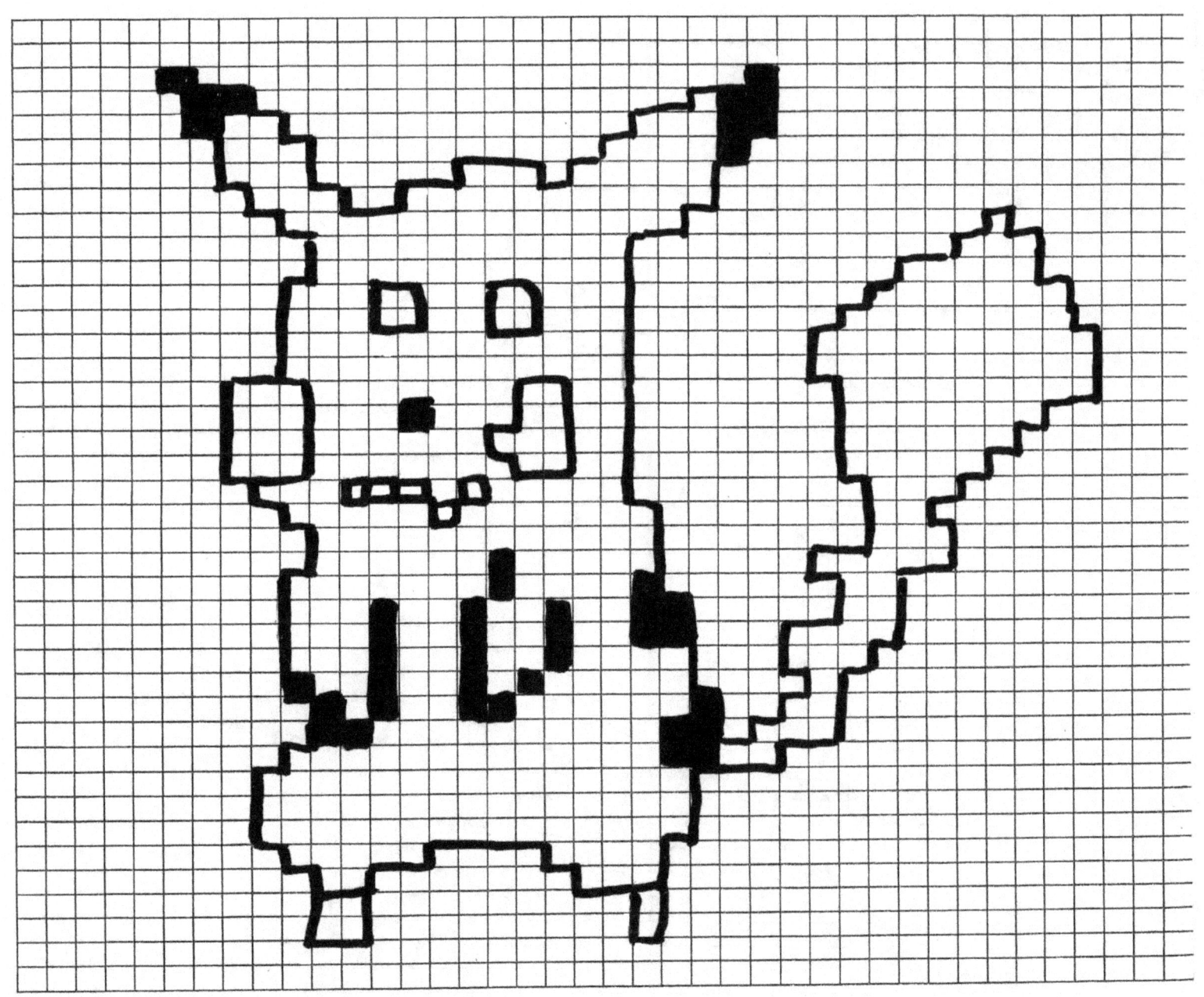

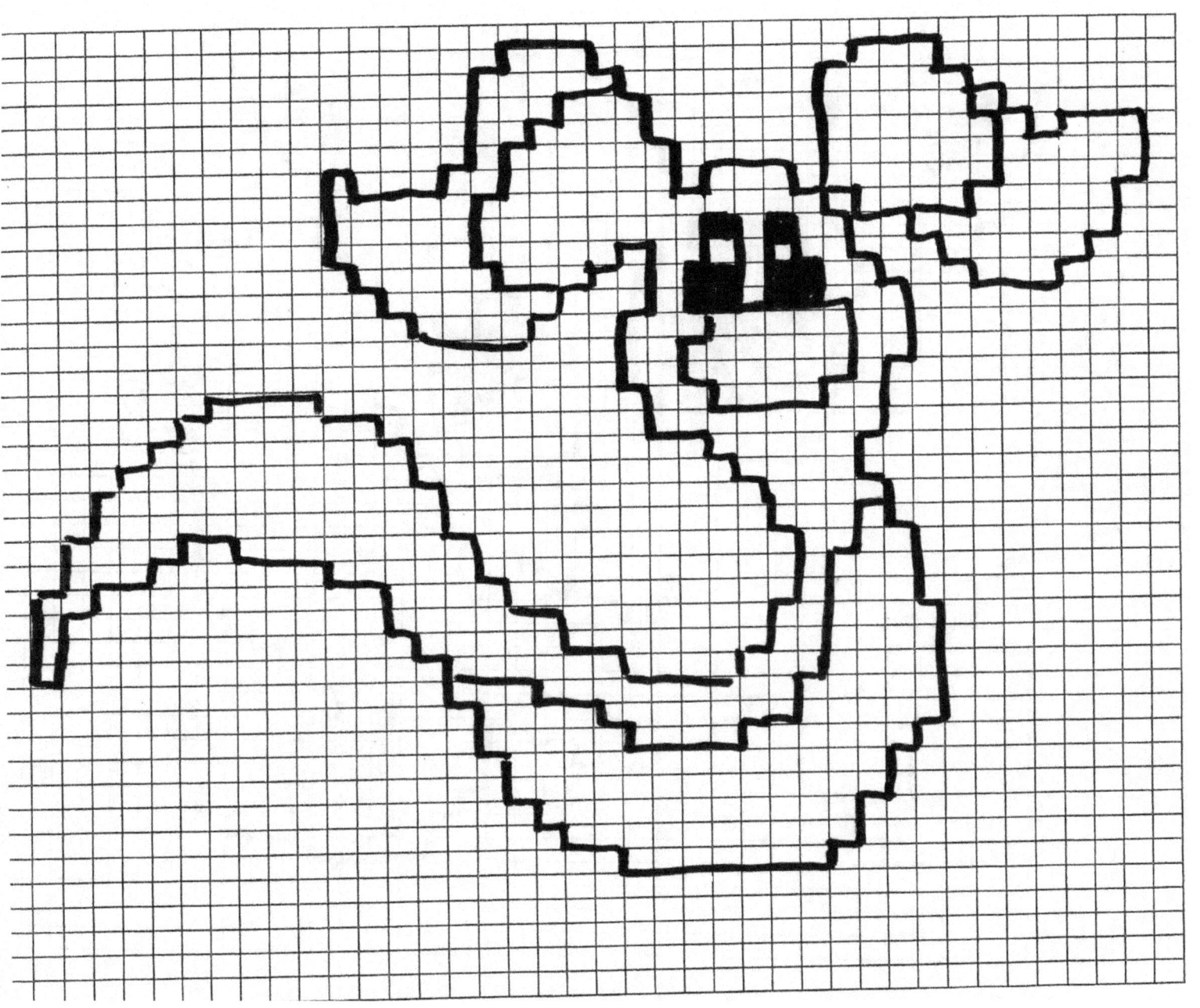

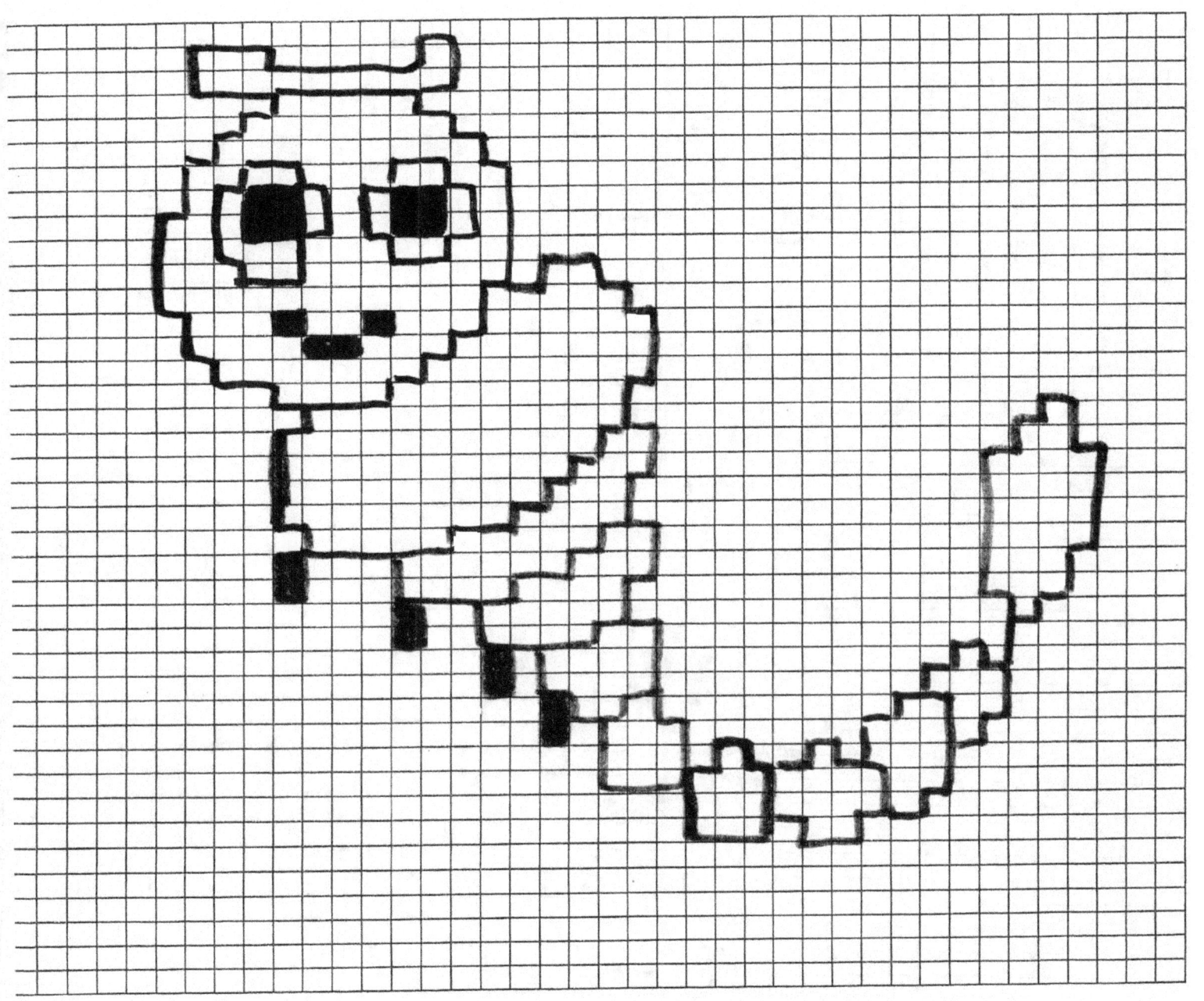

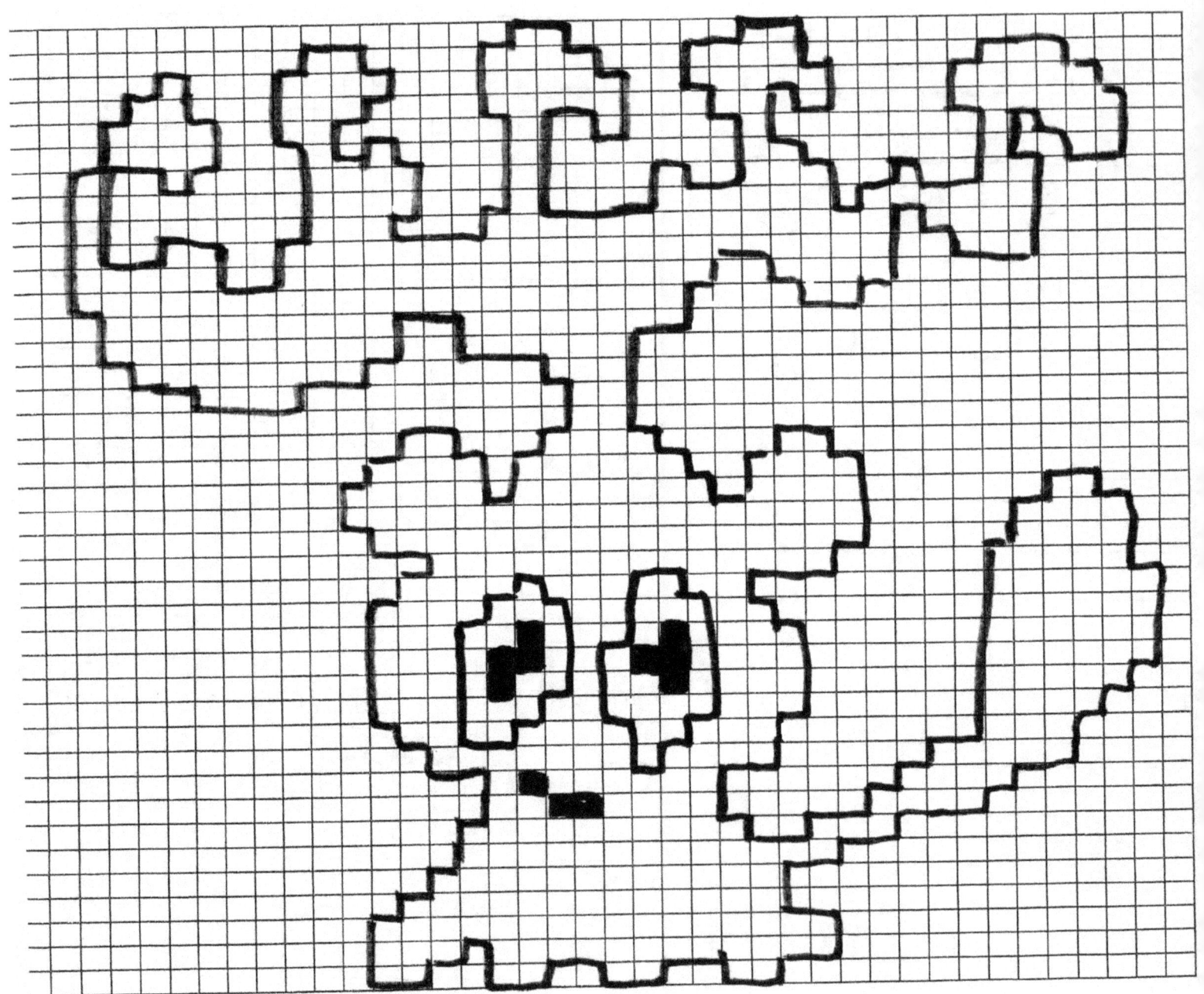

Animals, insects

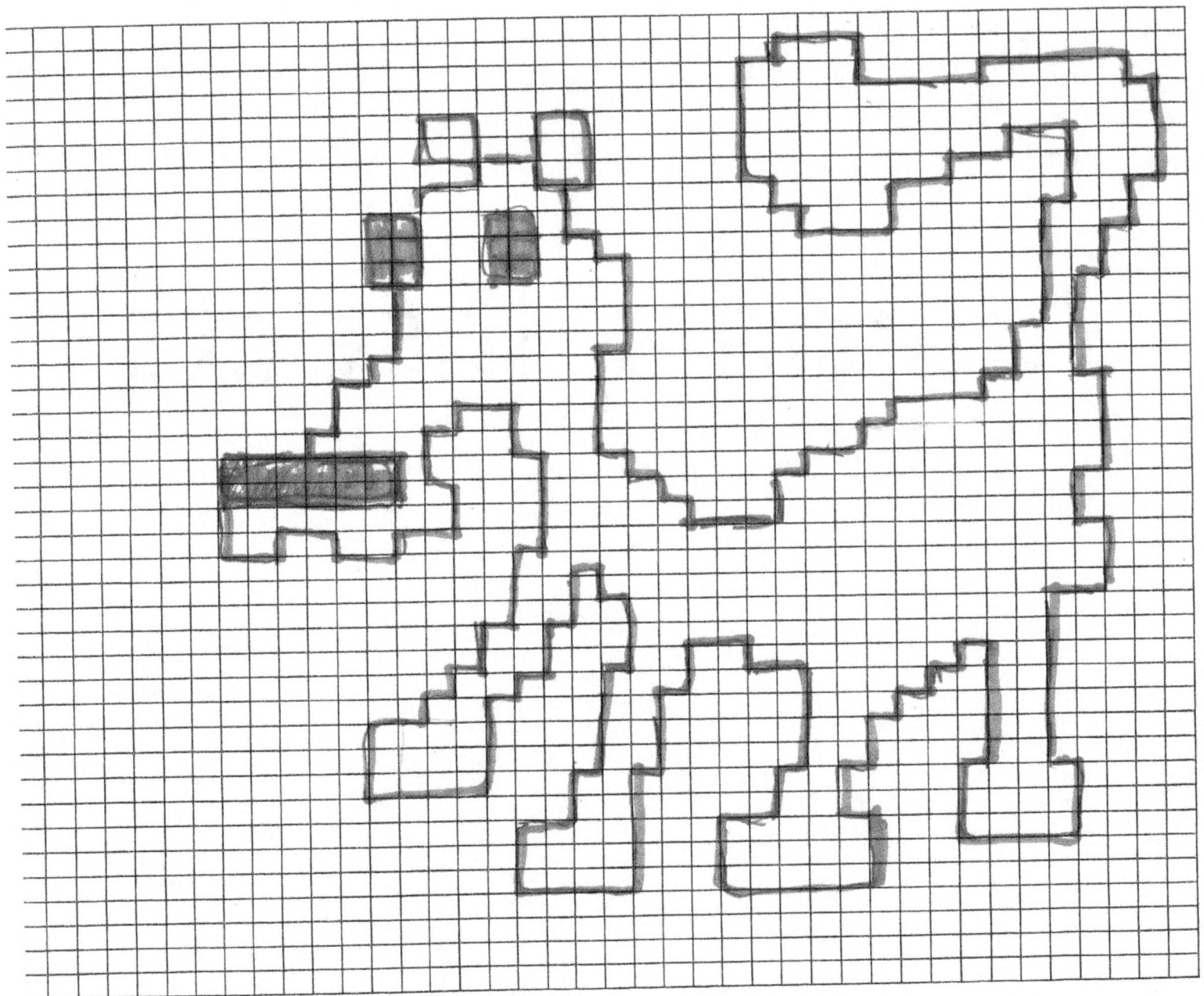

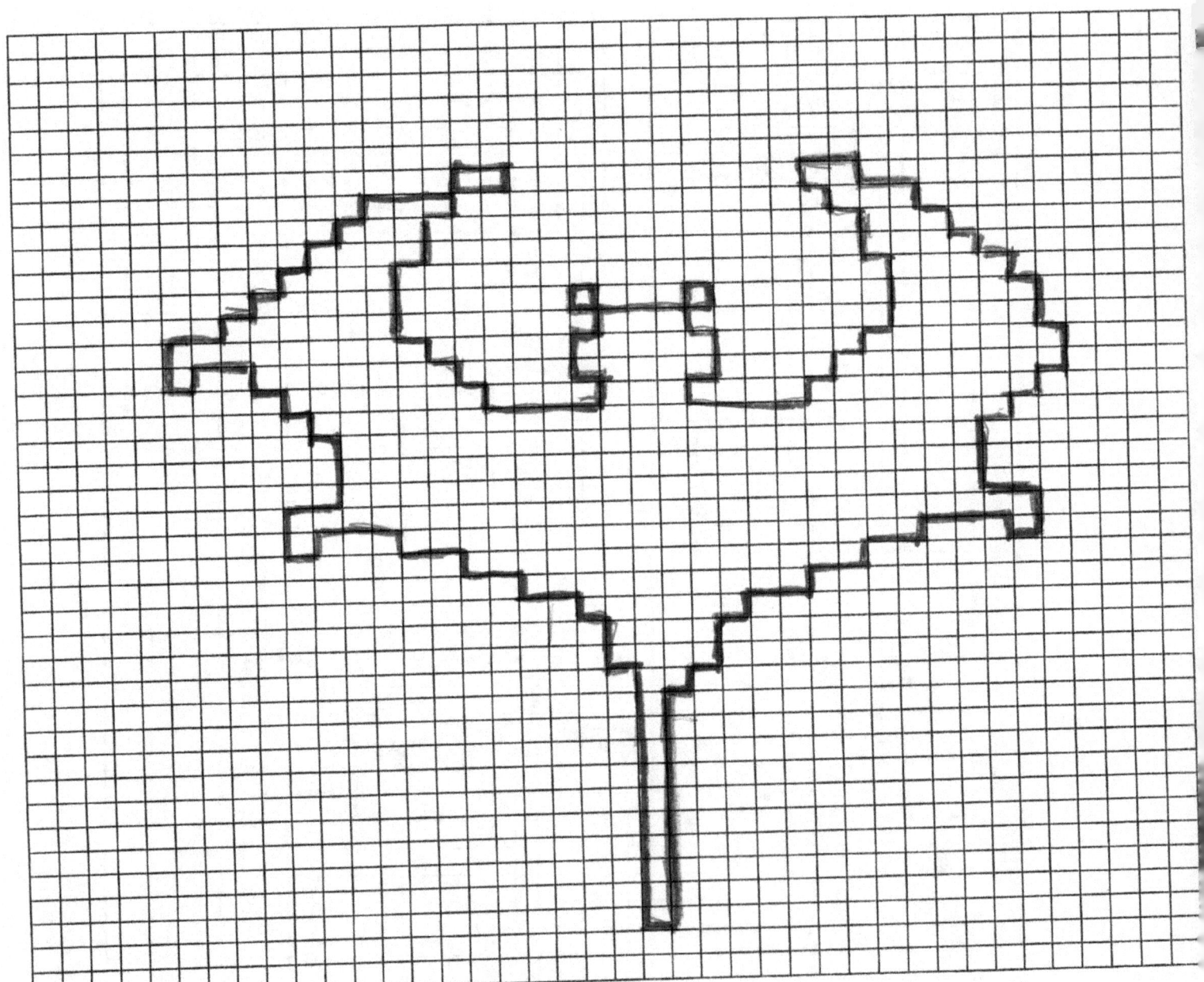

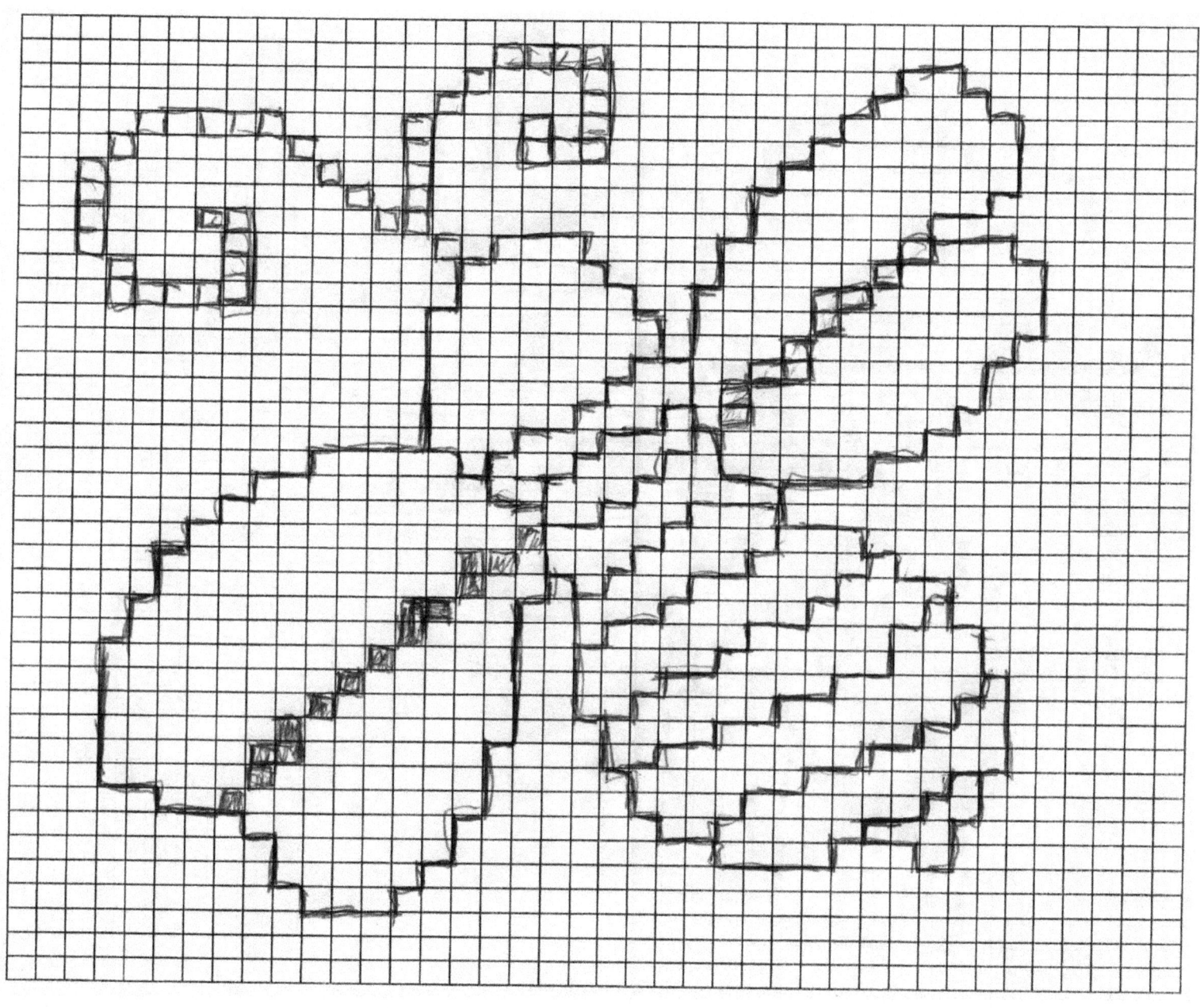

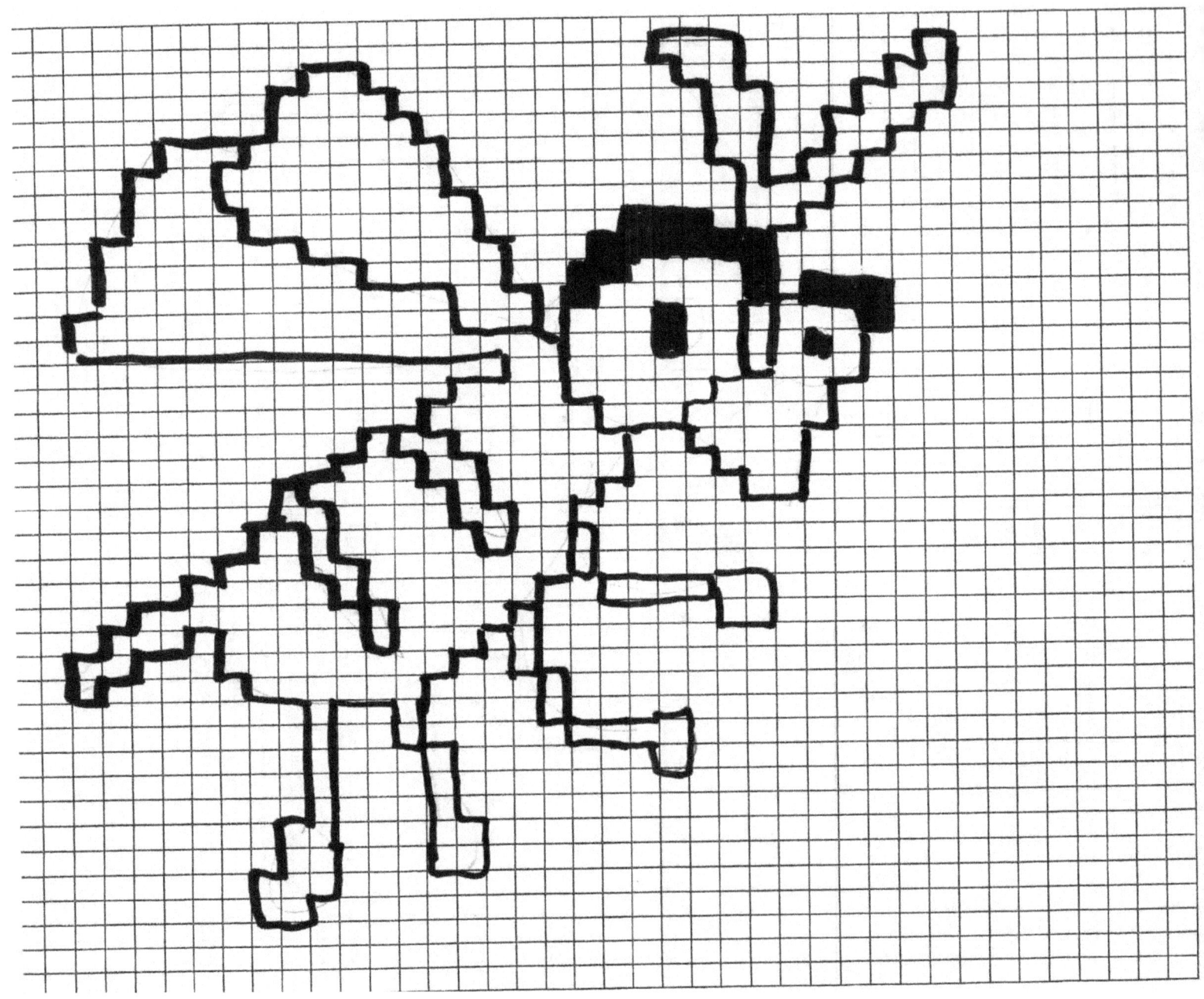

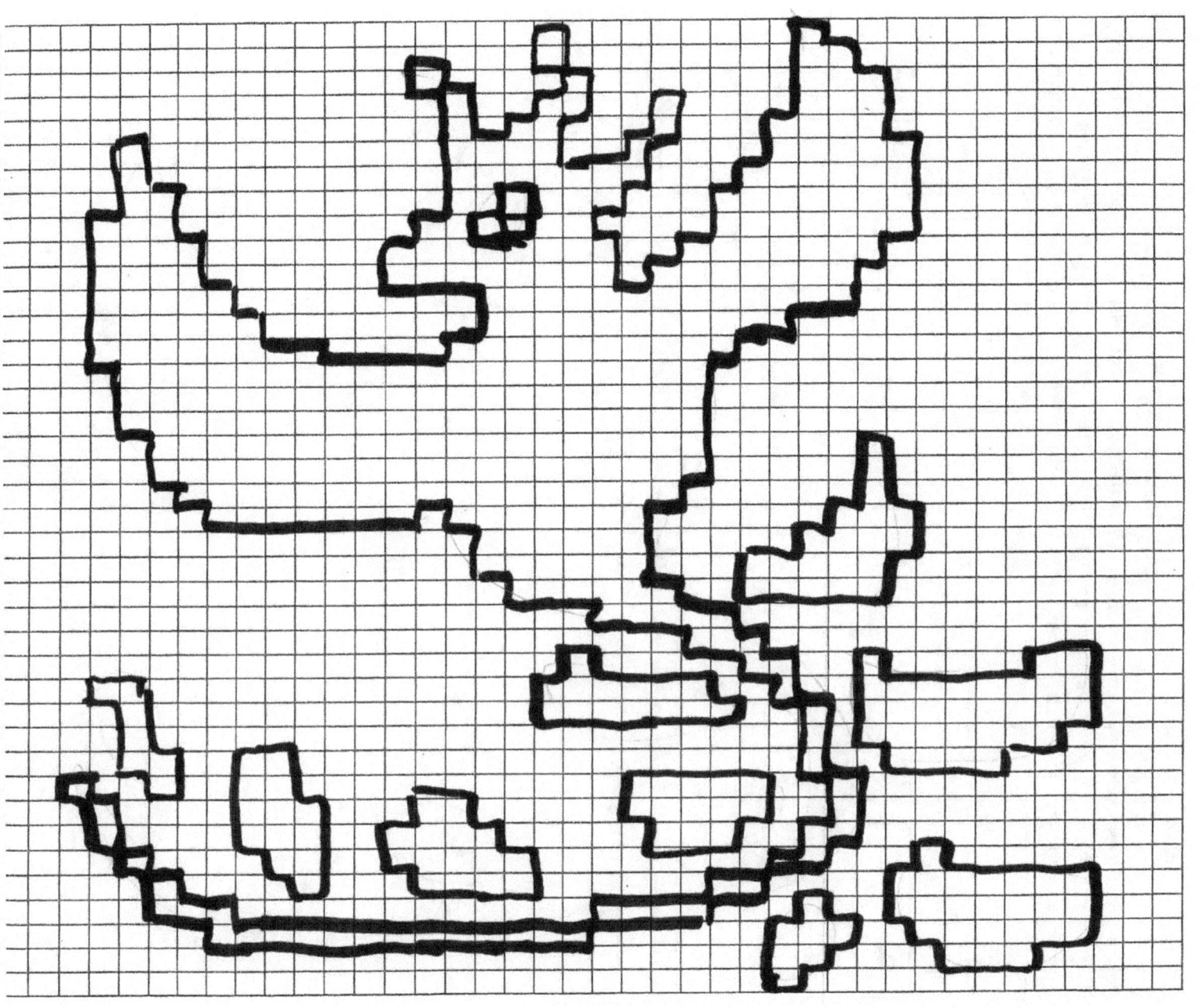

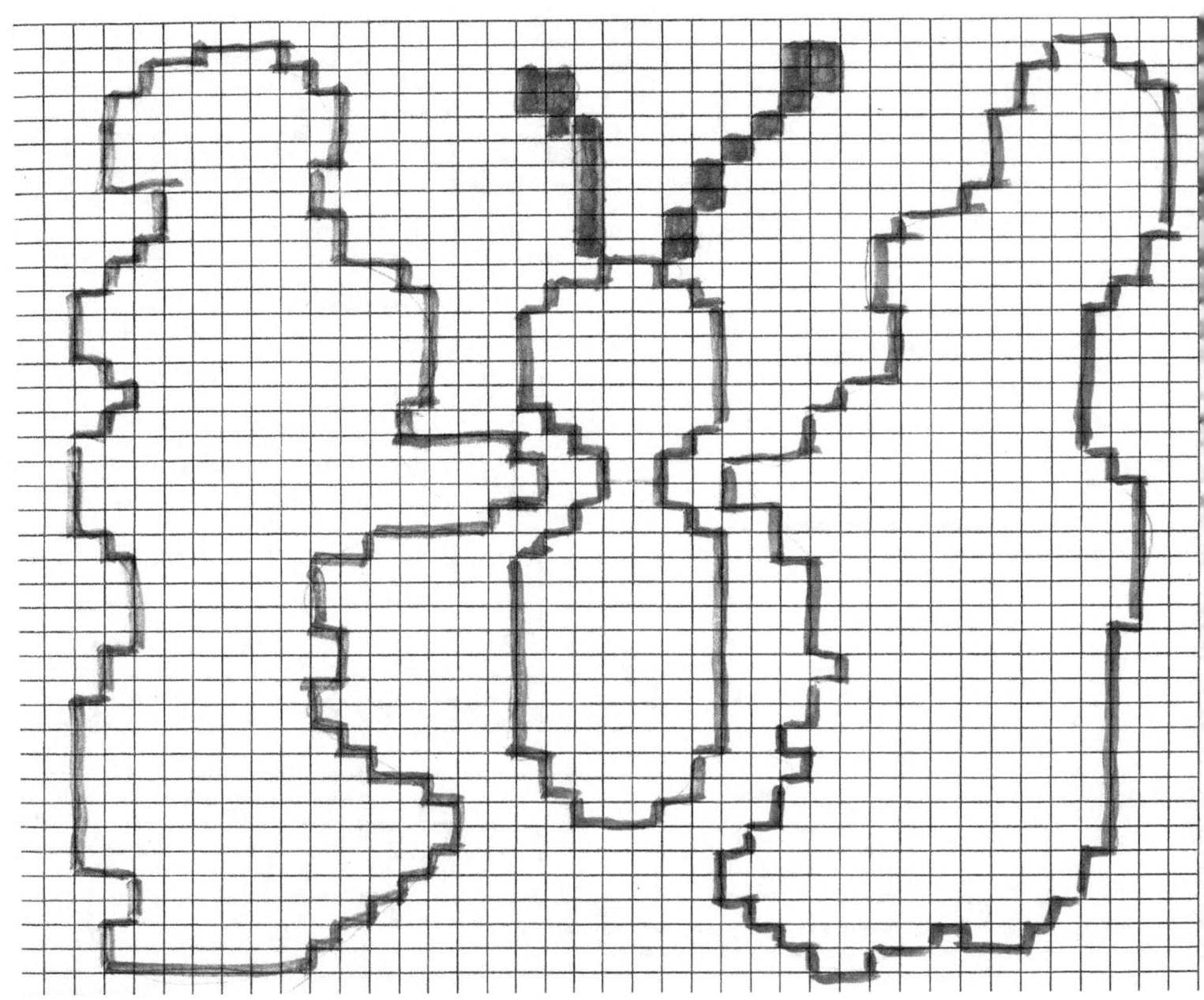

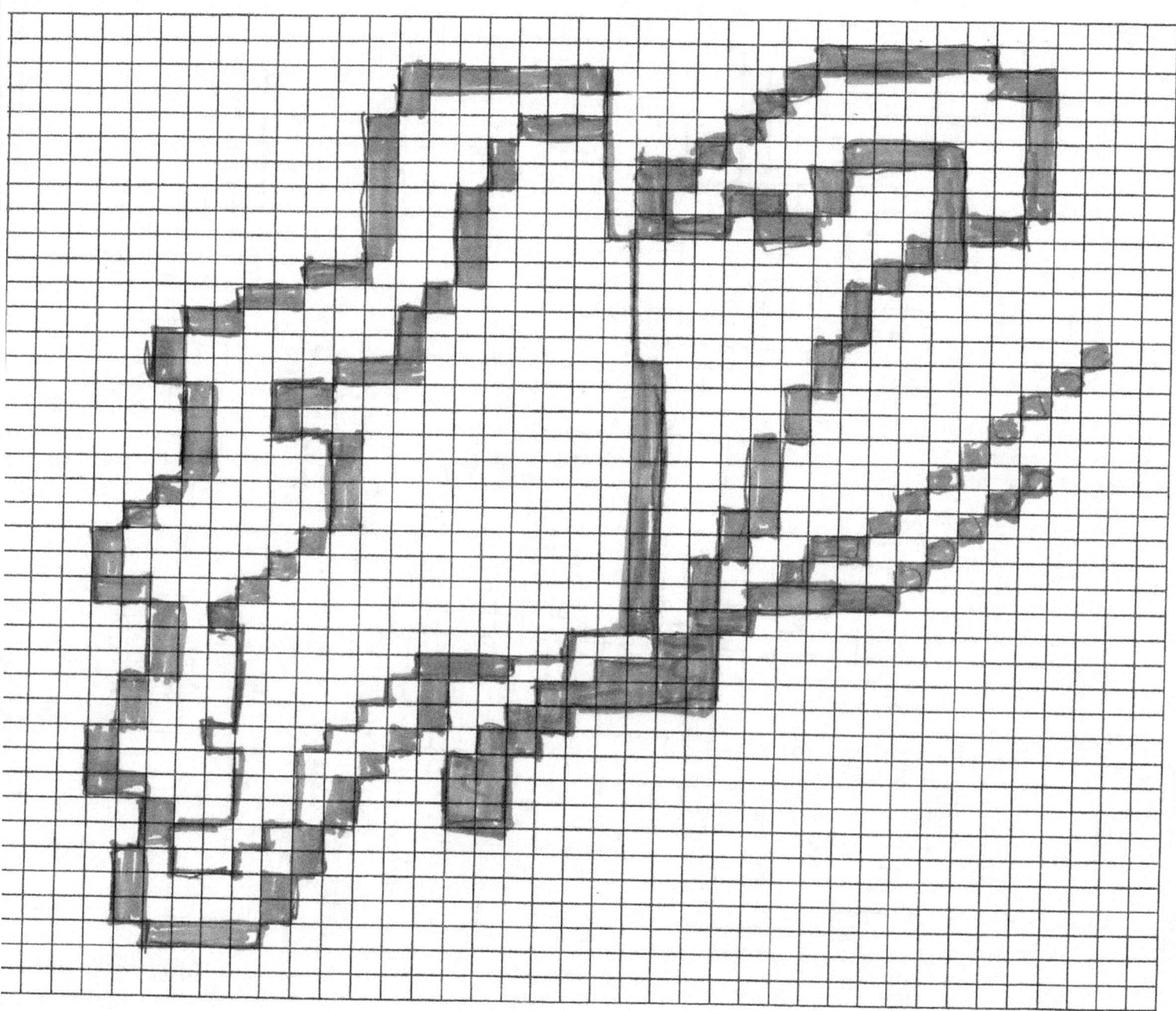

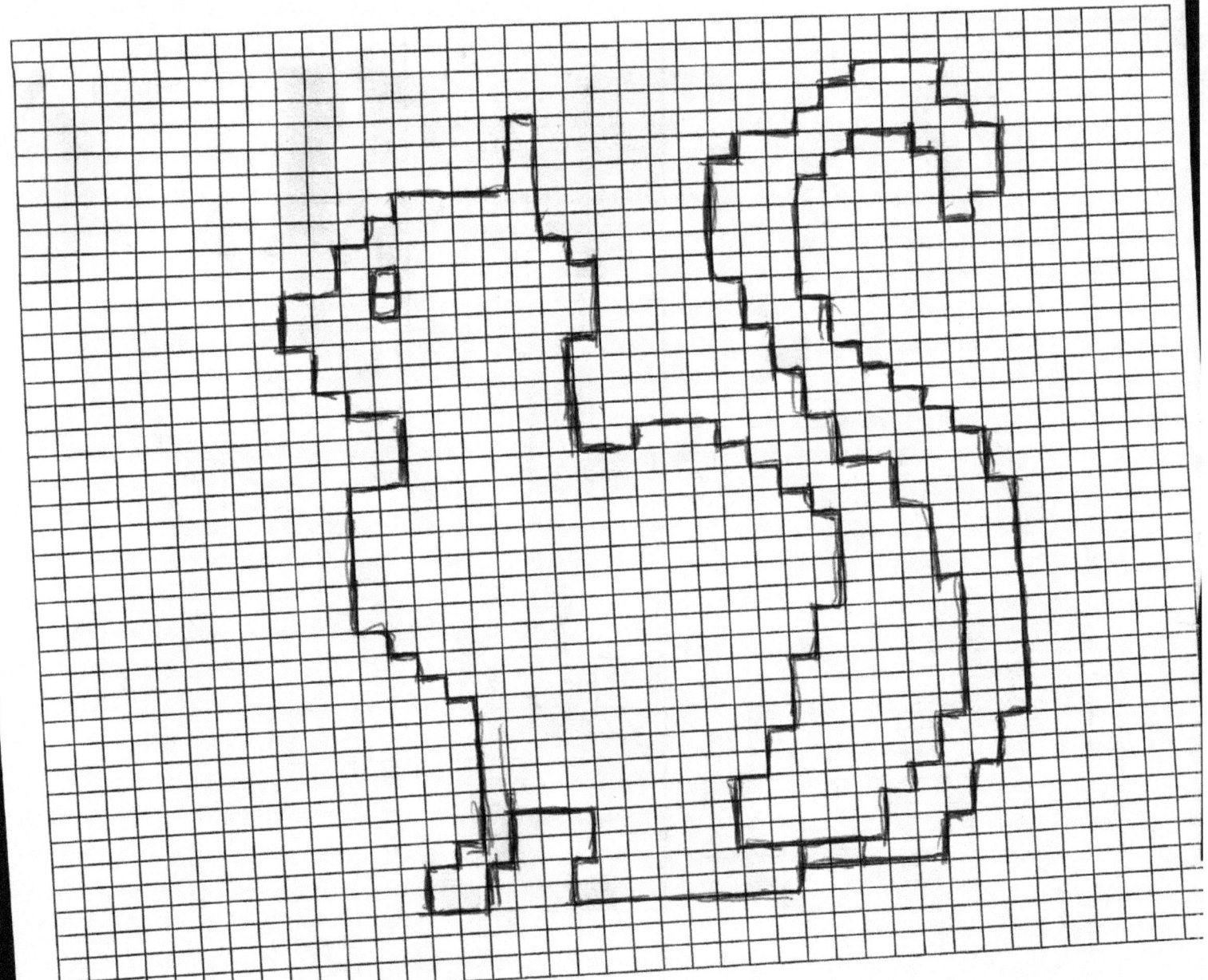

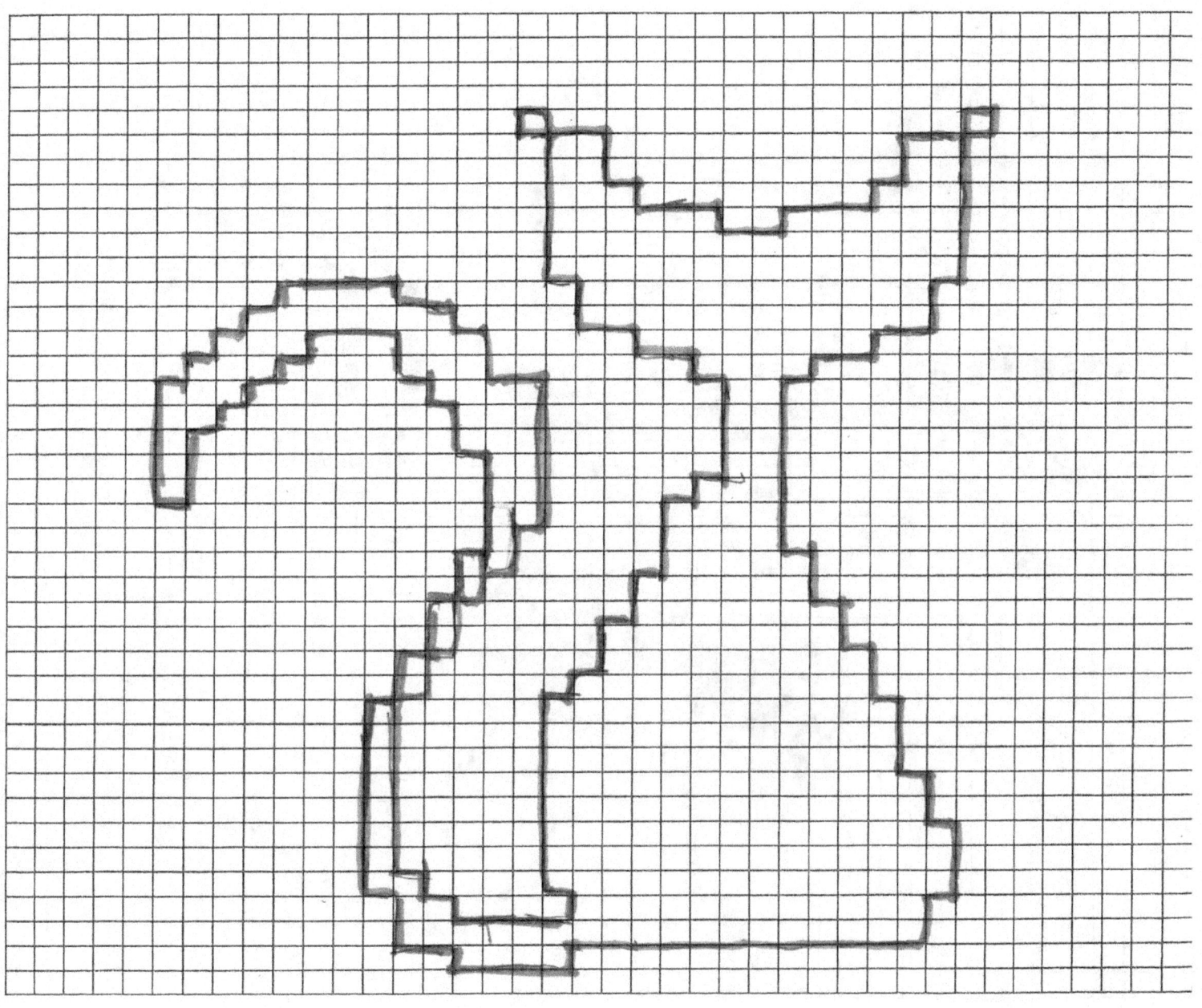

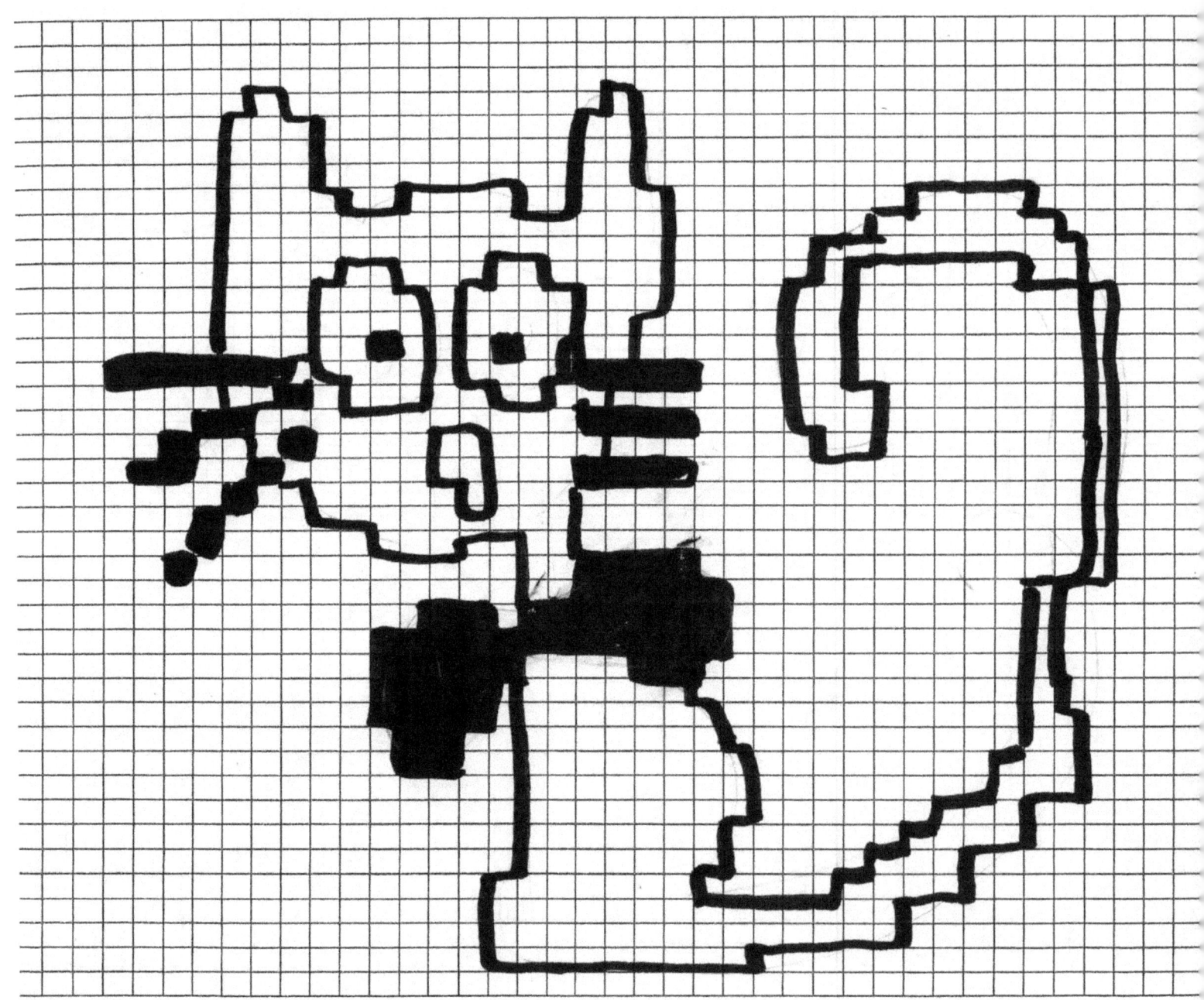

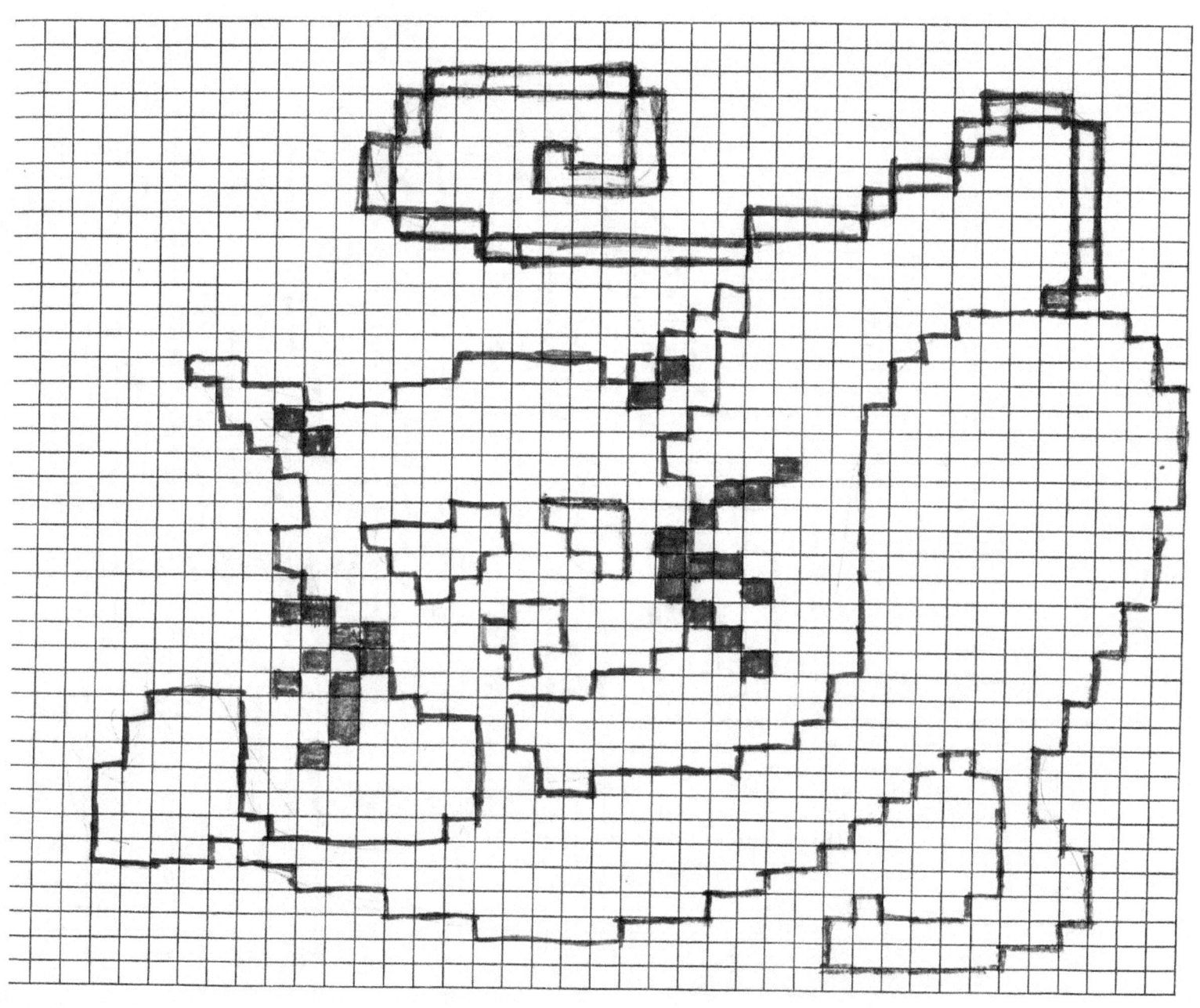

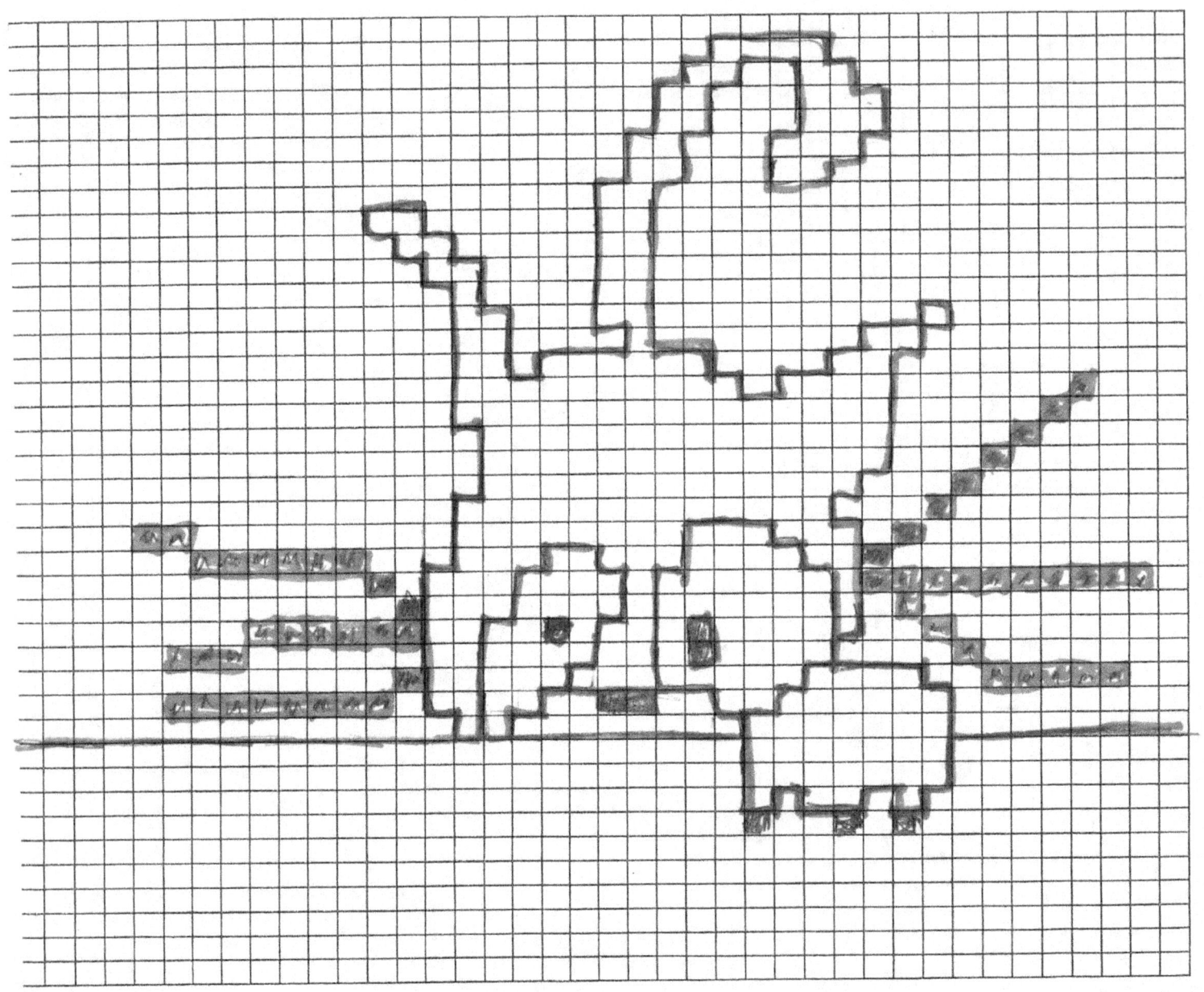

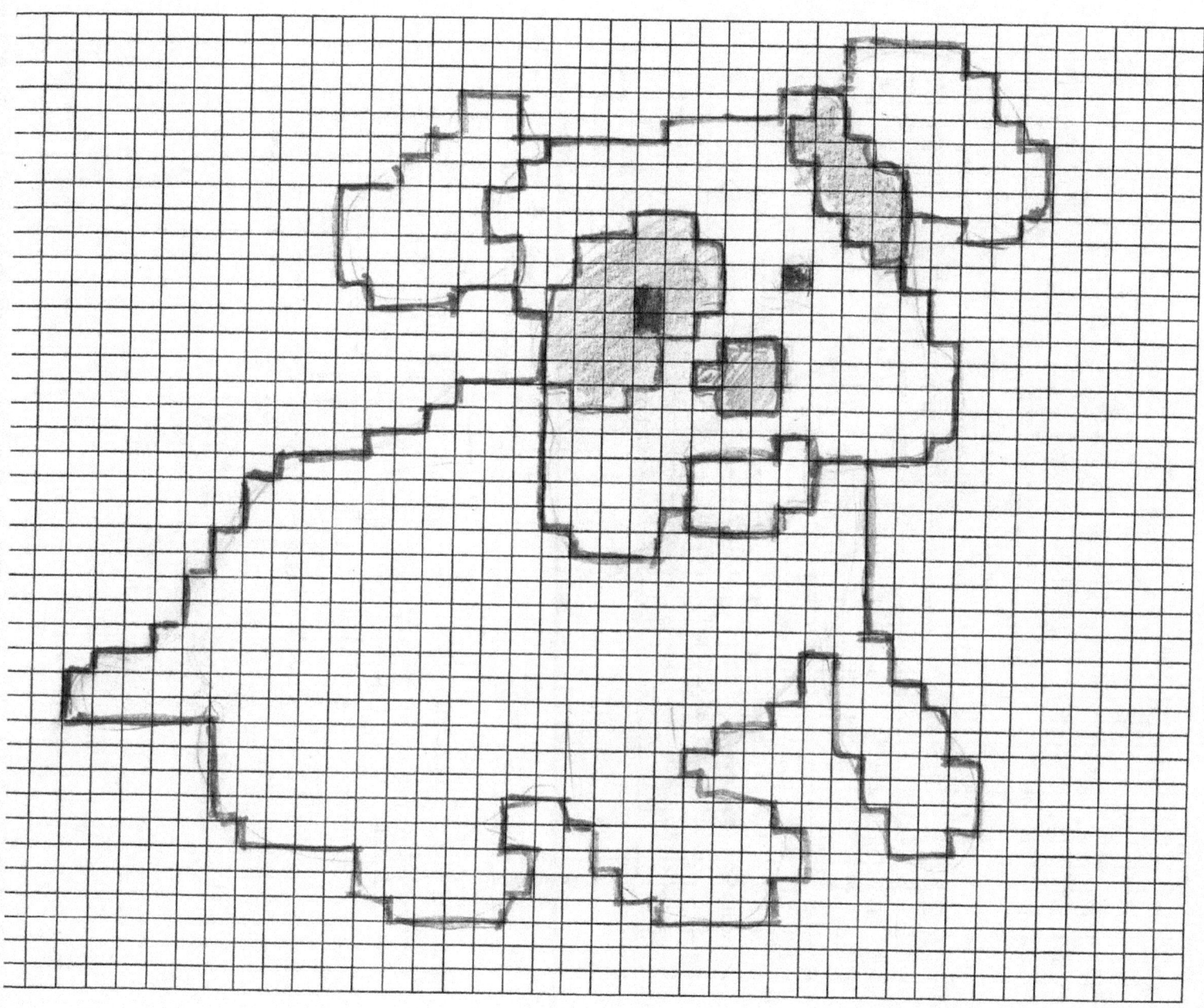

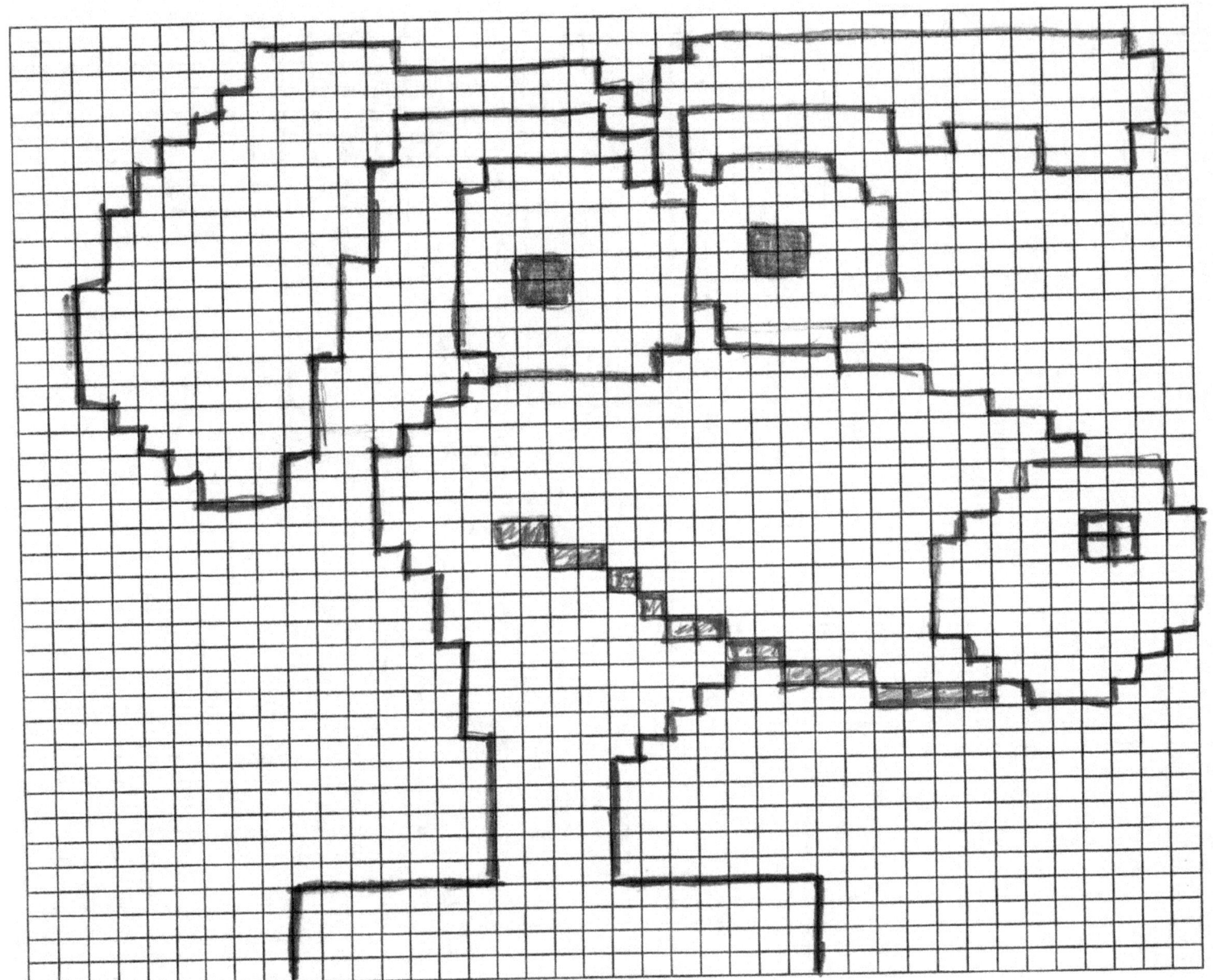

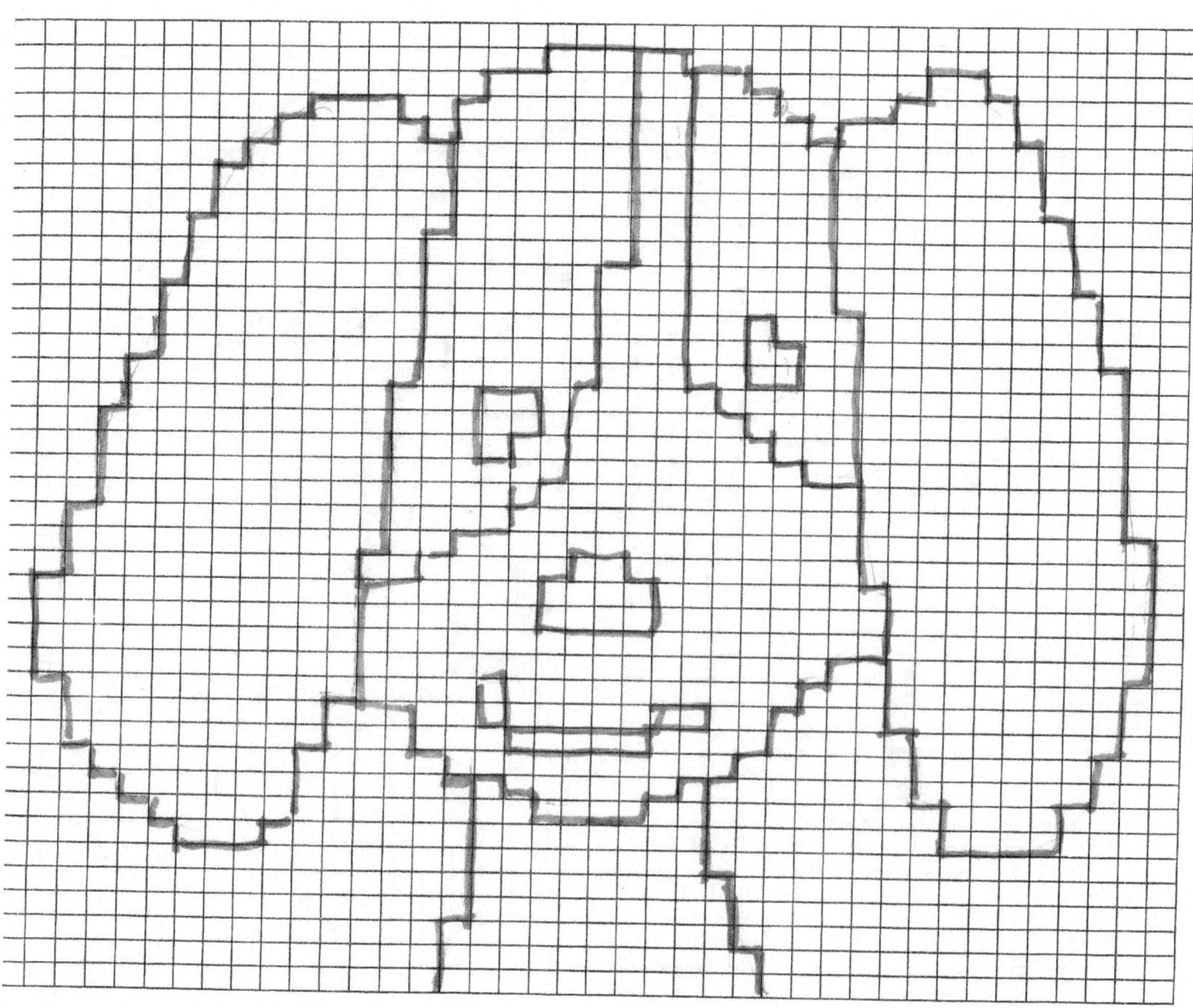

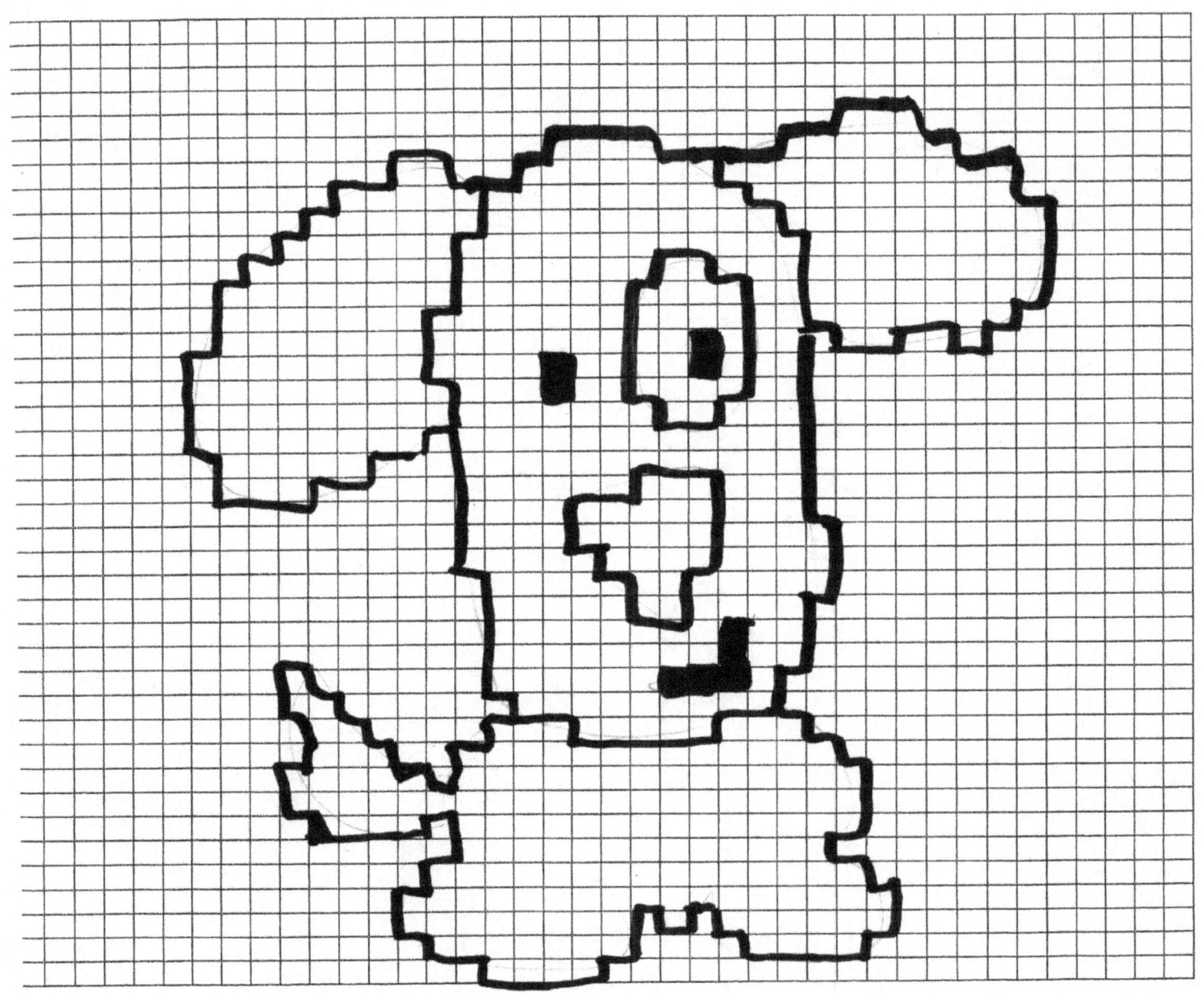

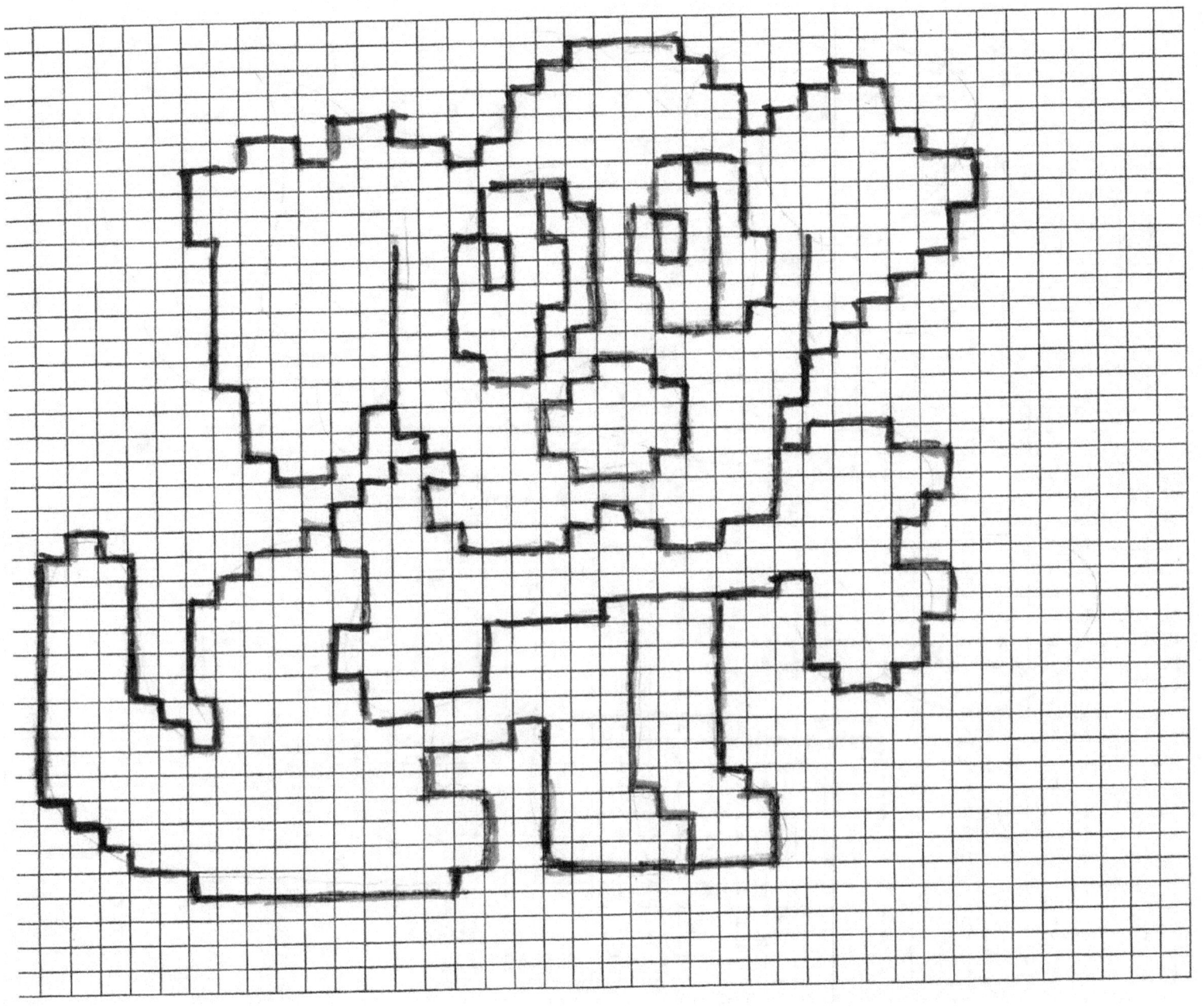

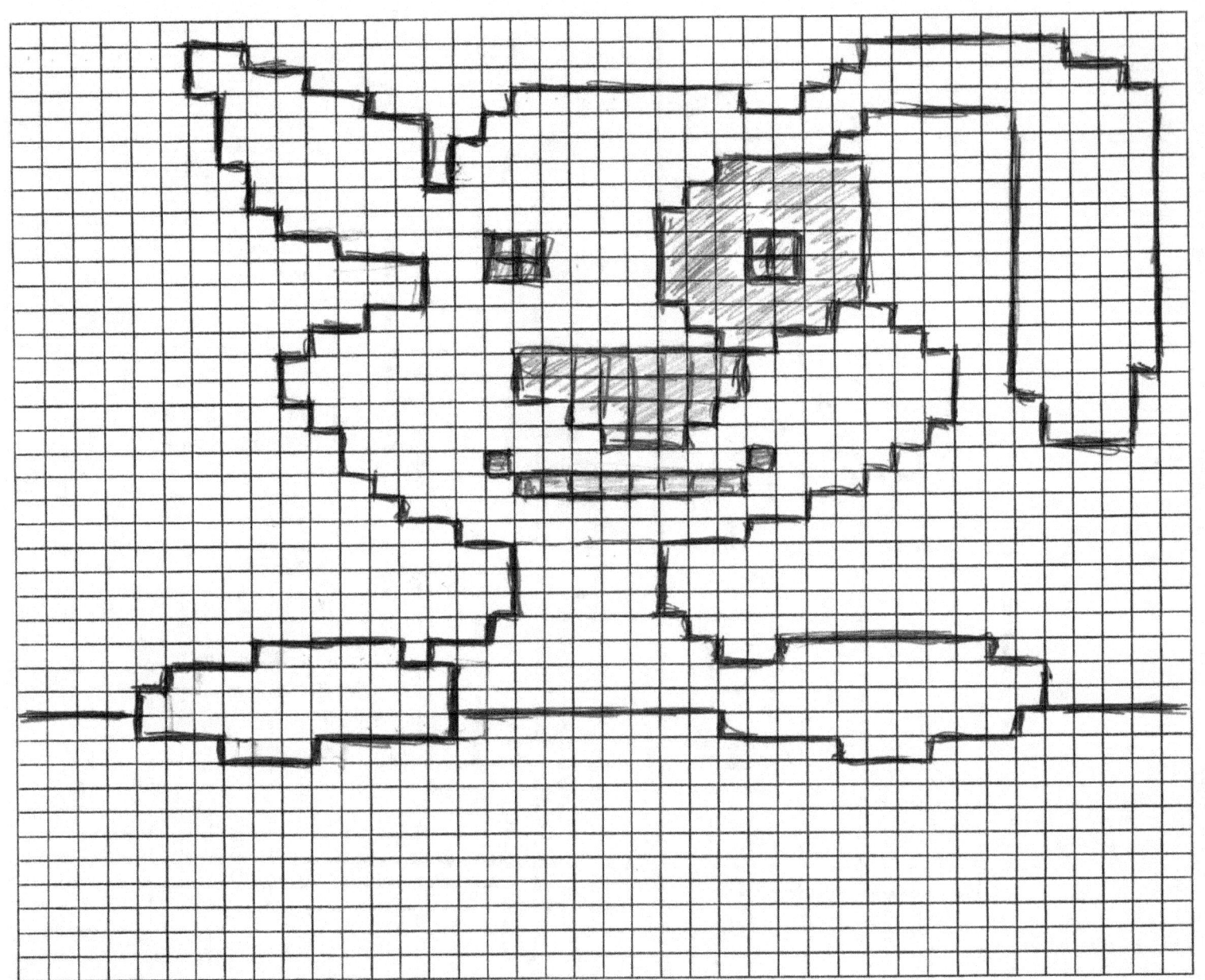

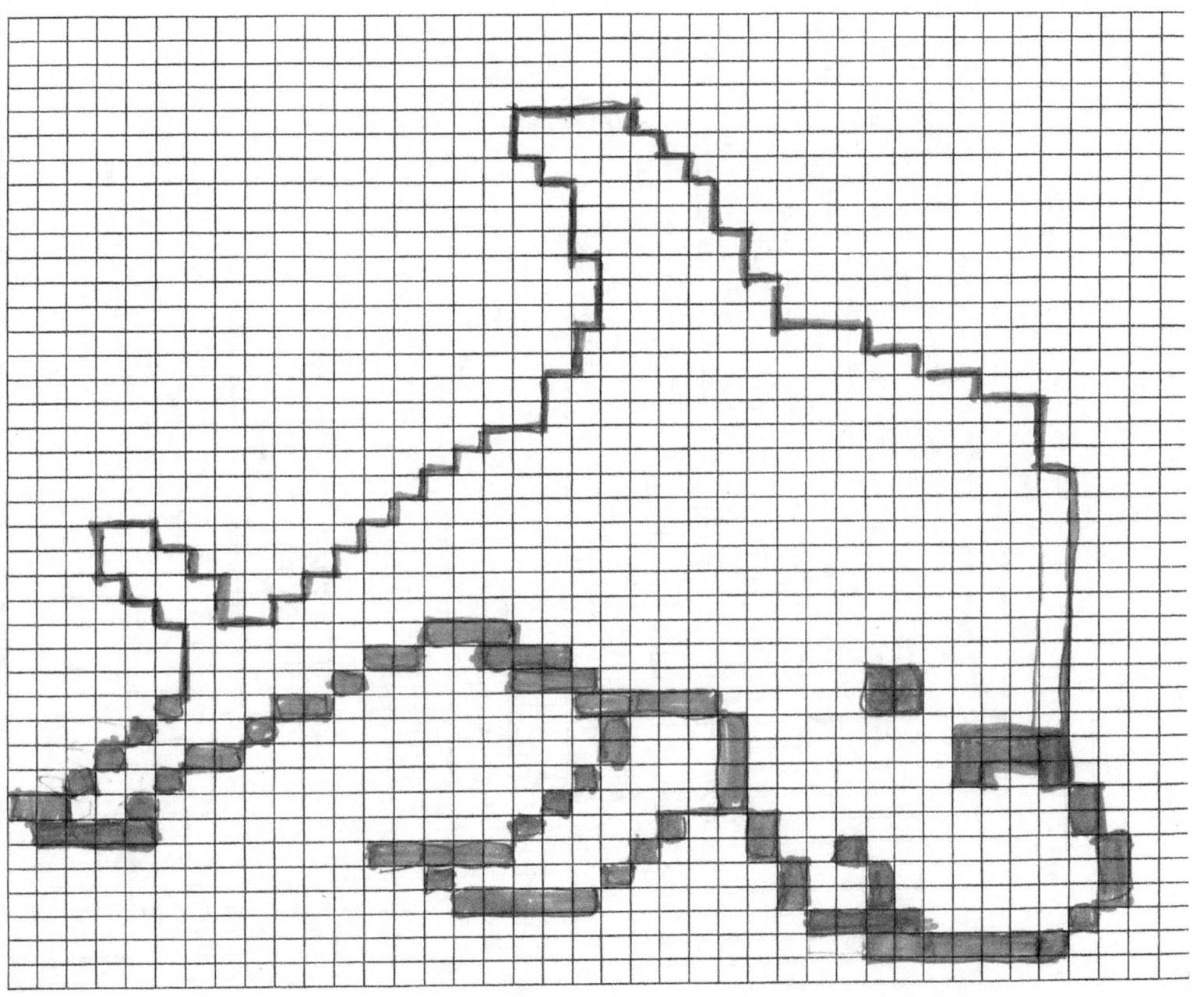

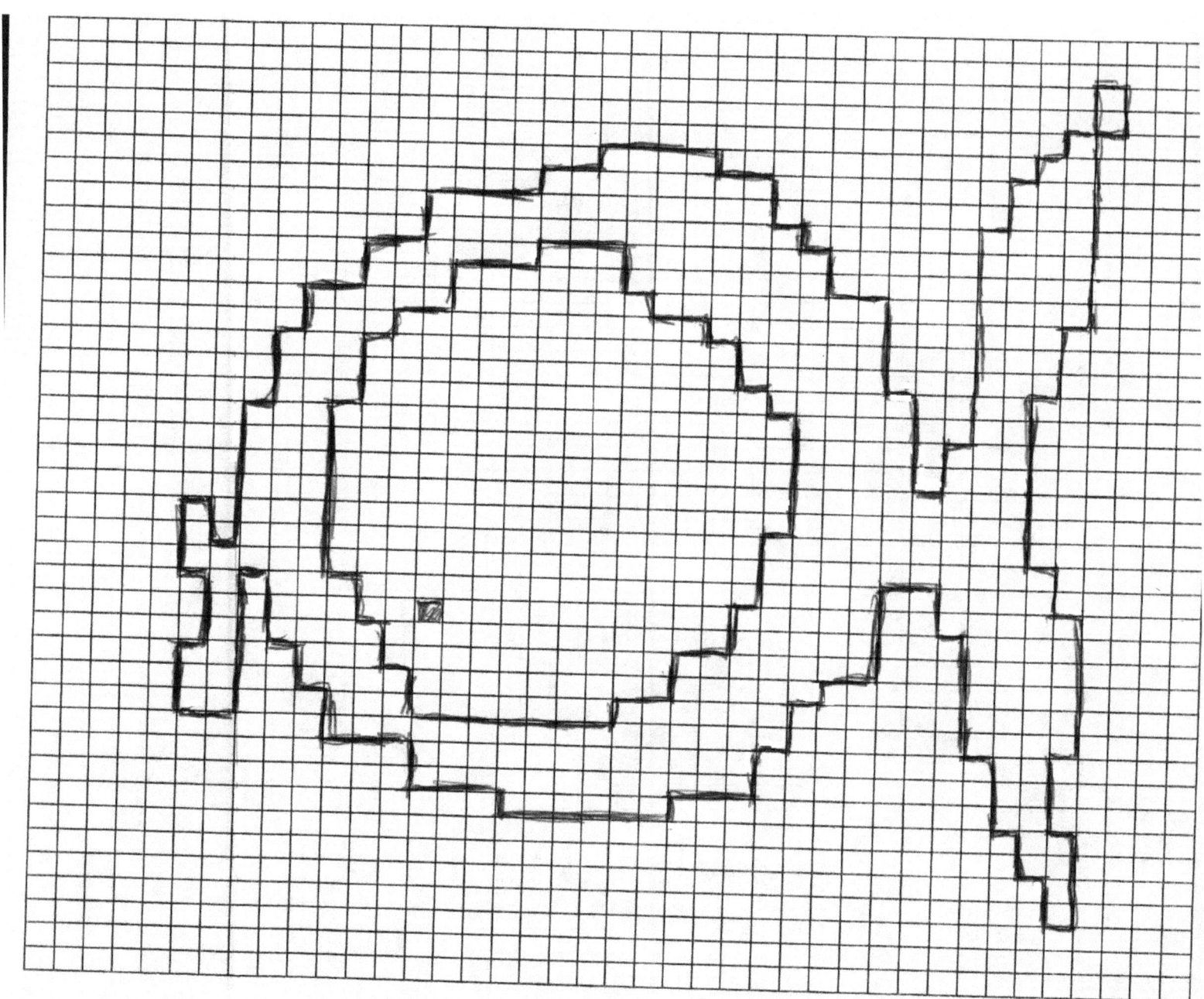

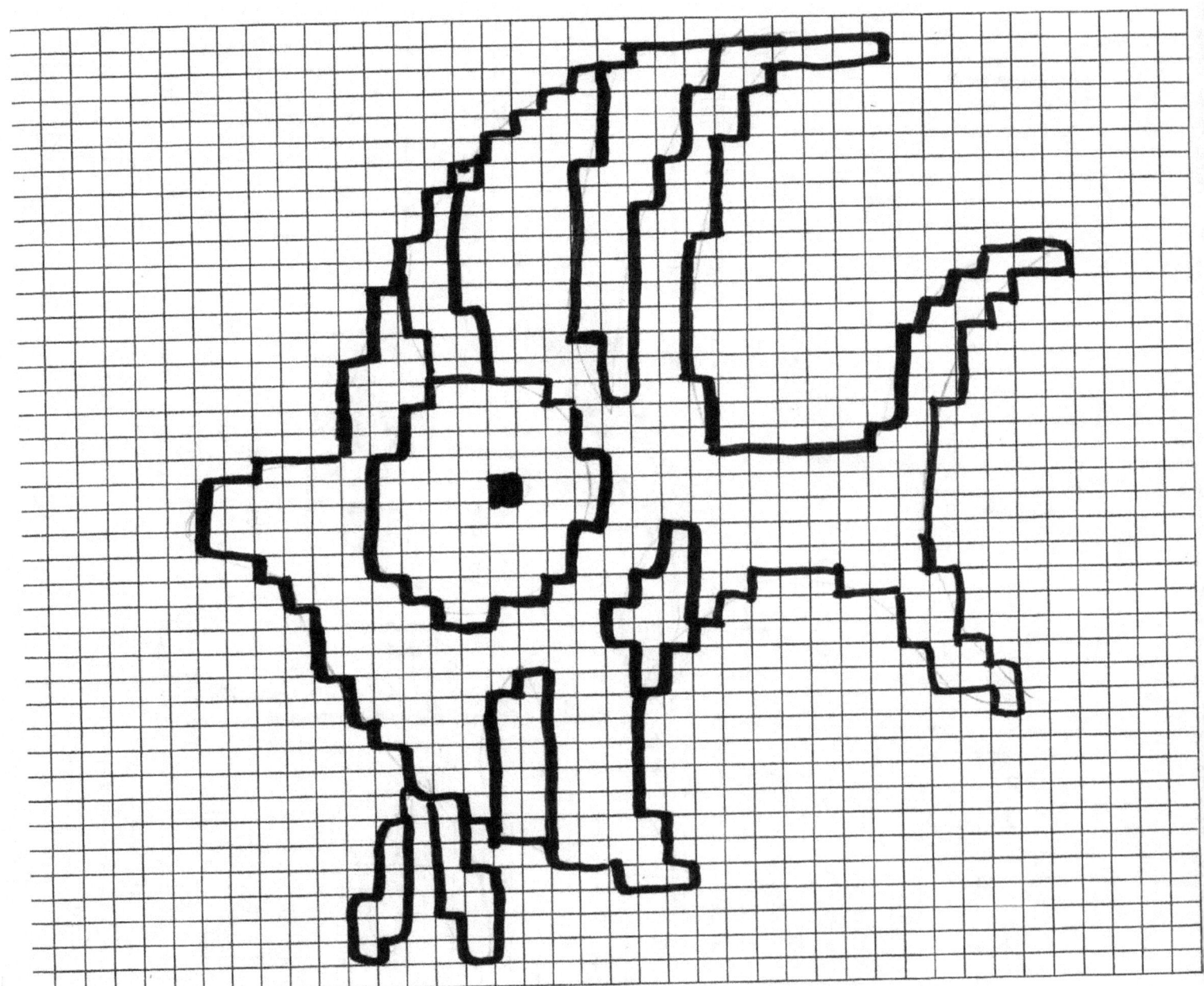

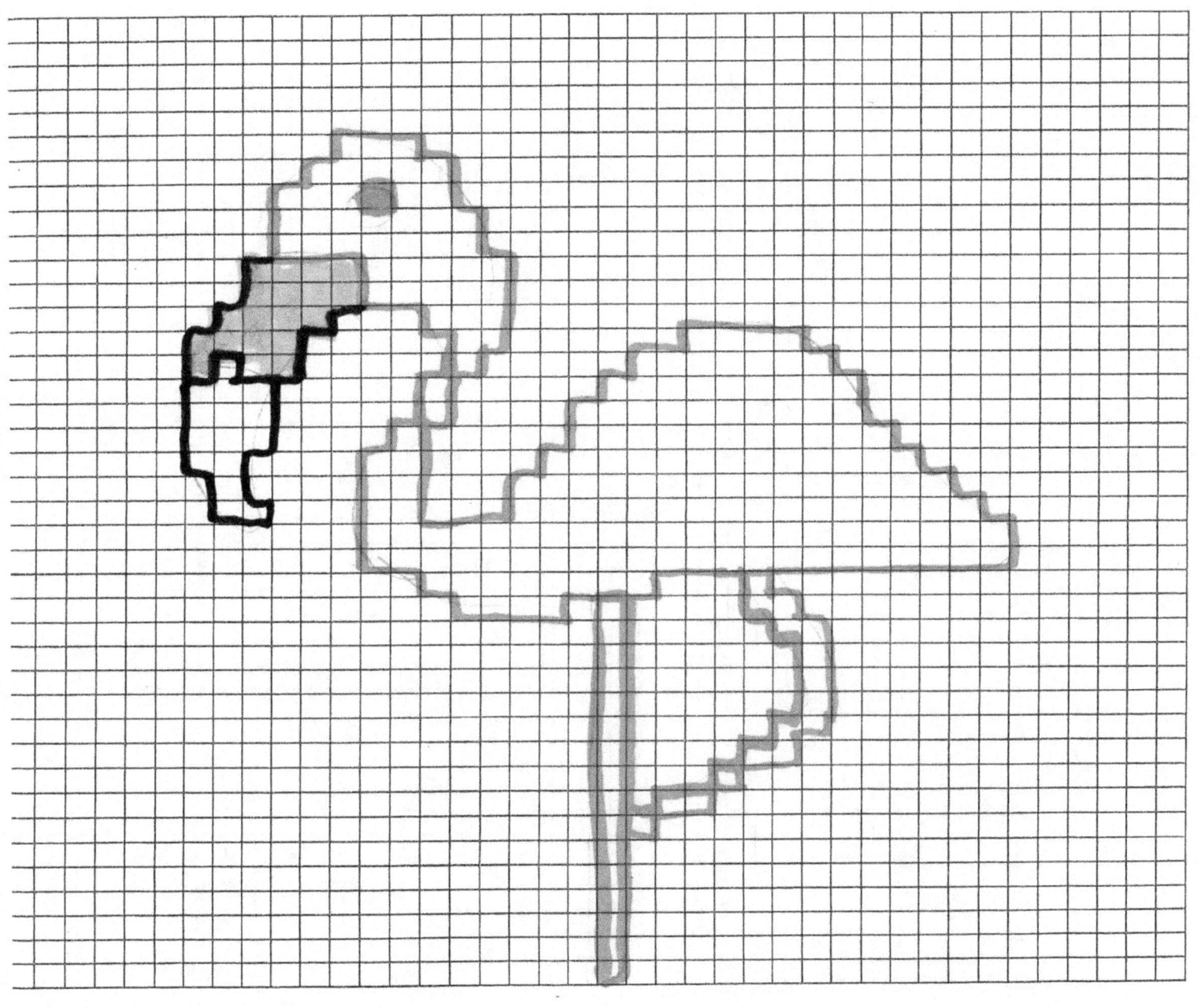

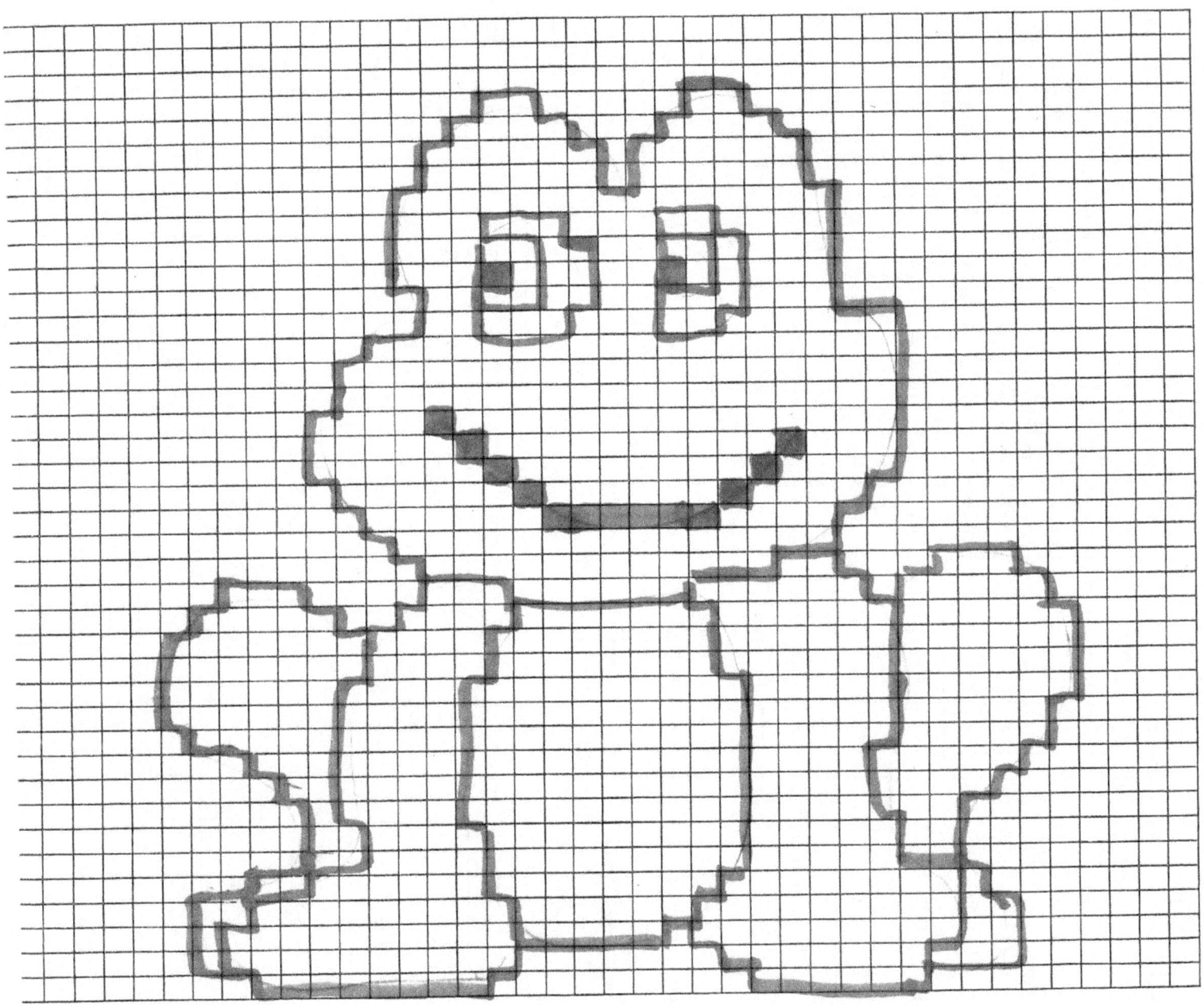

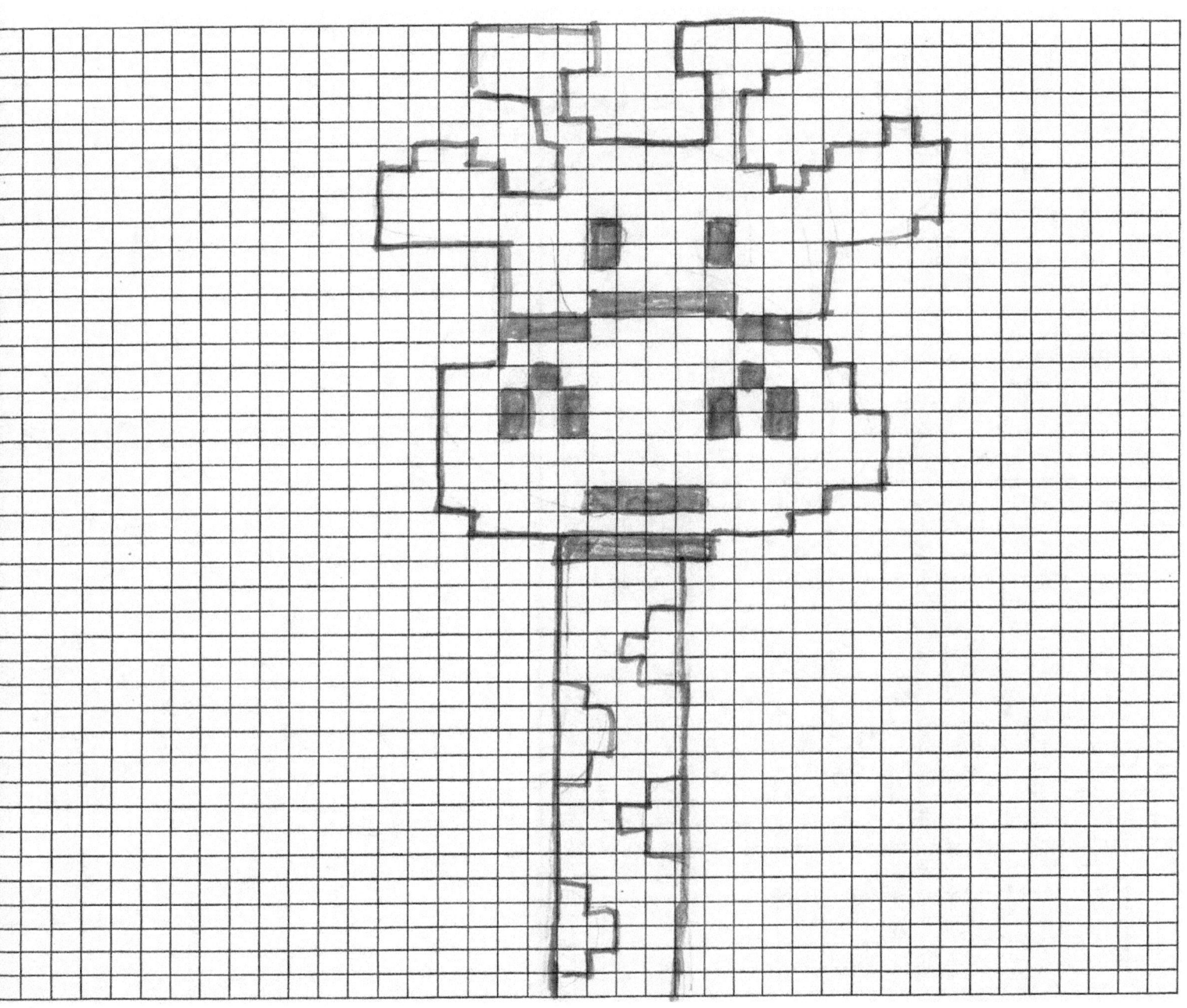

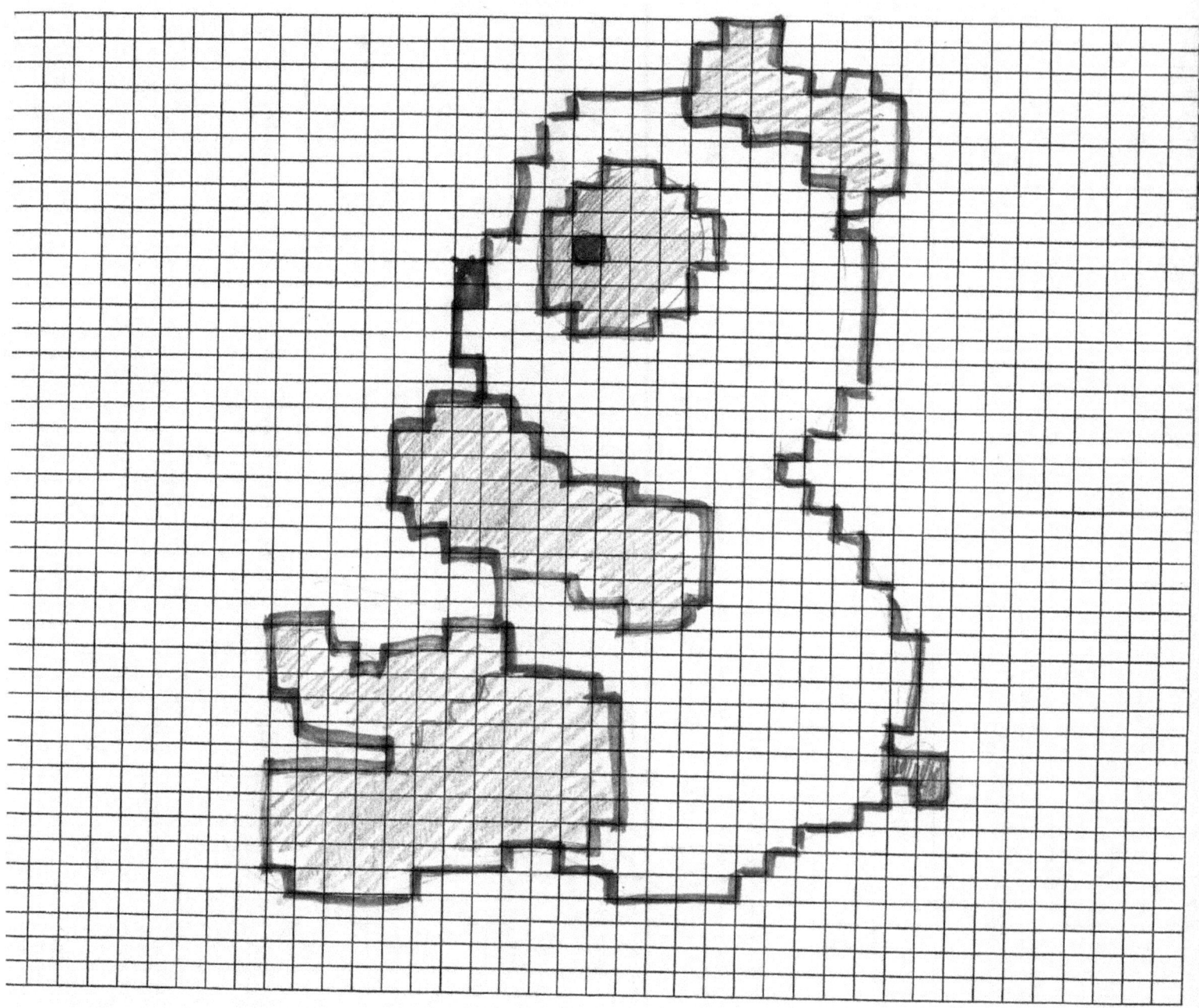

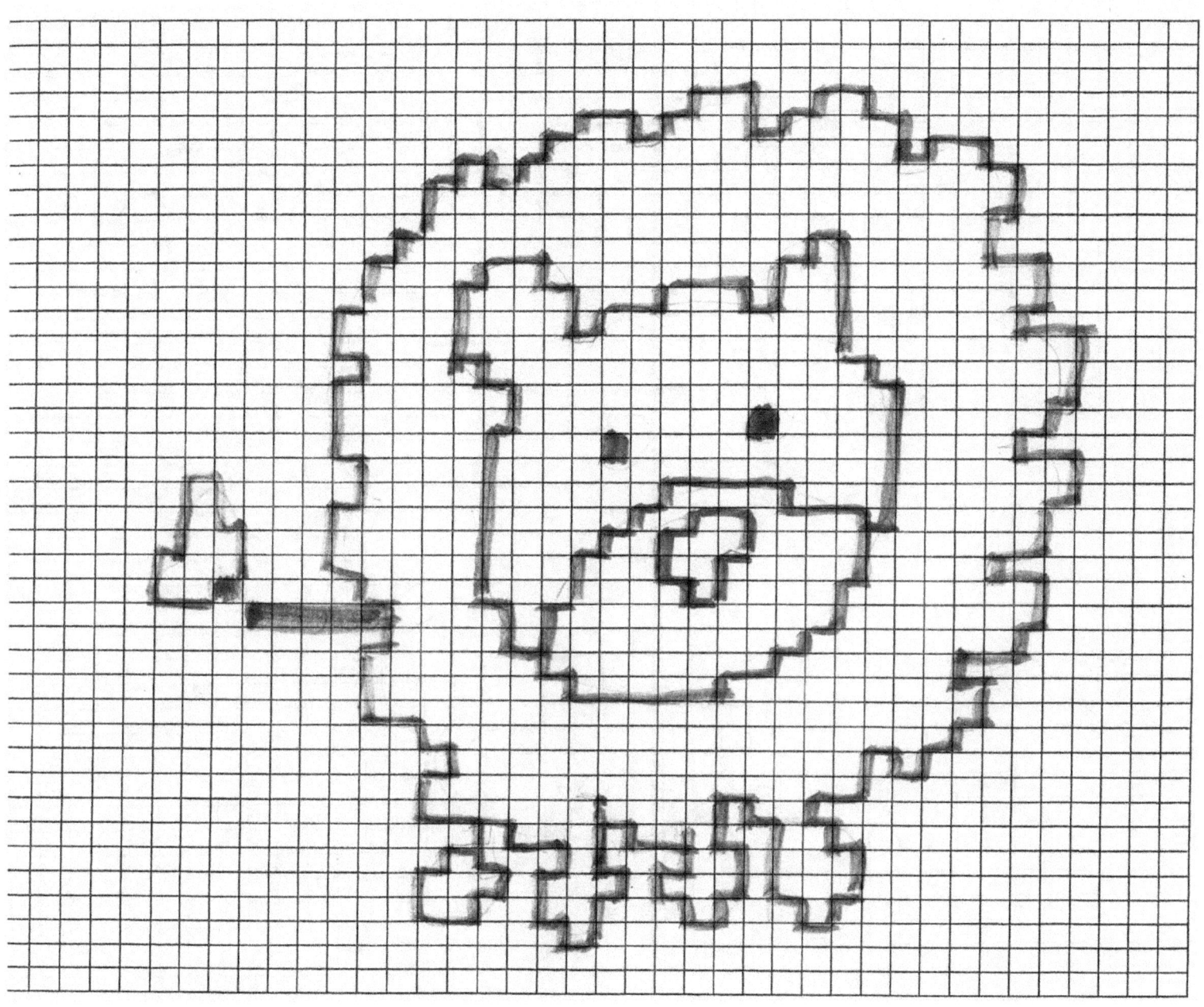

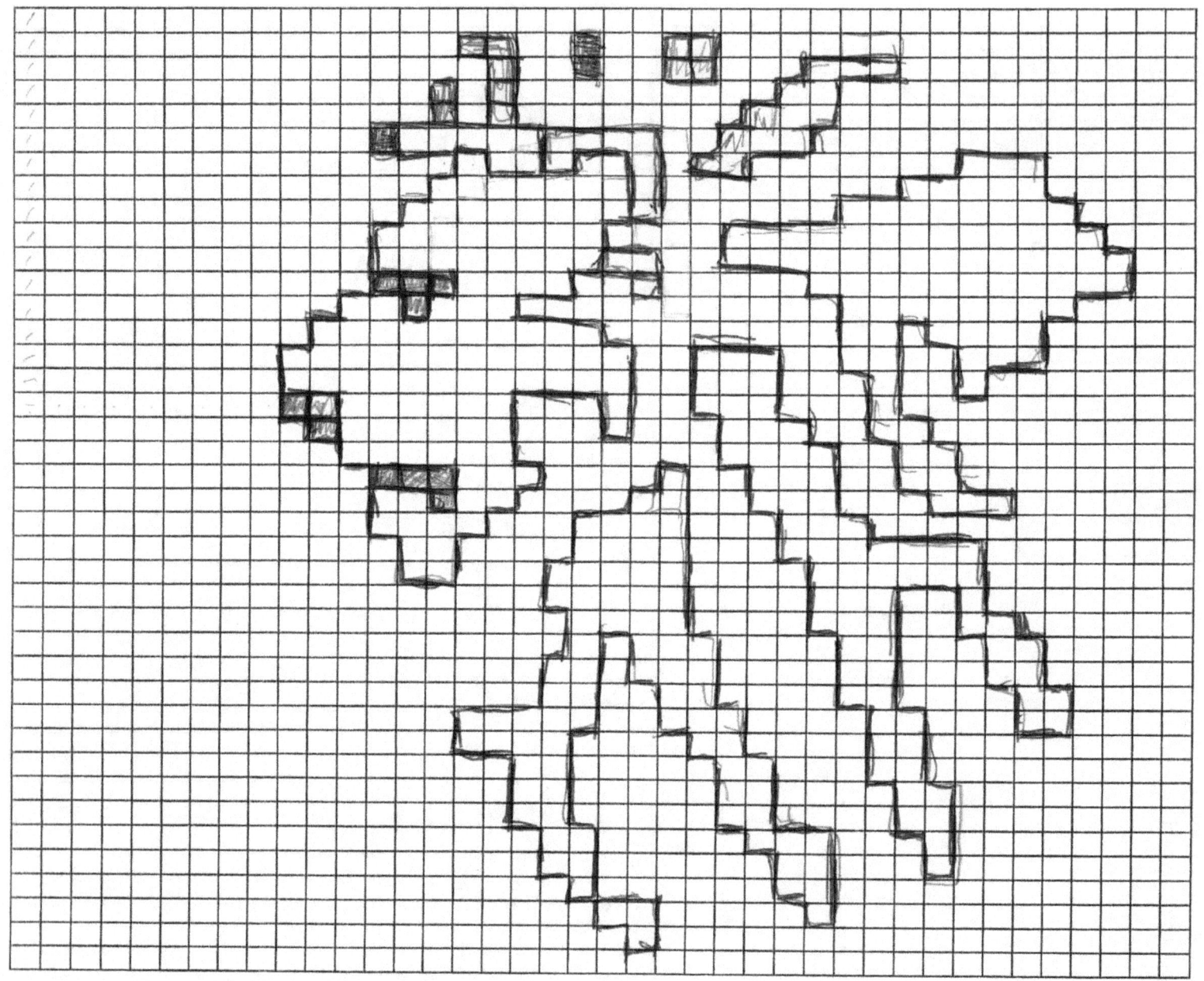

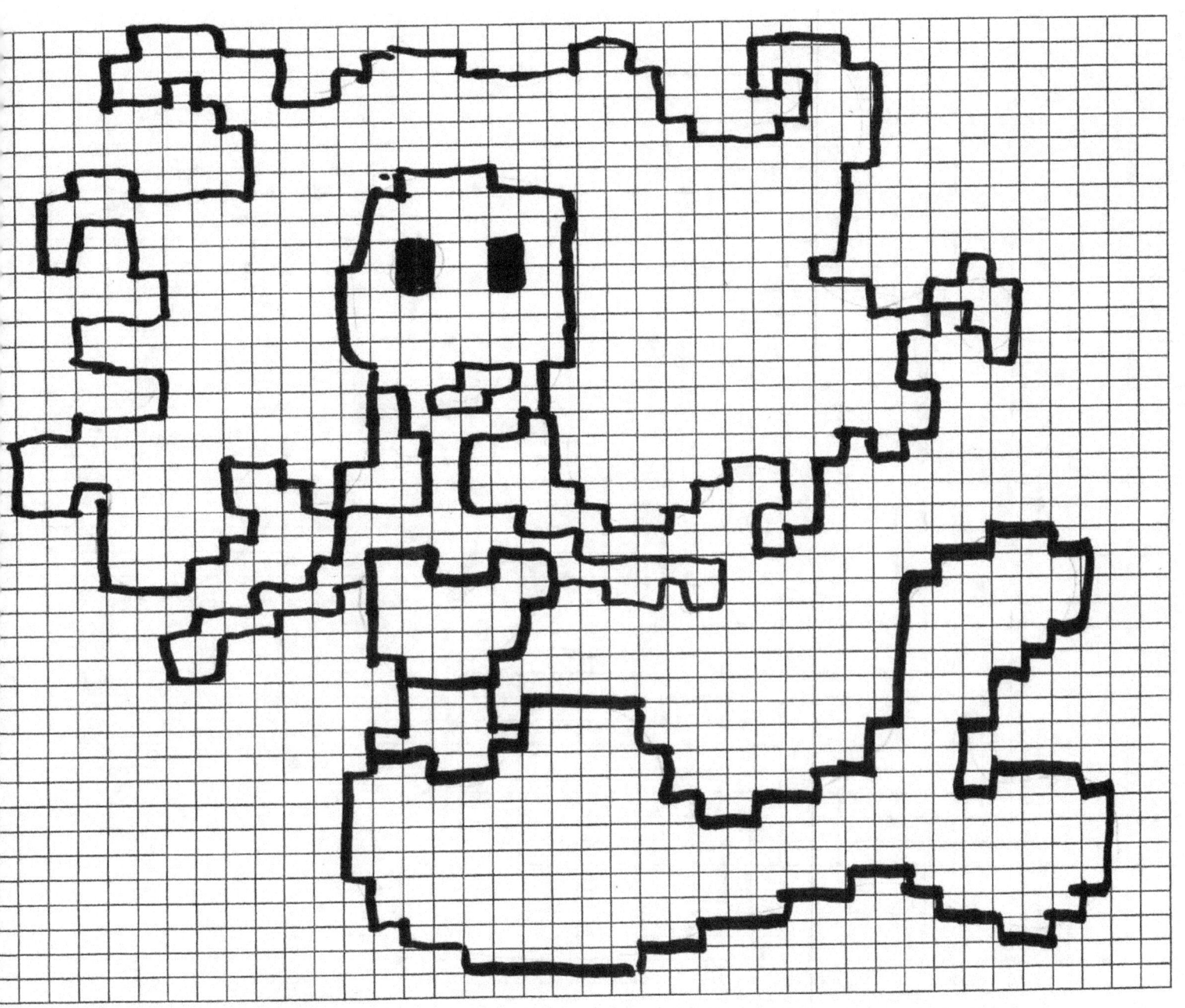

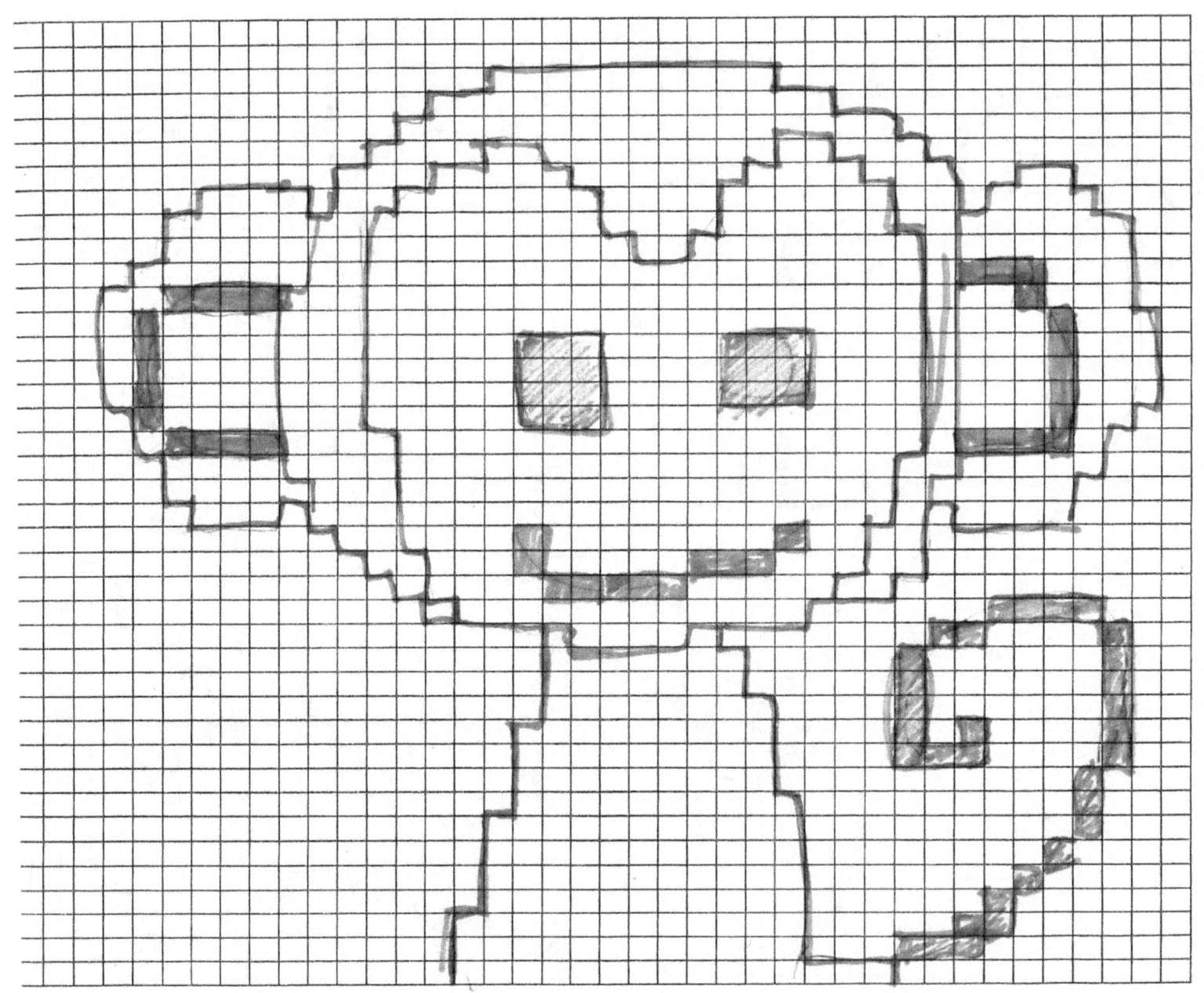

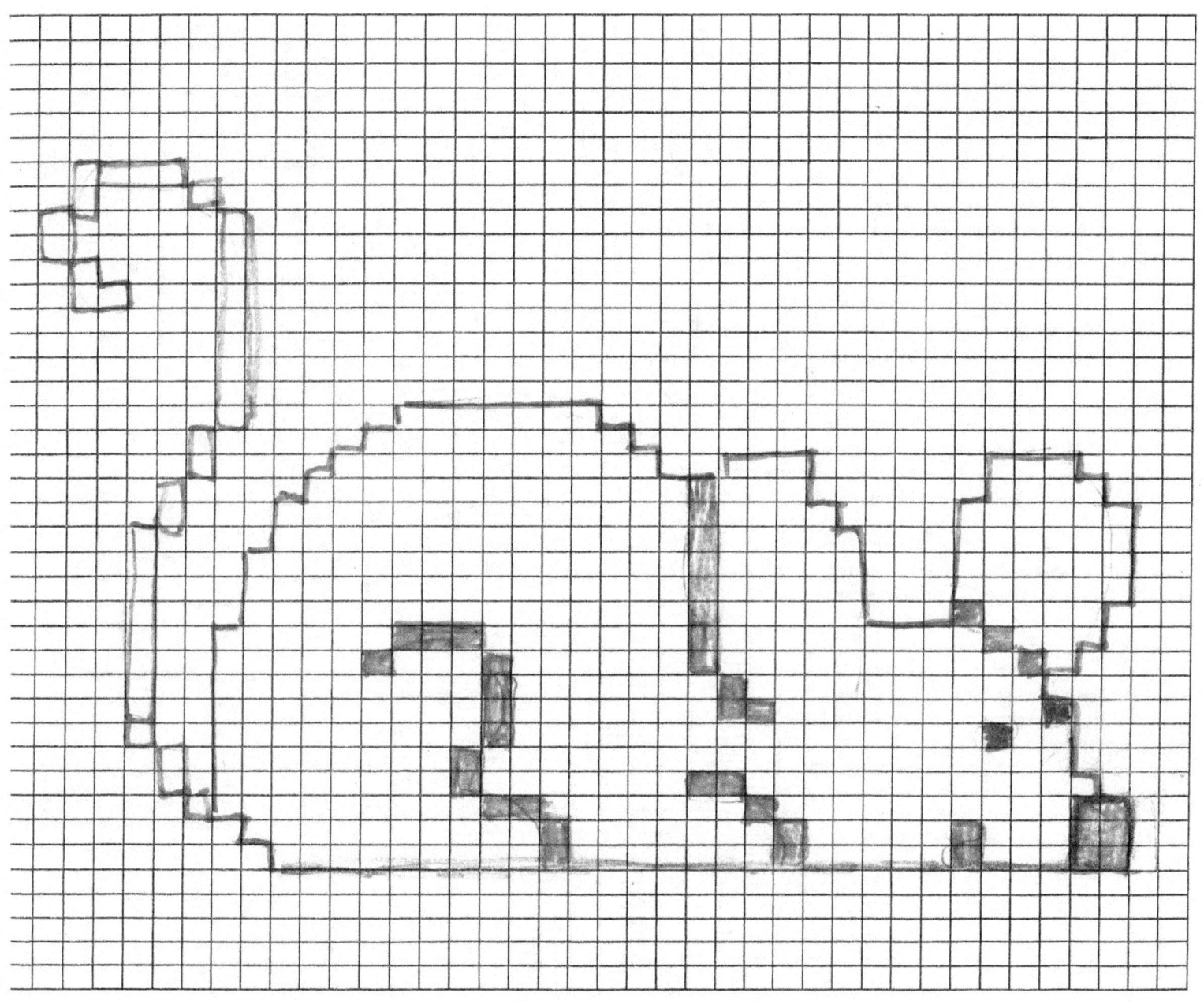

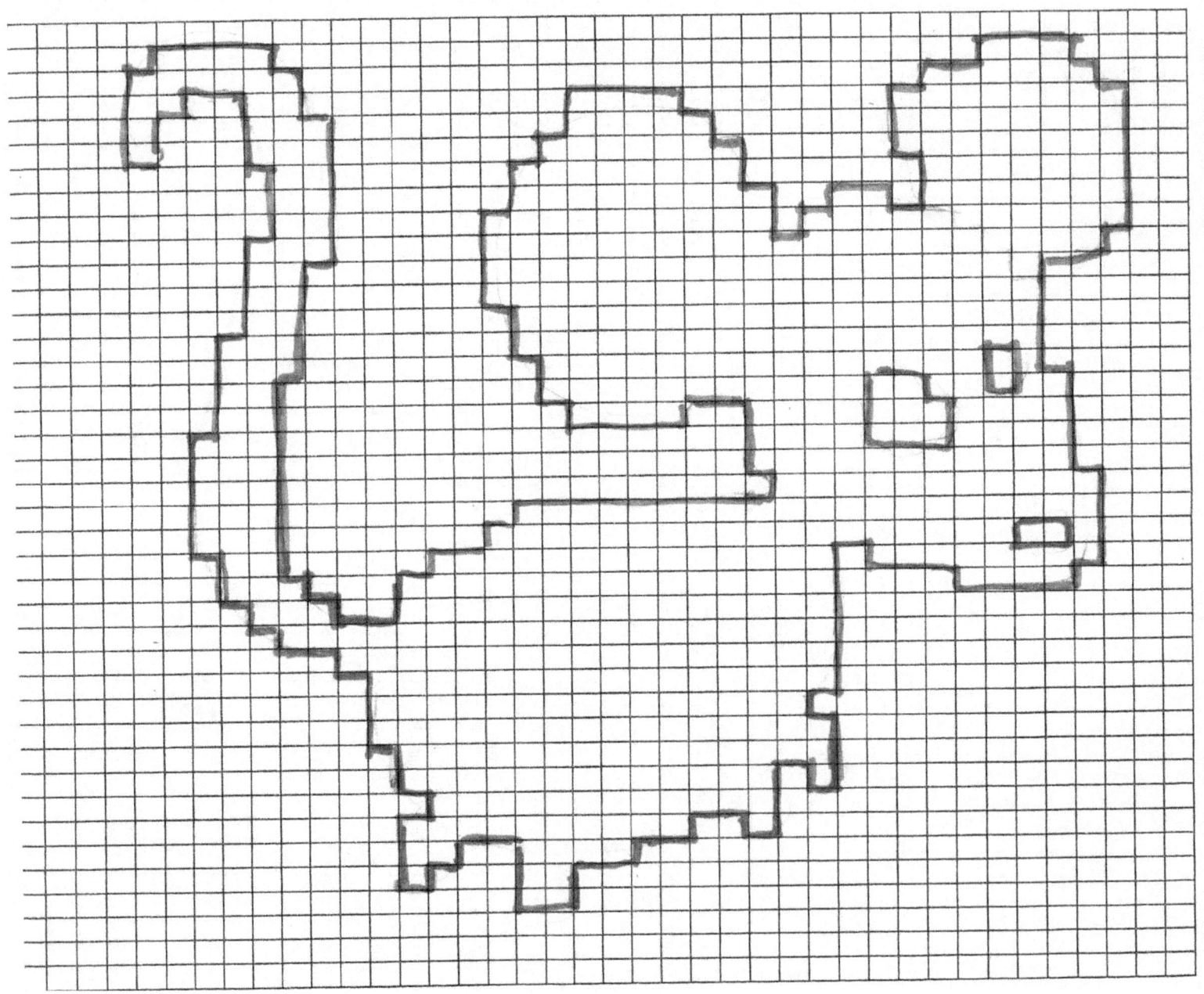

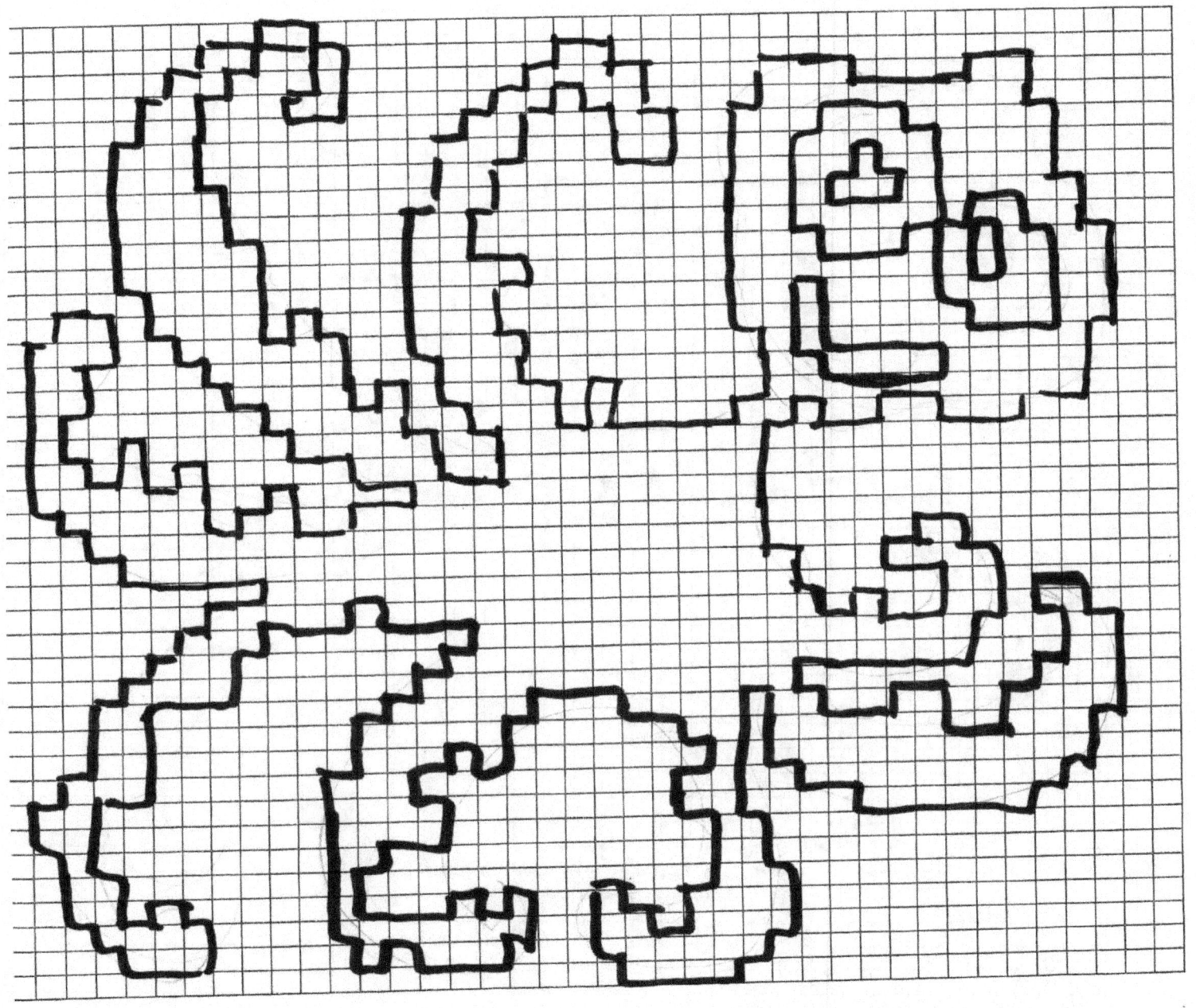

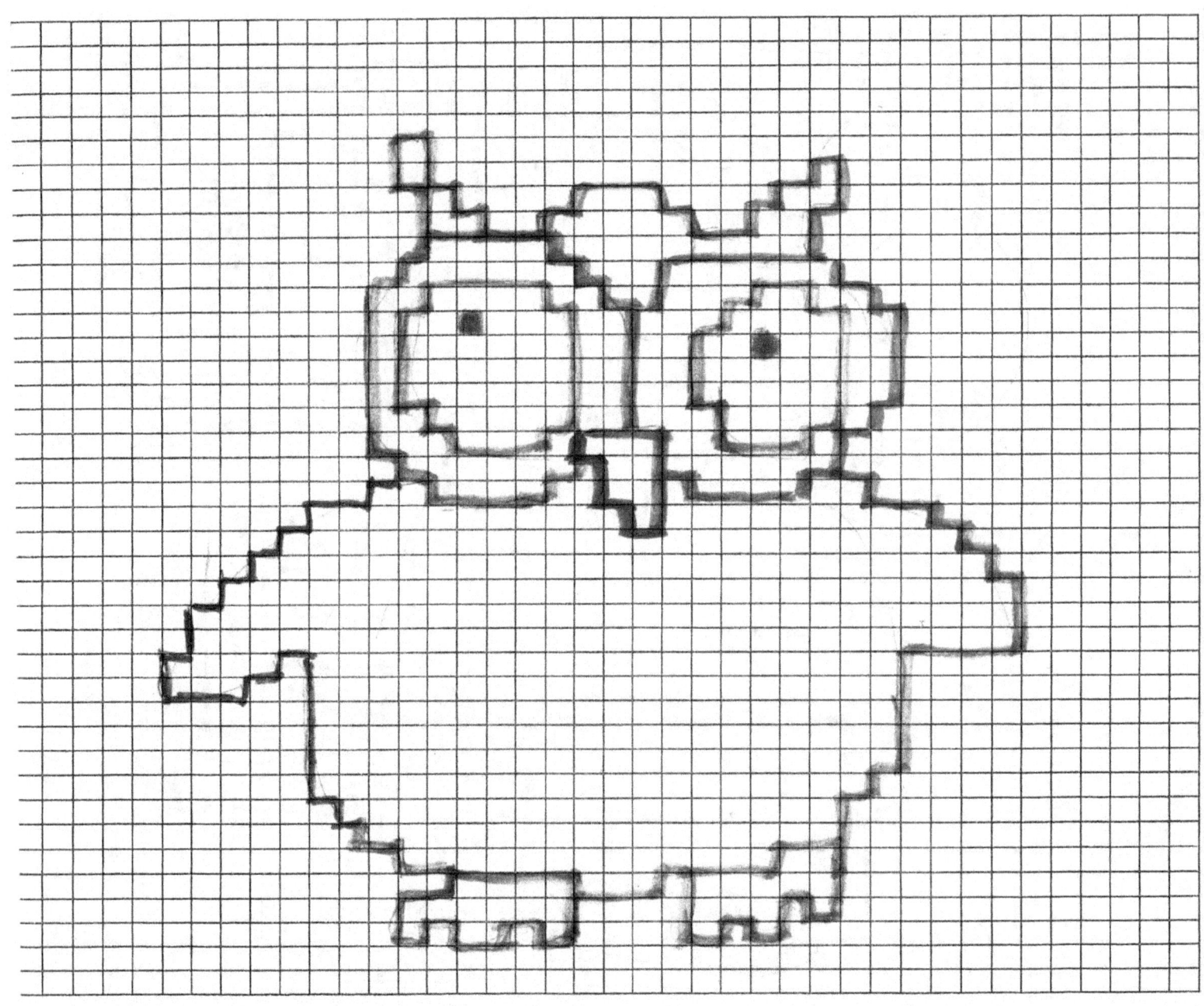

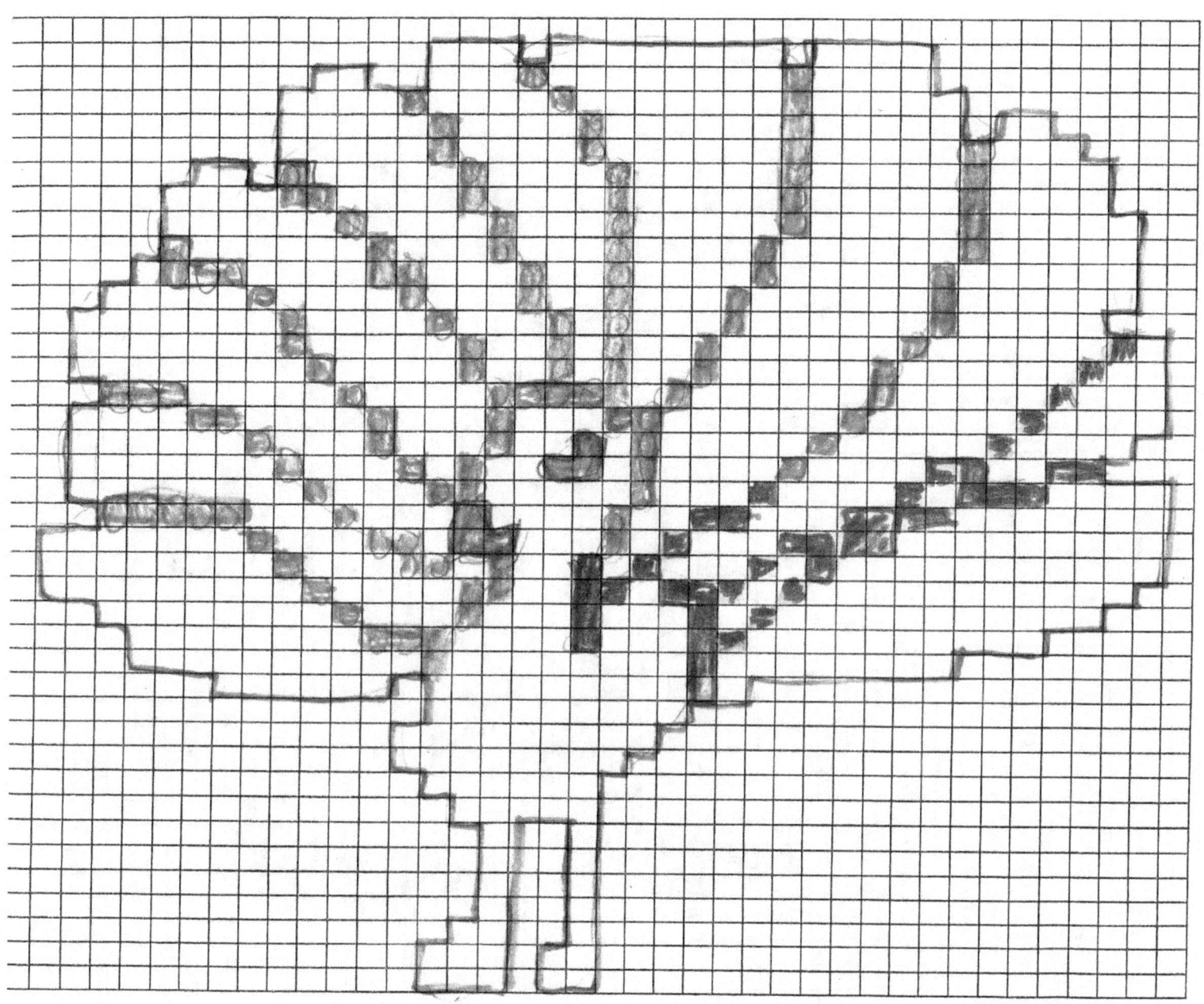

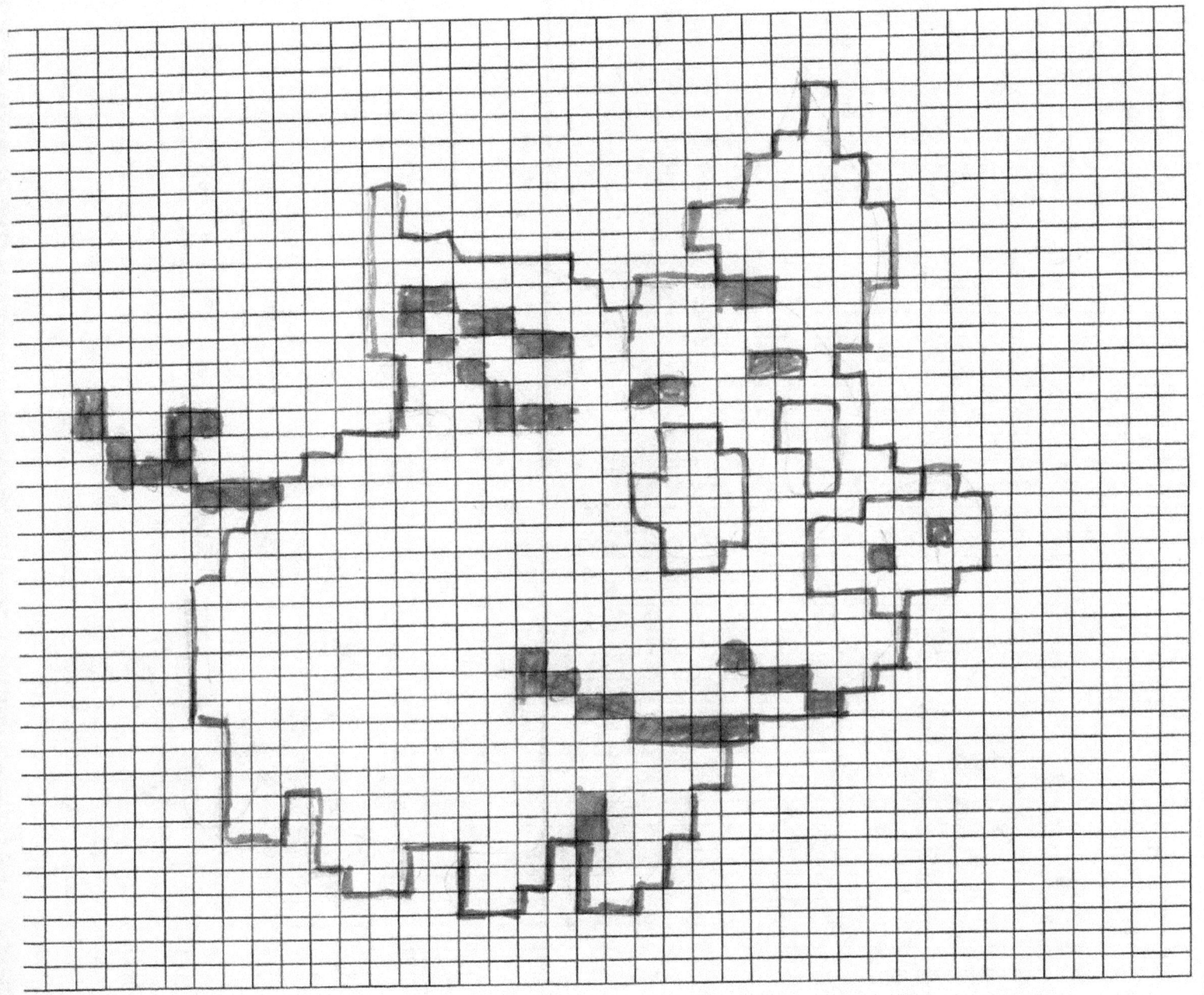

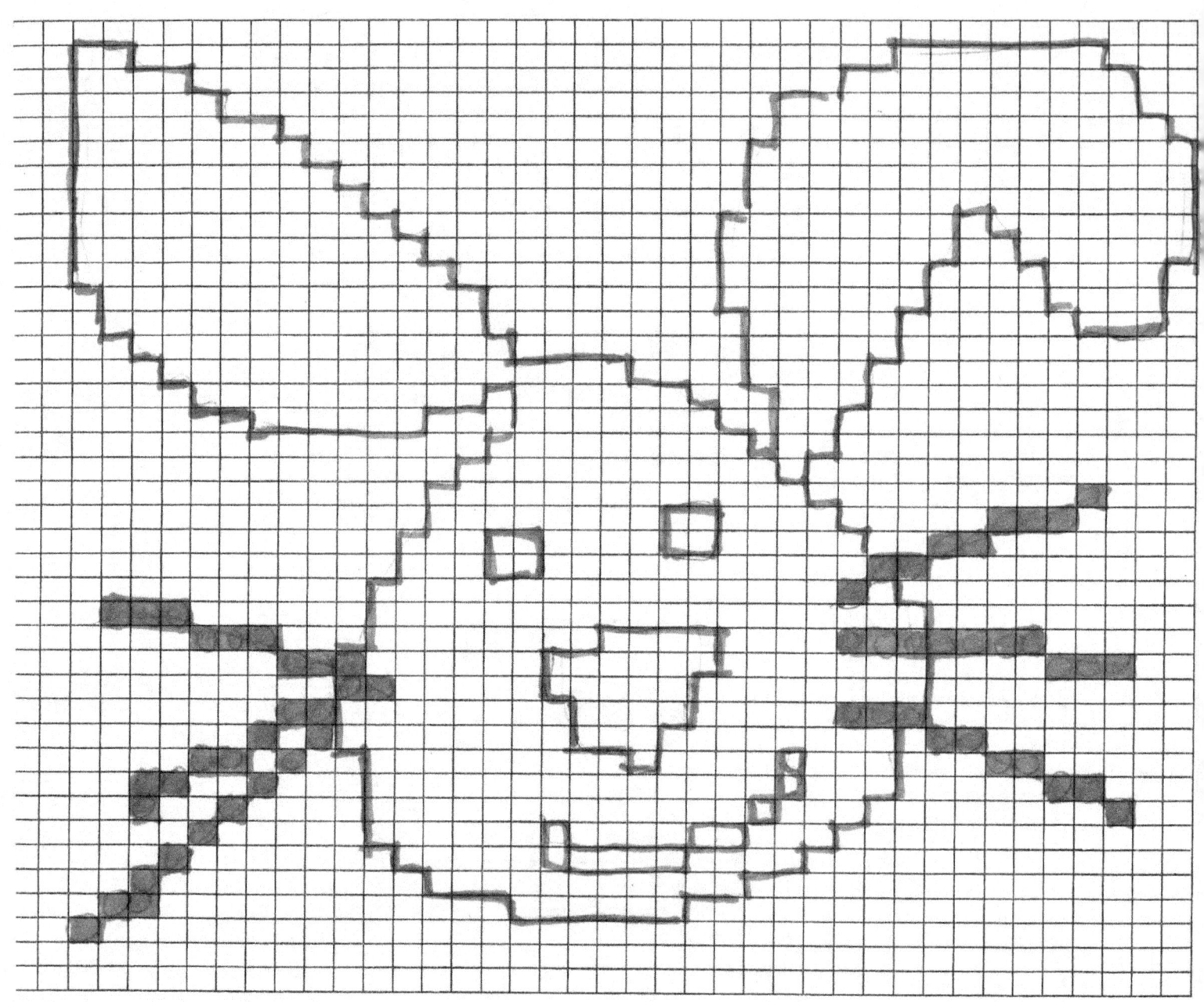

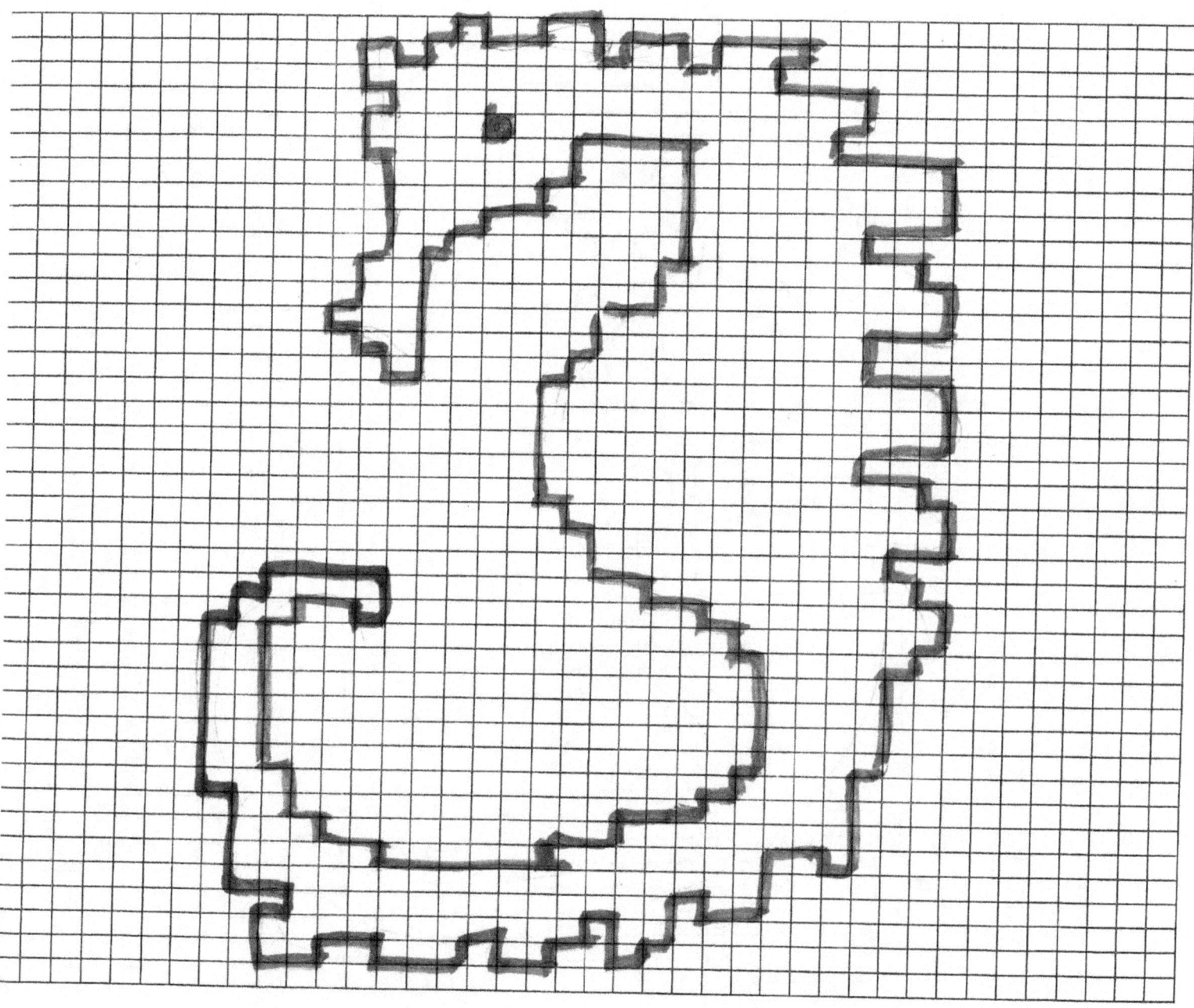

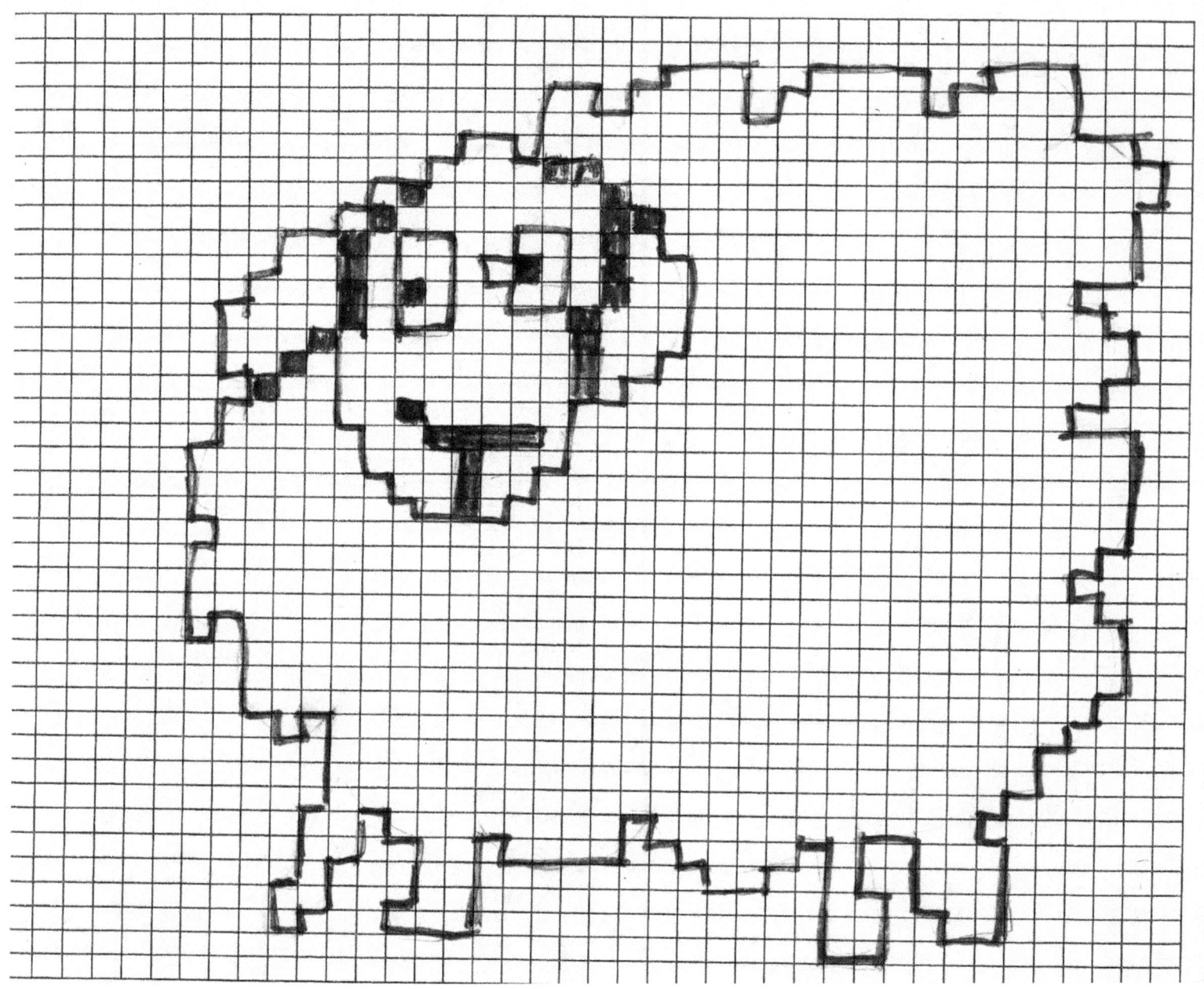

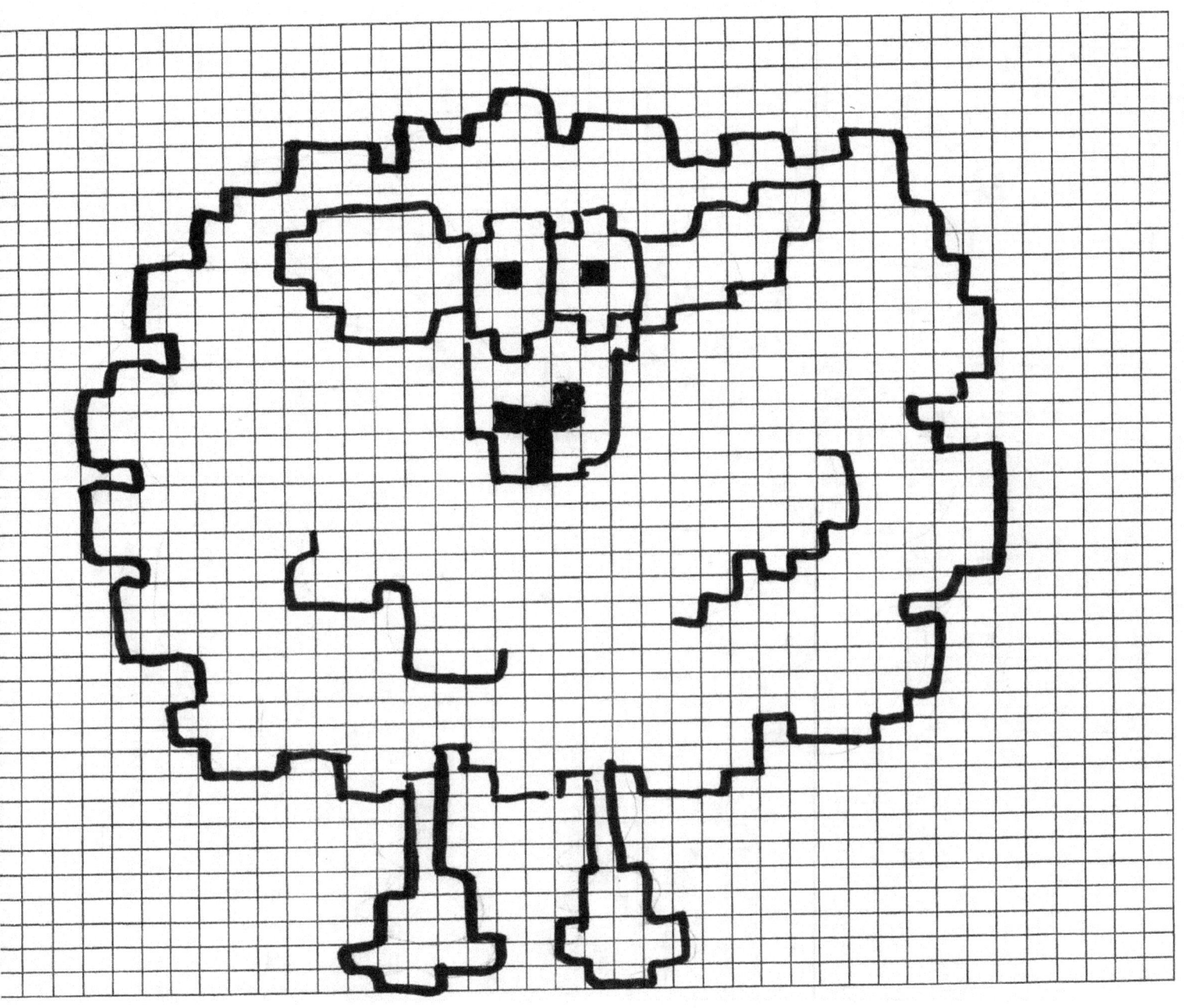

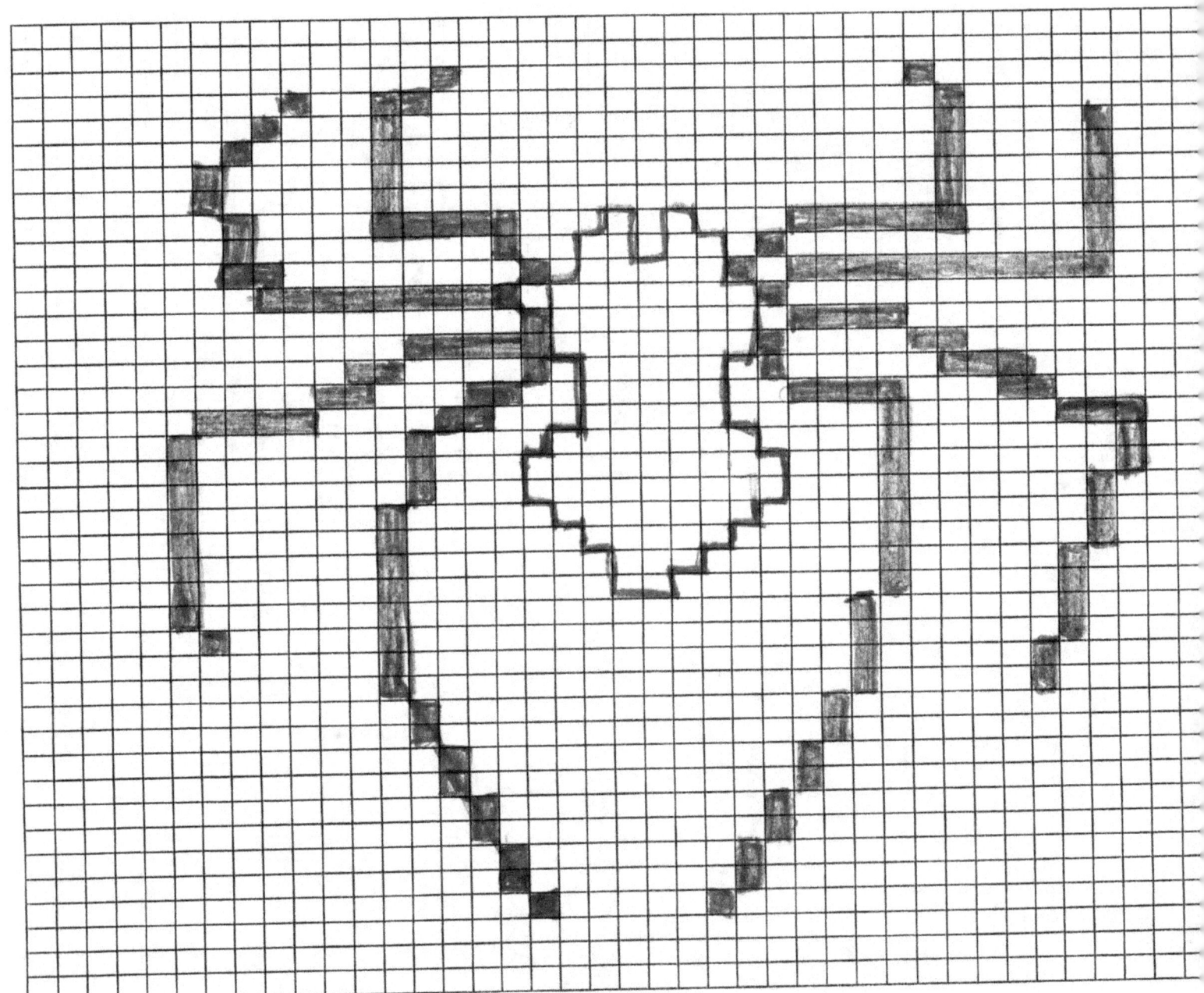

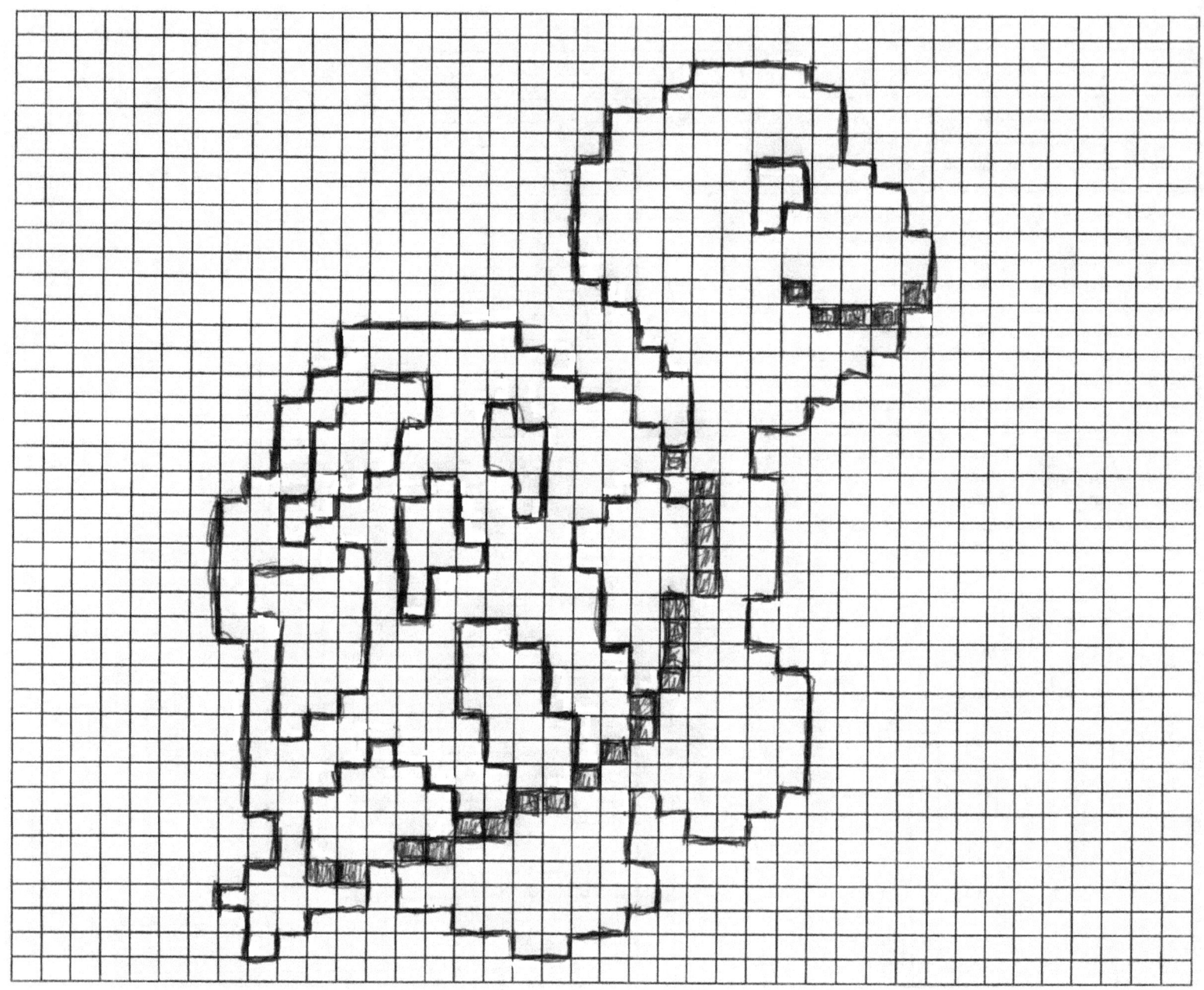

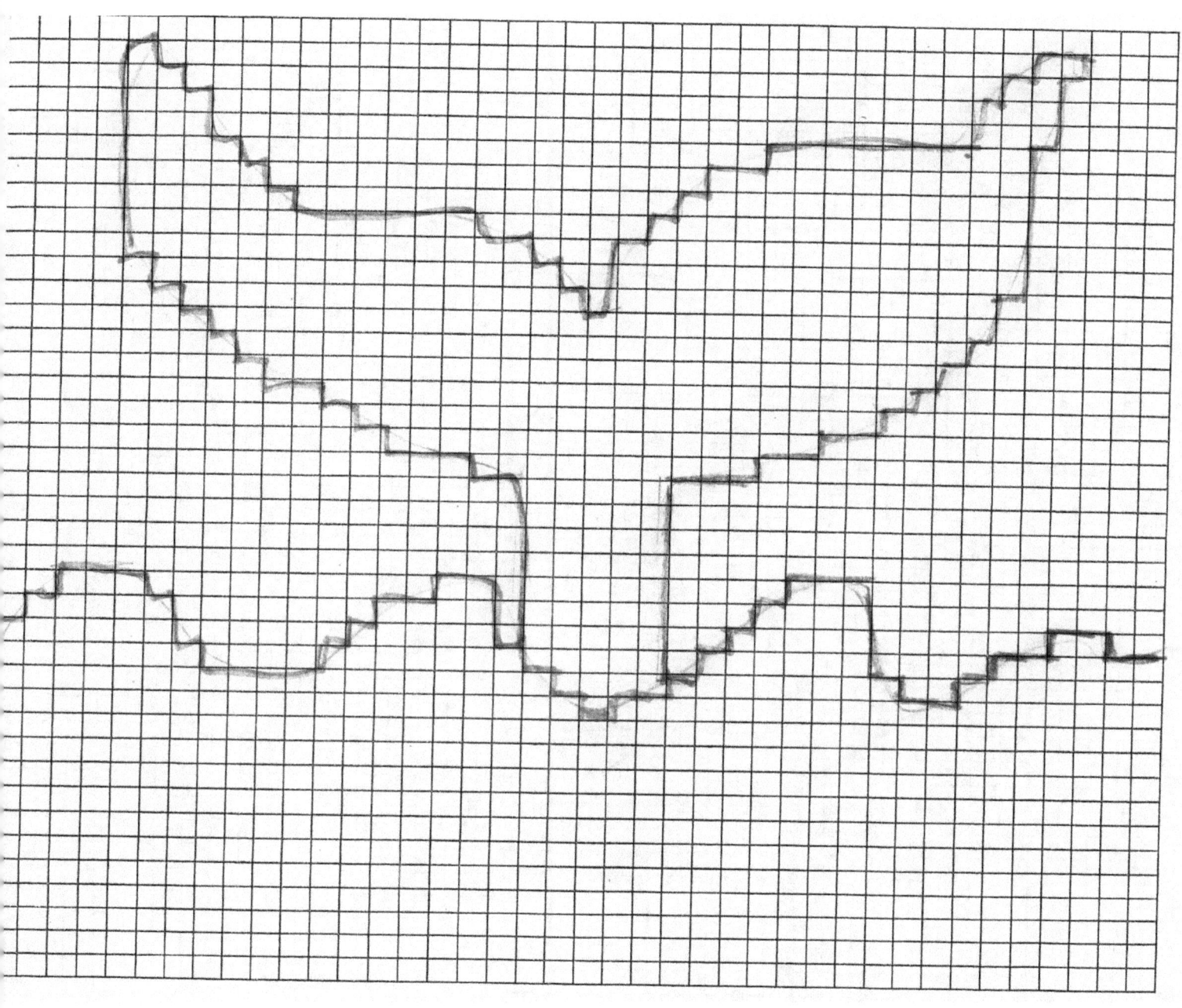

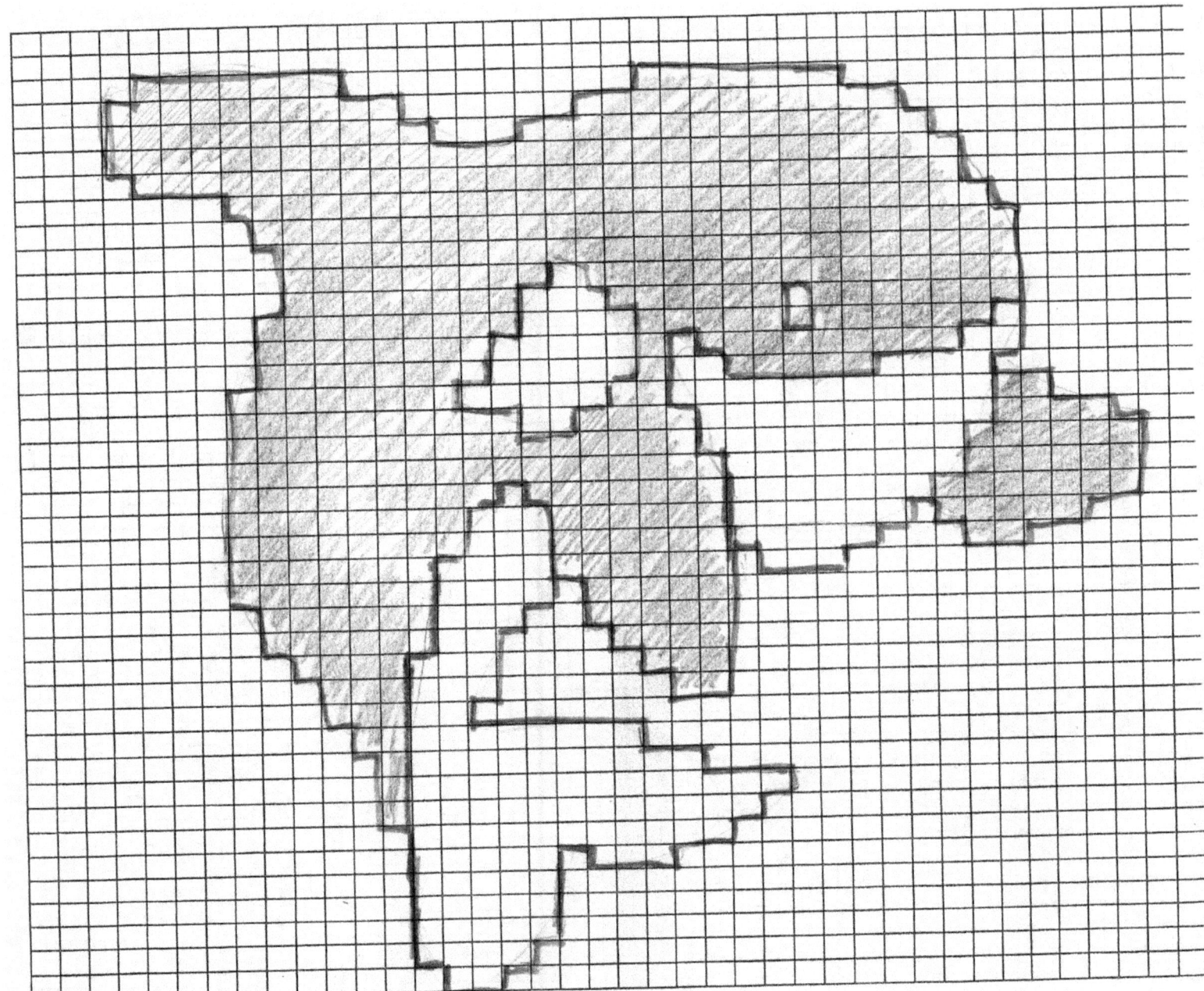

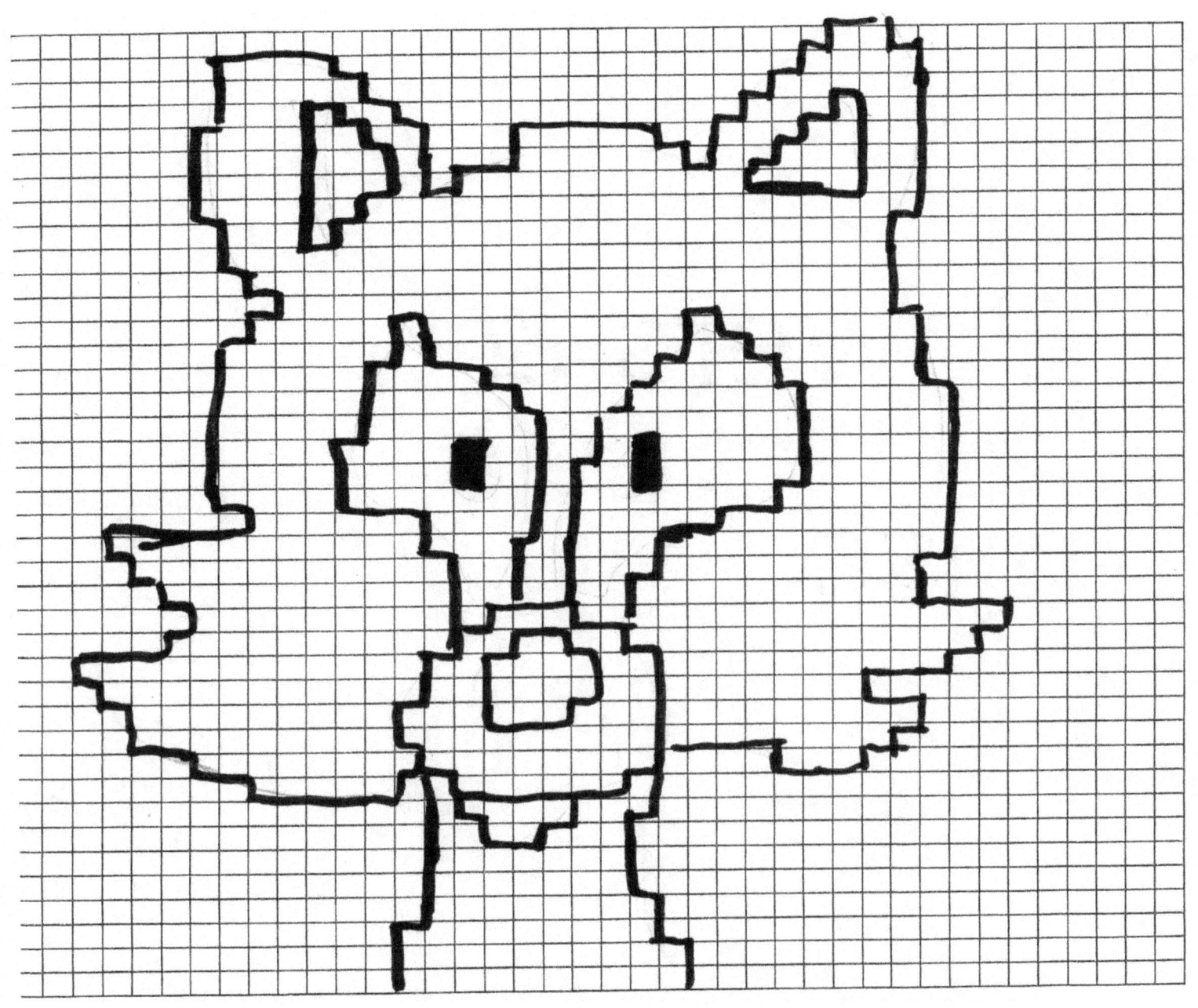

Flowers & misc.

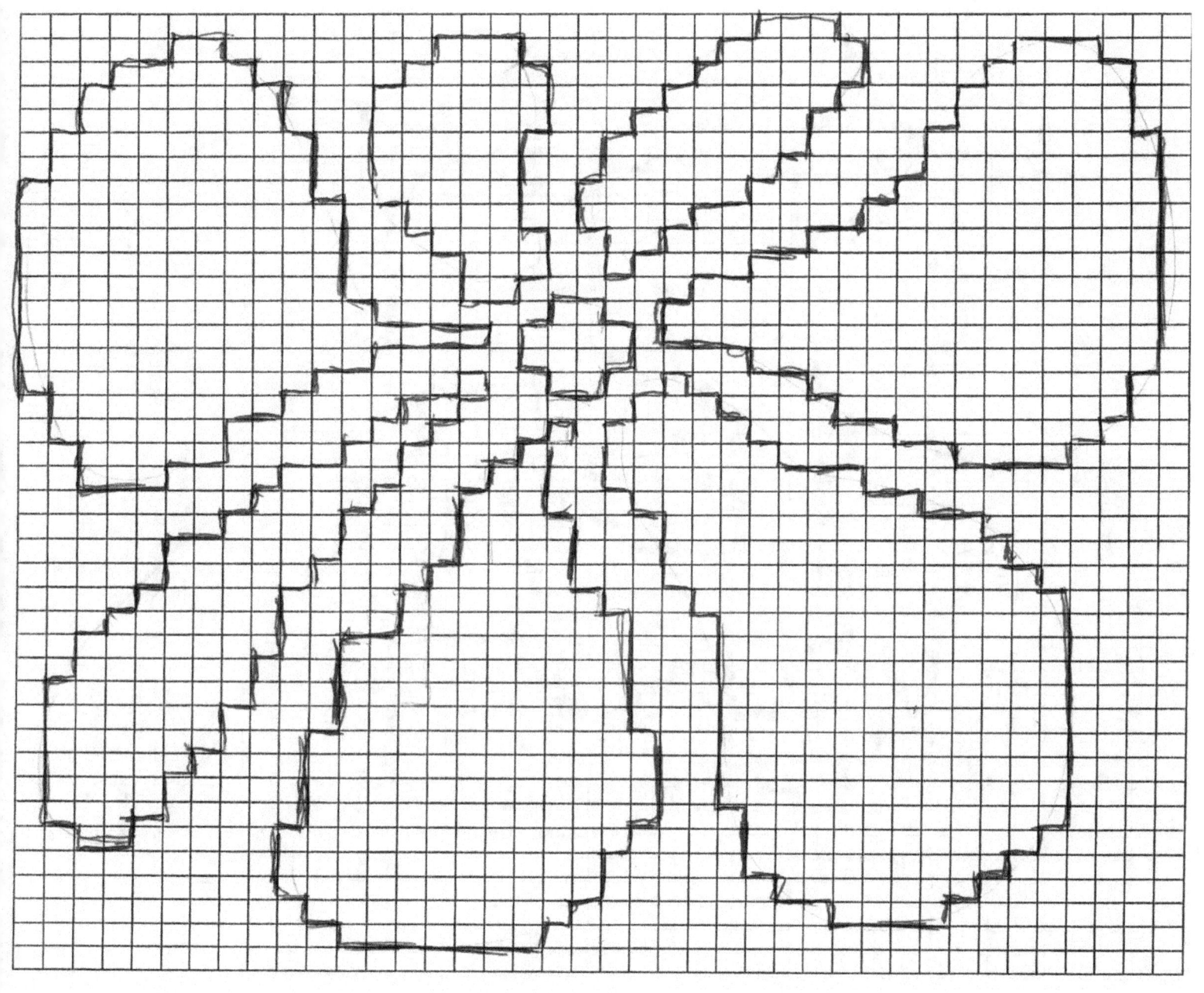

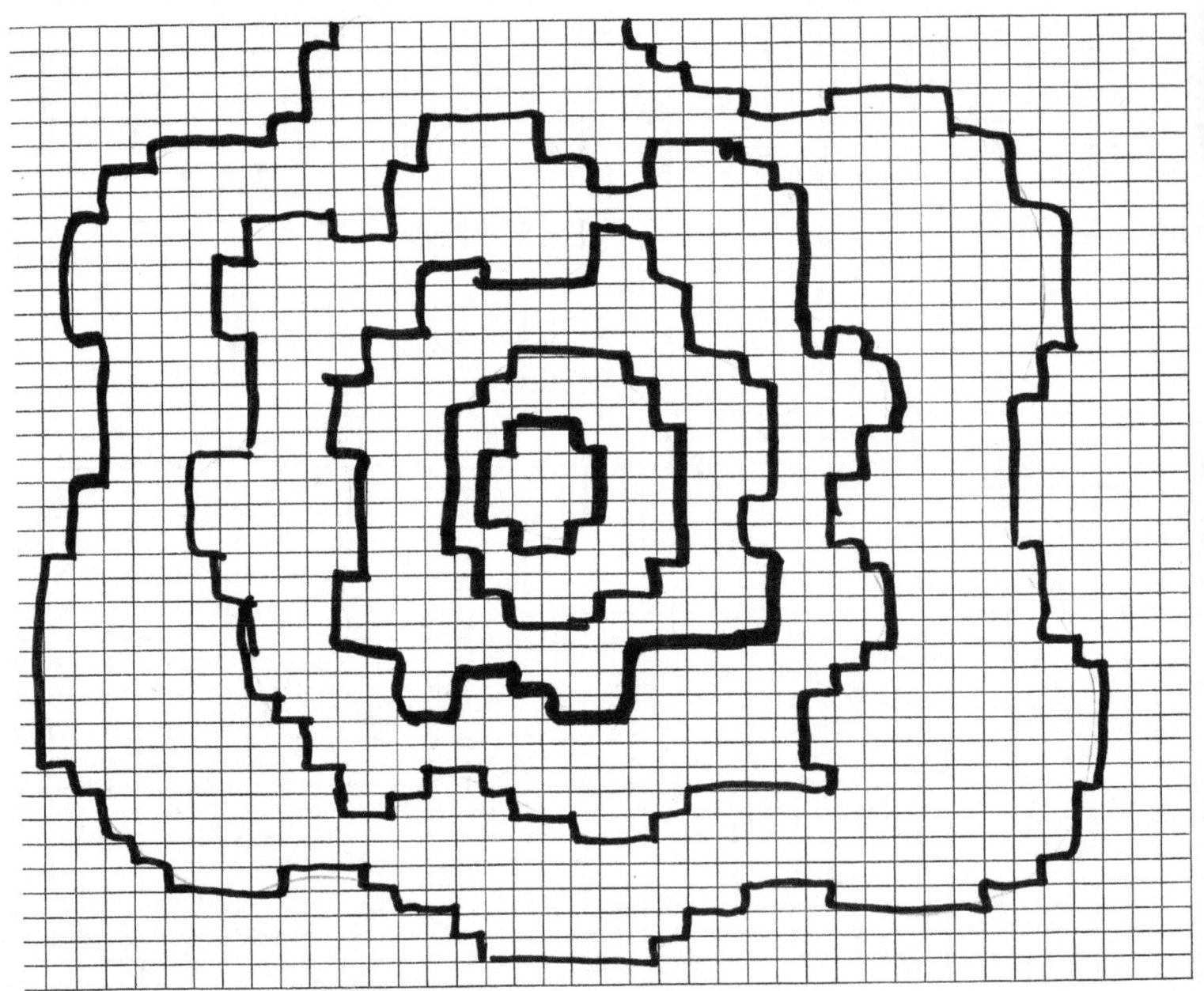

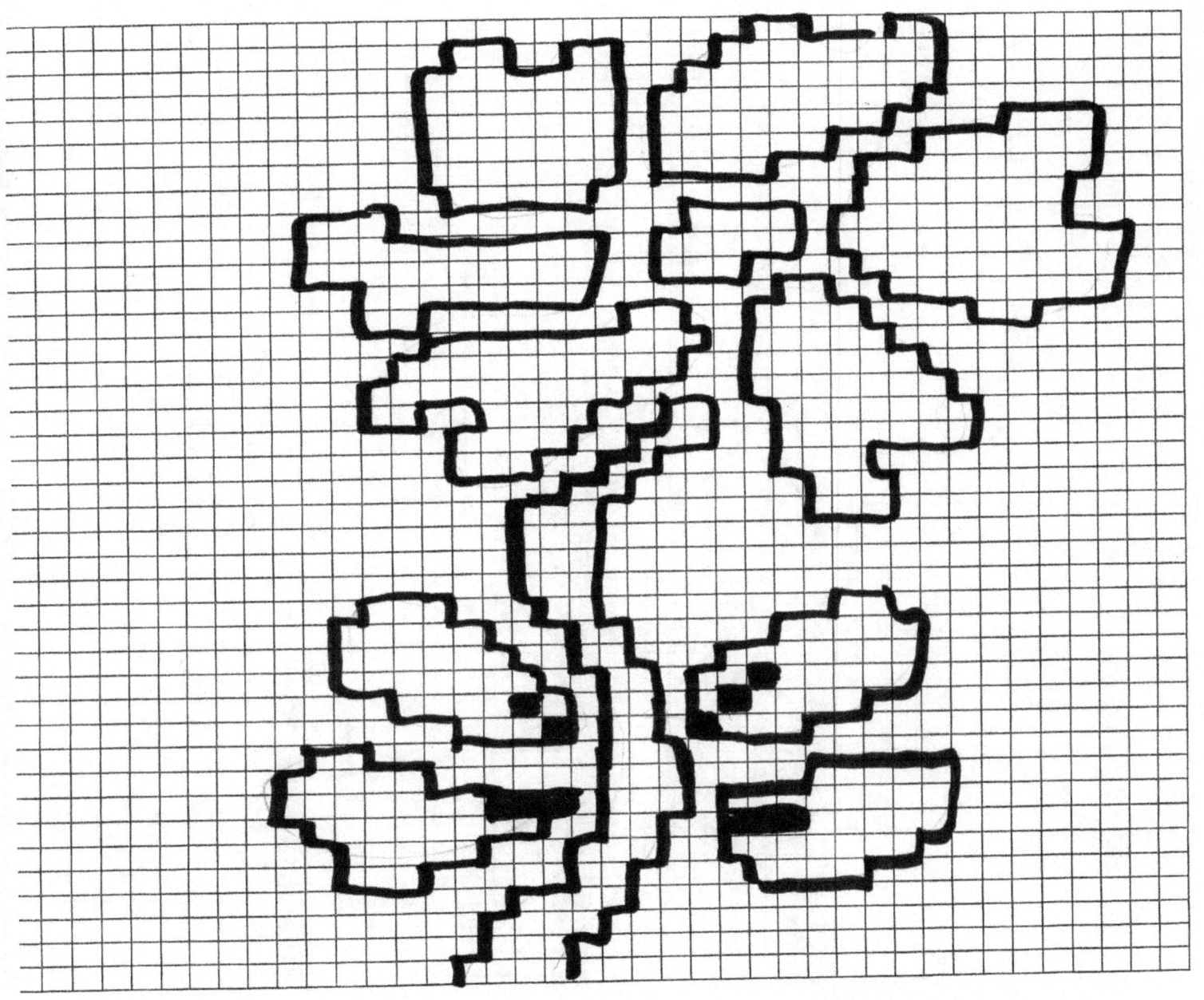

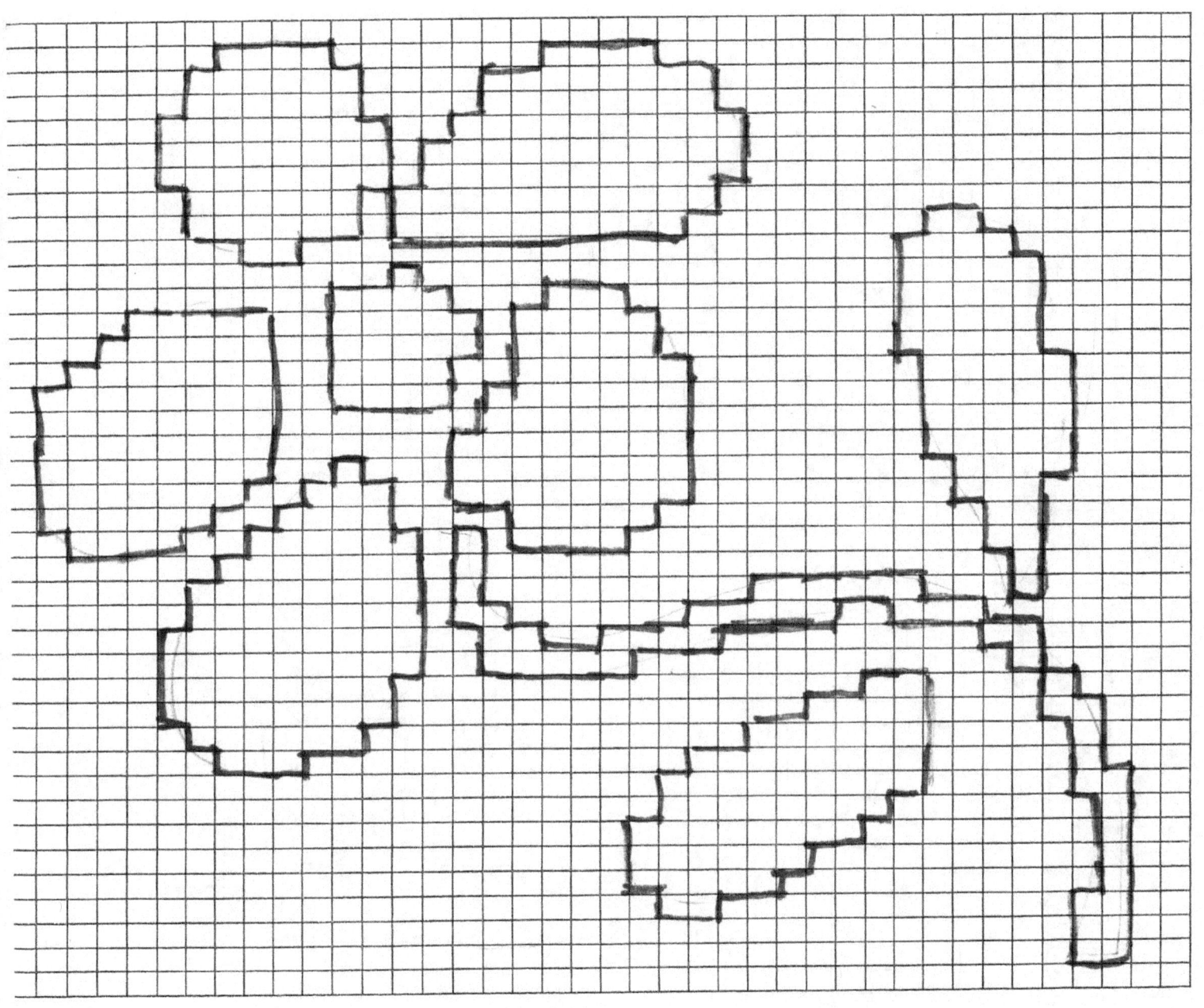

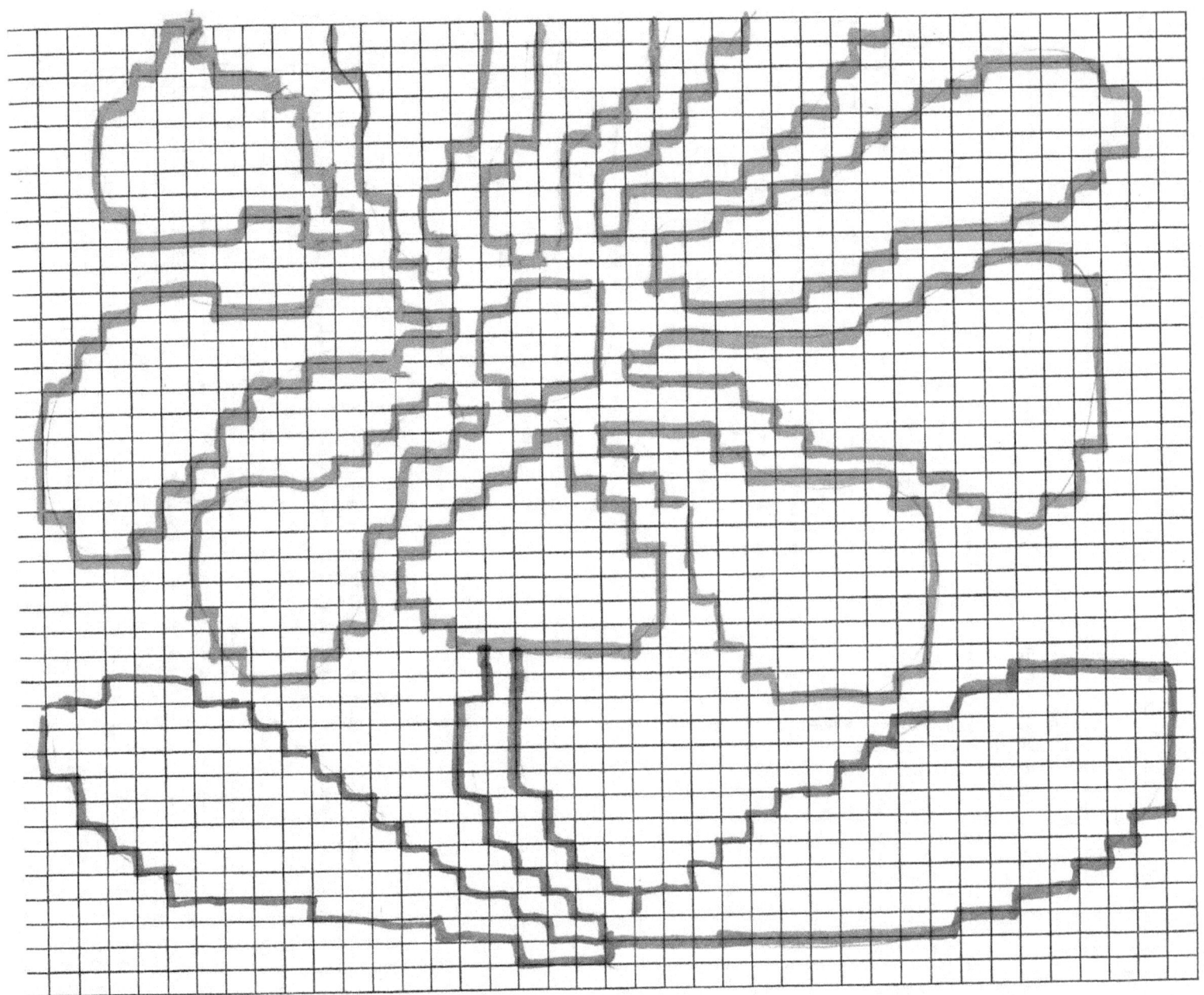

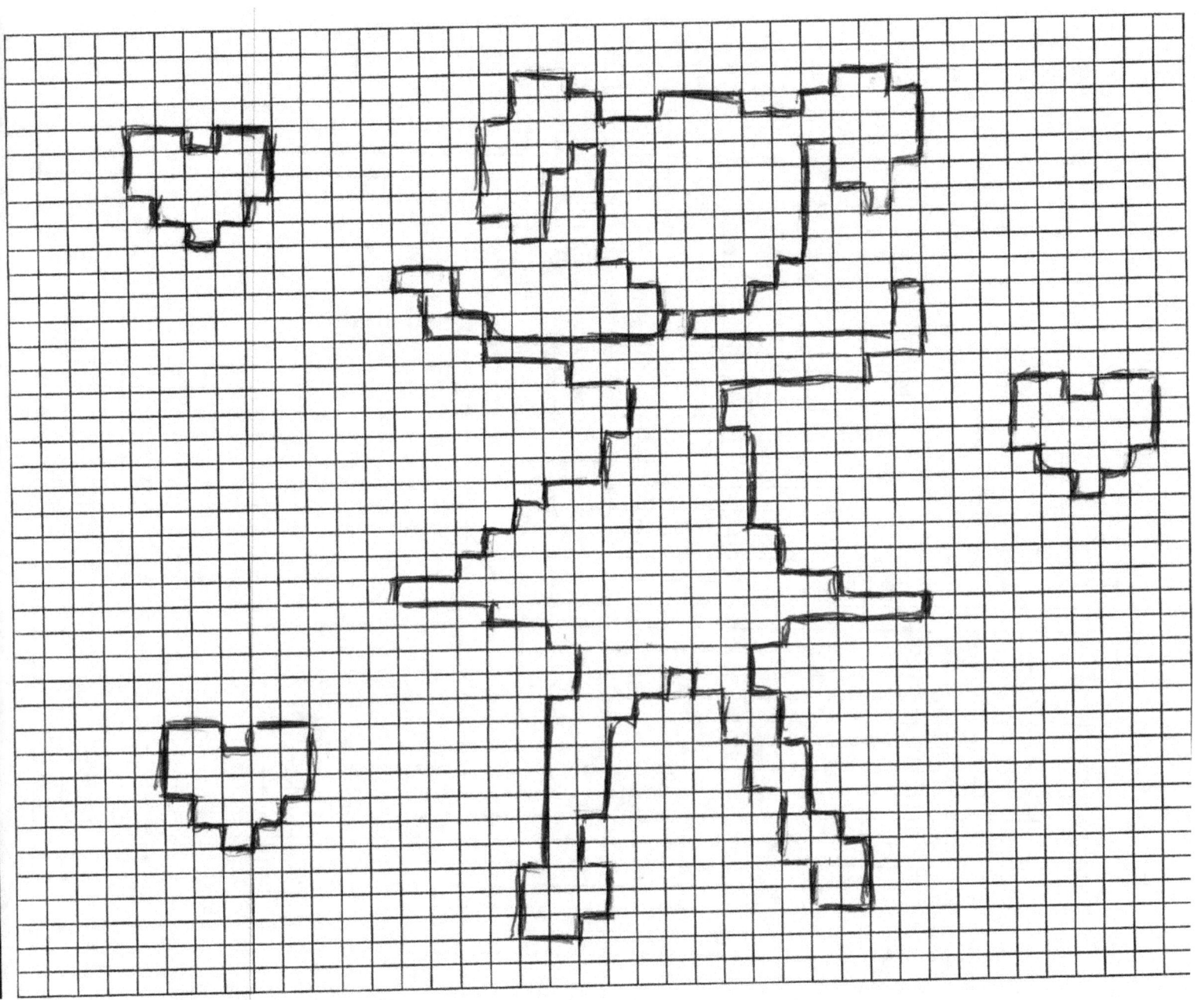

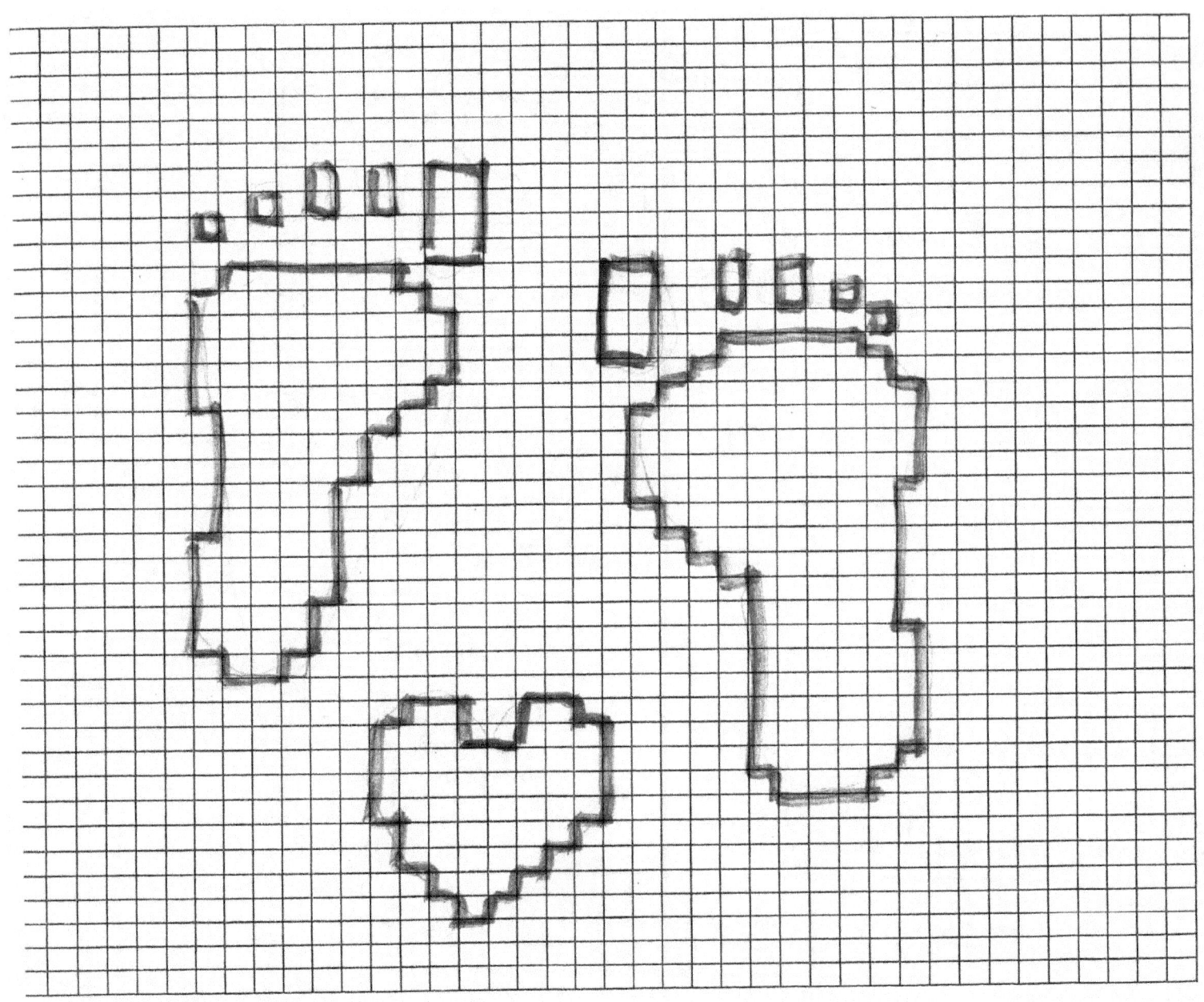

Numbers

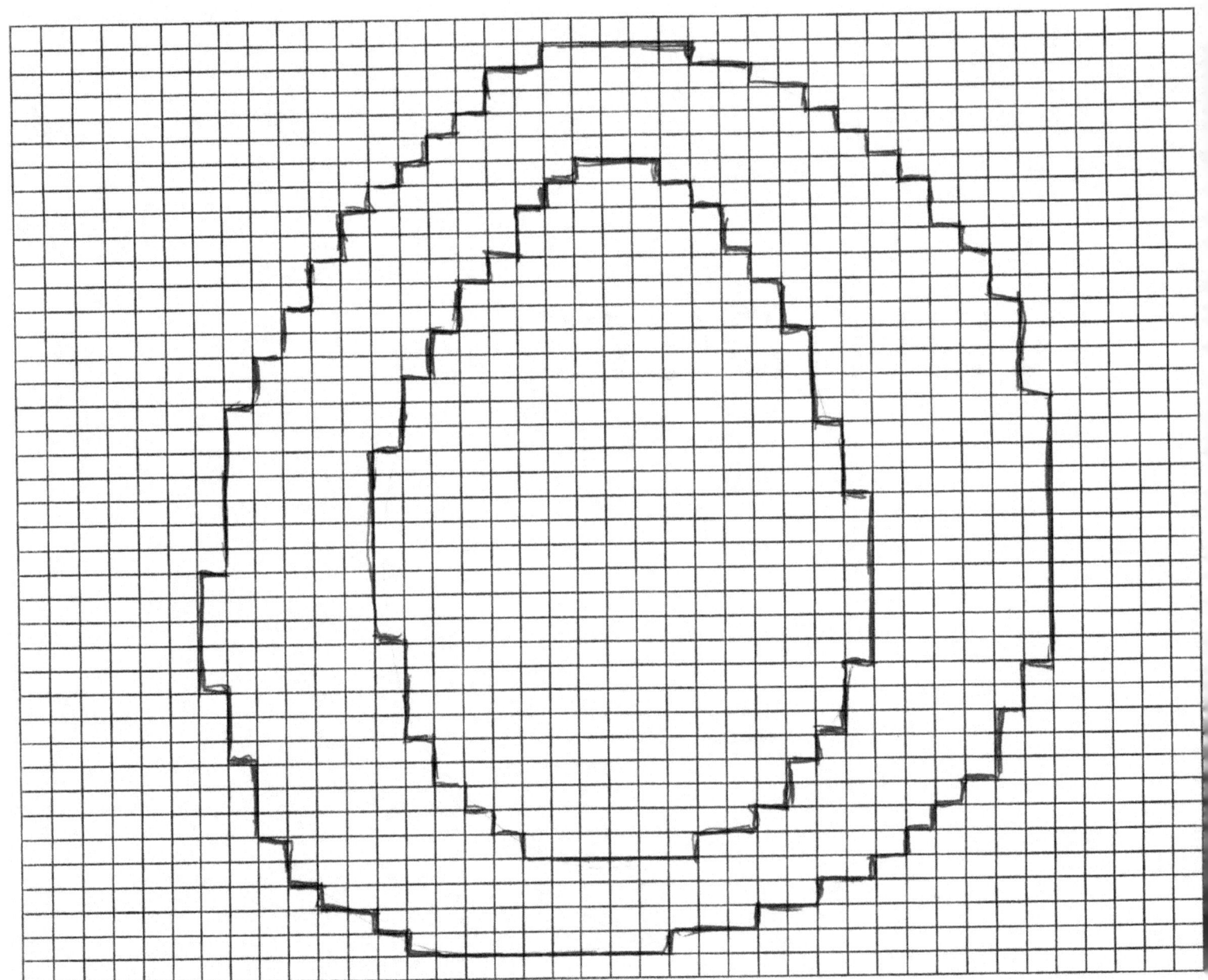

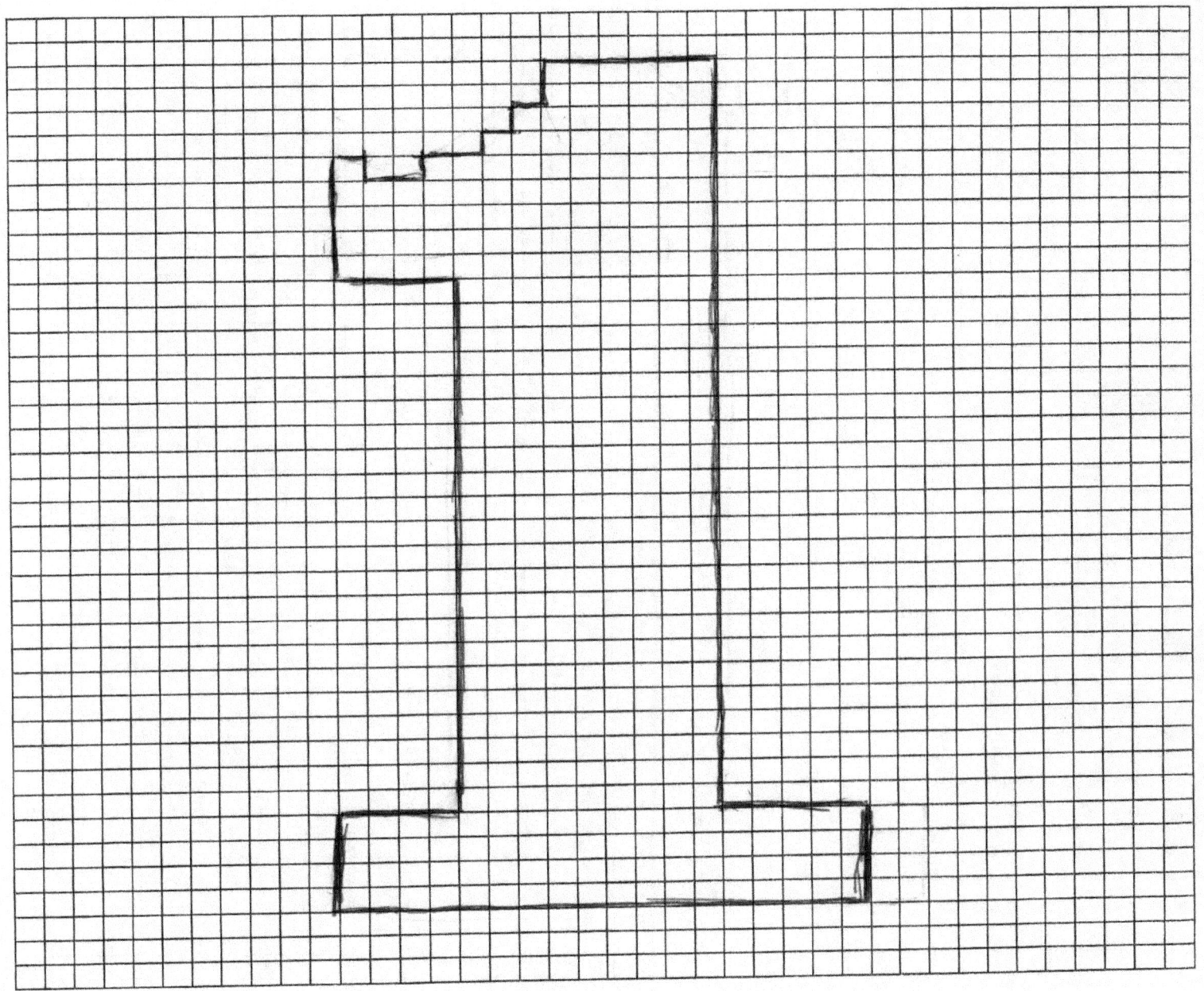

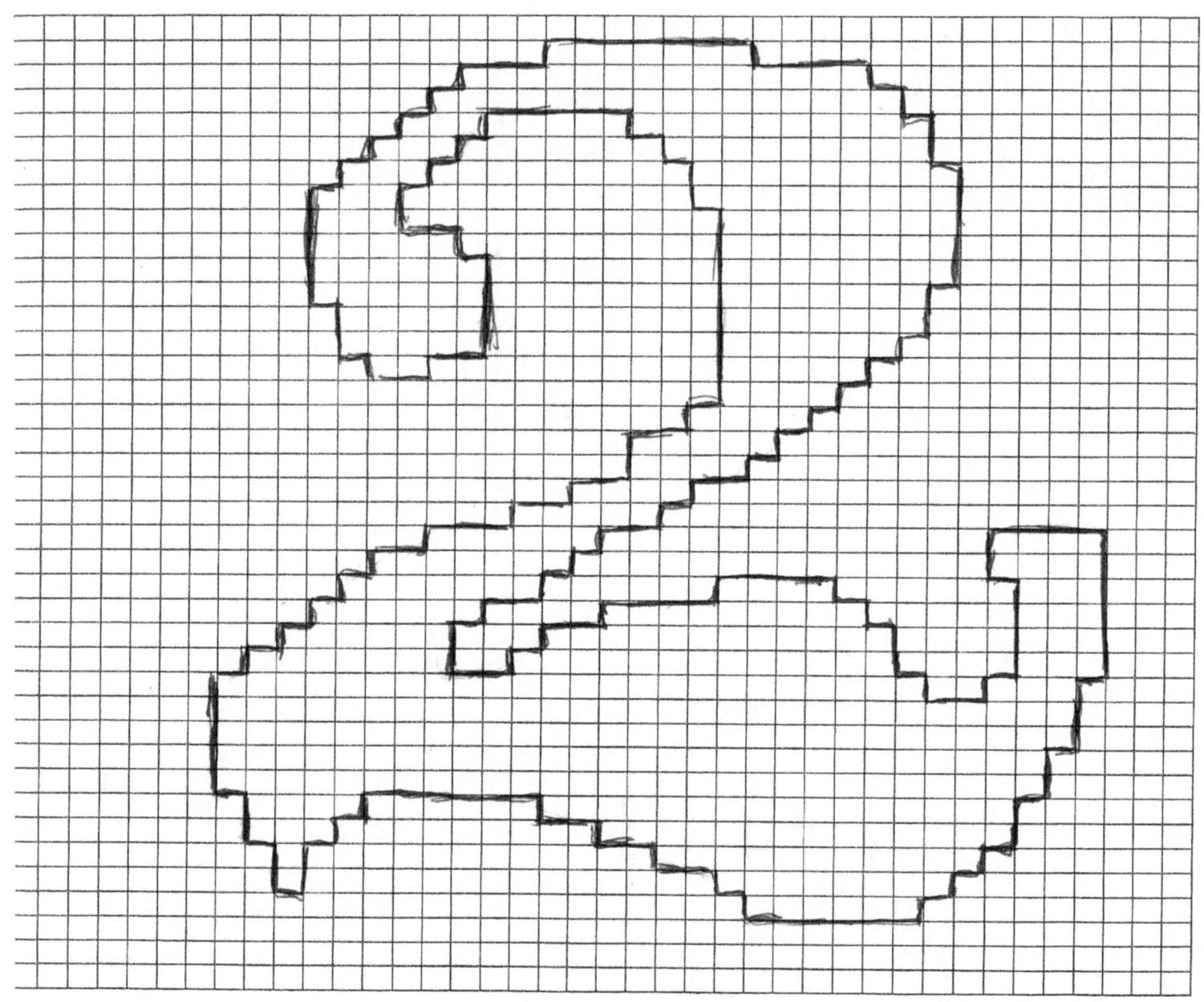

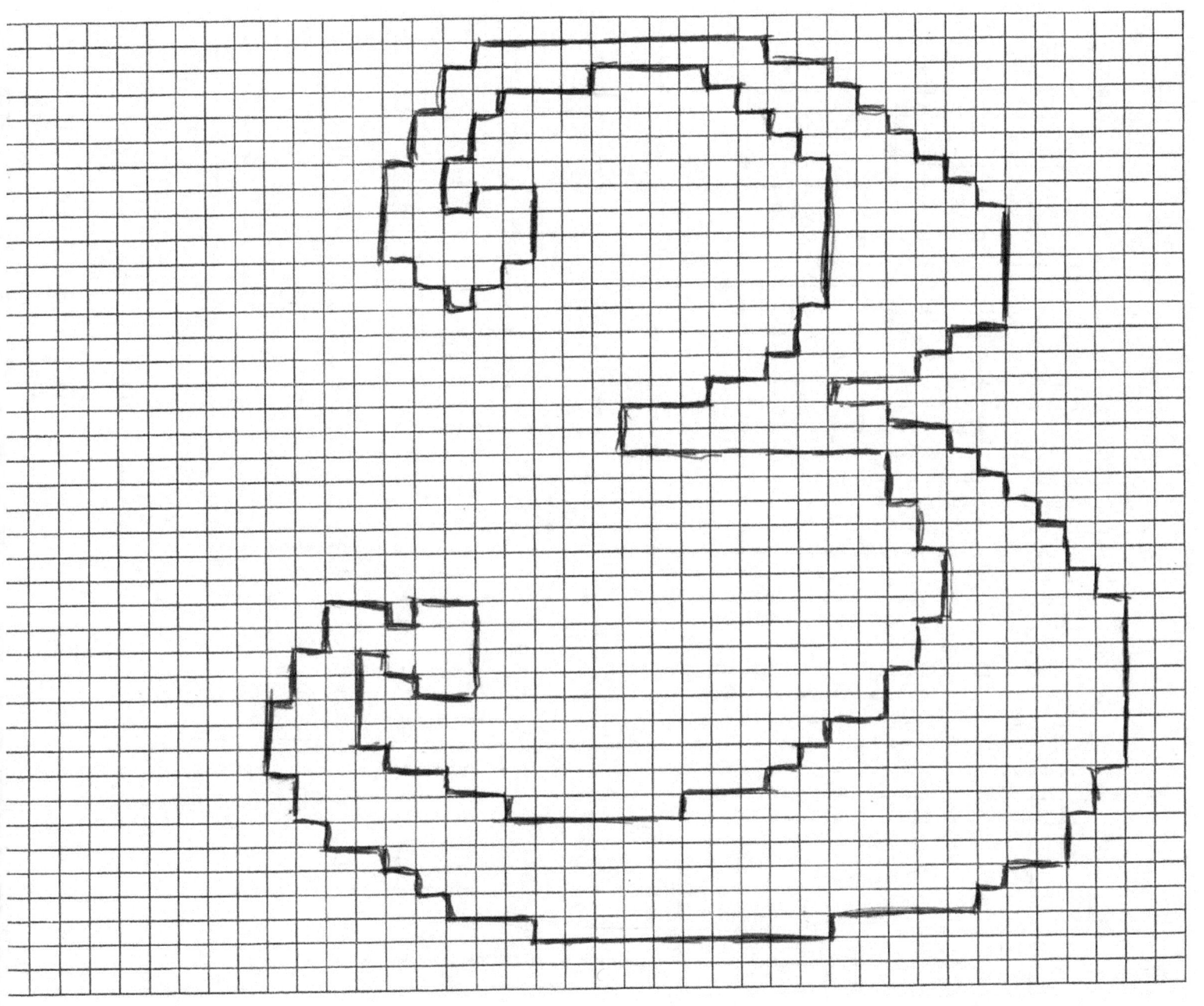

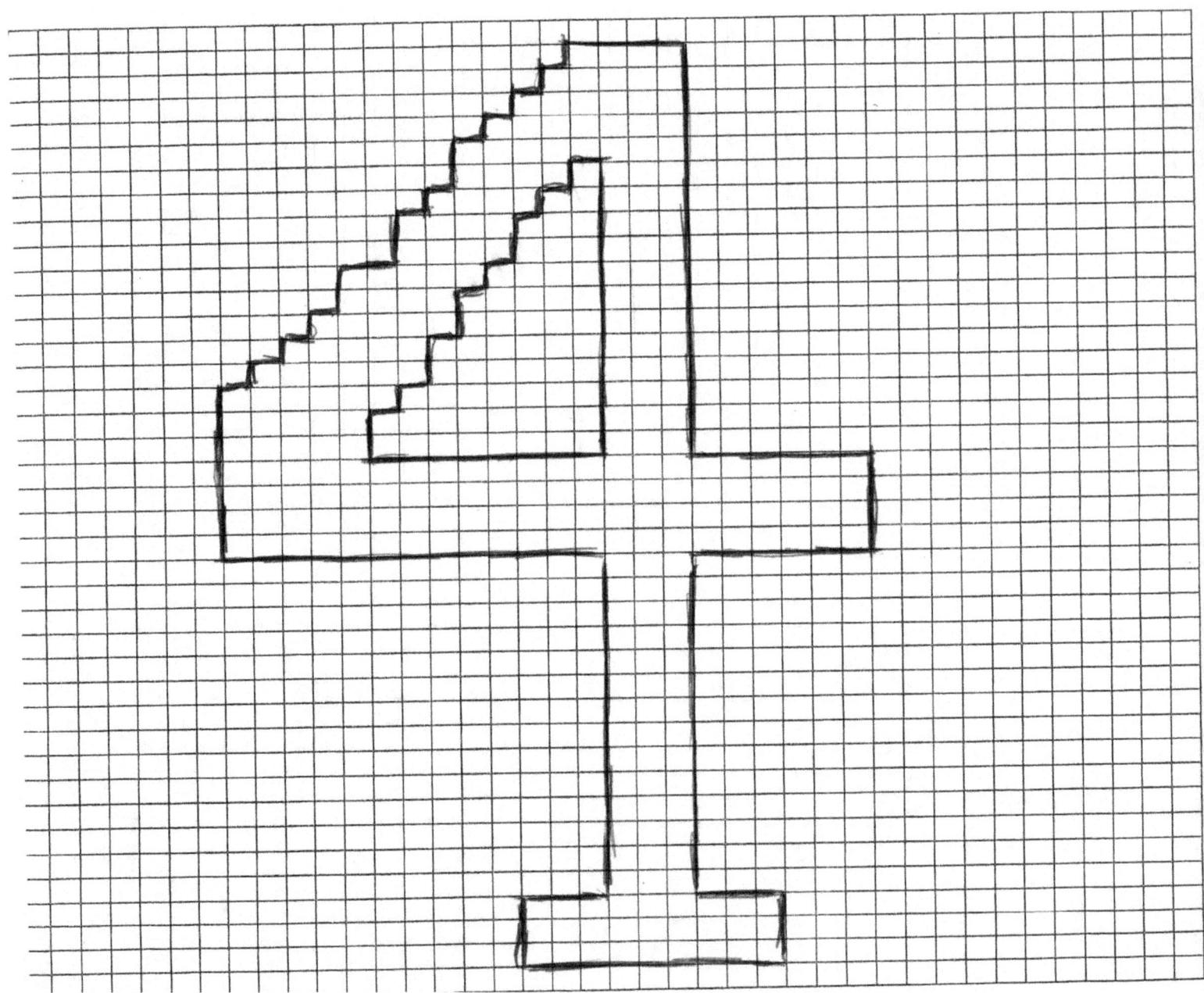

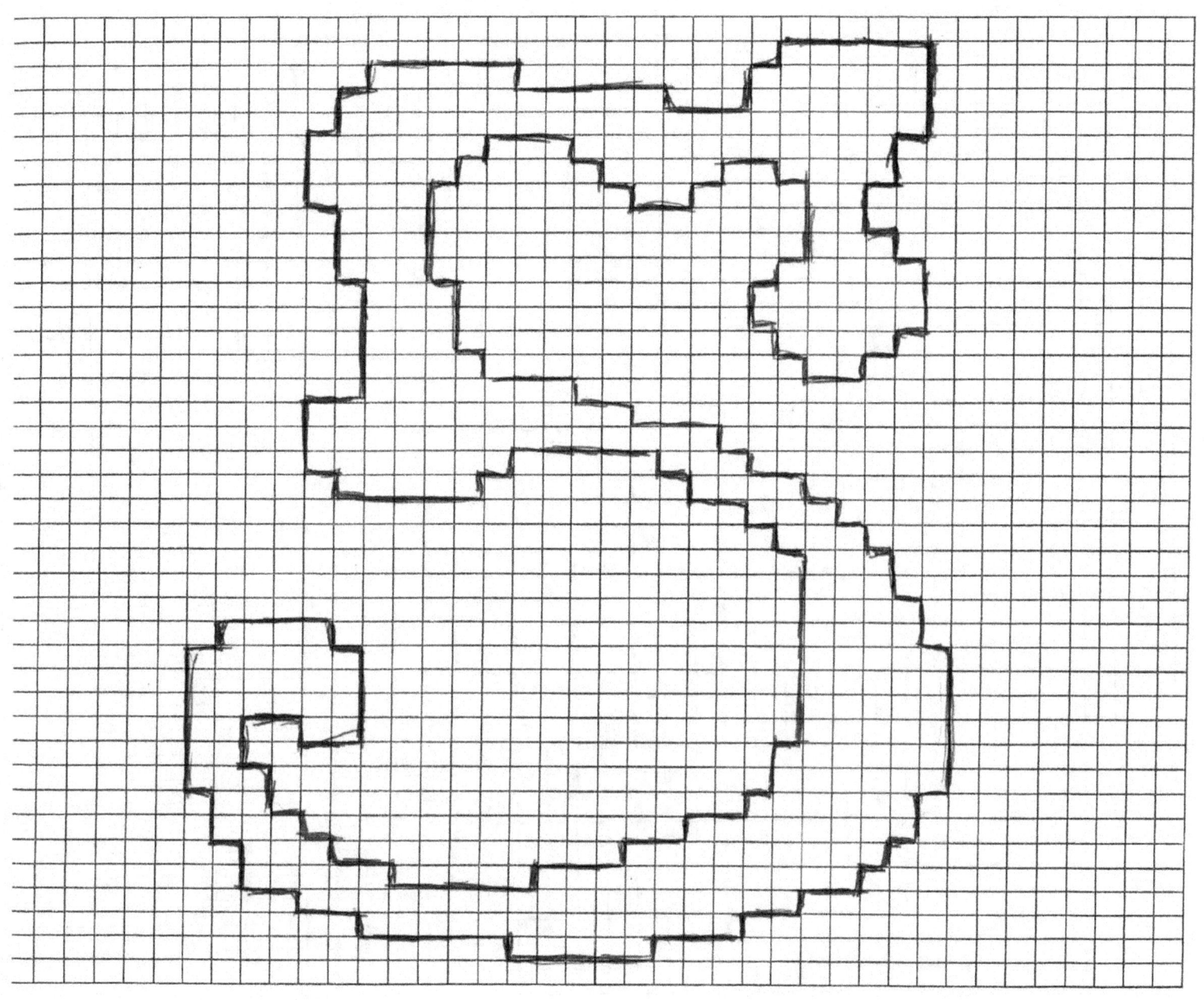

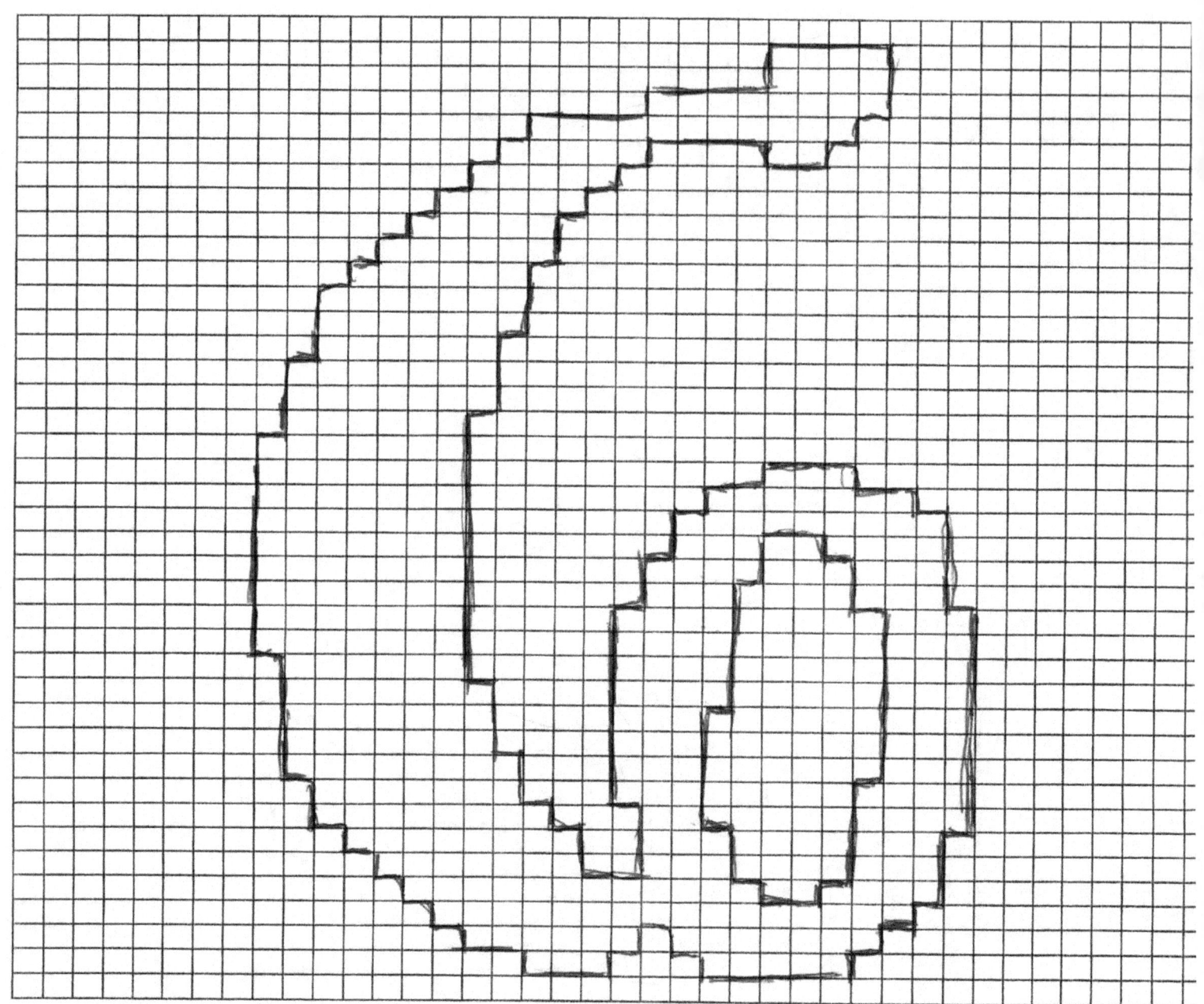

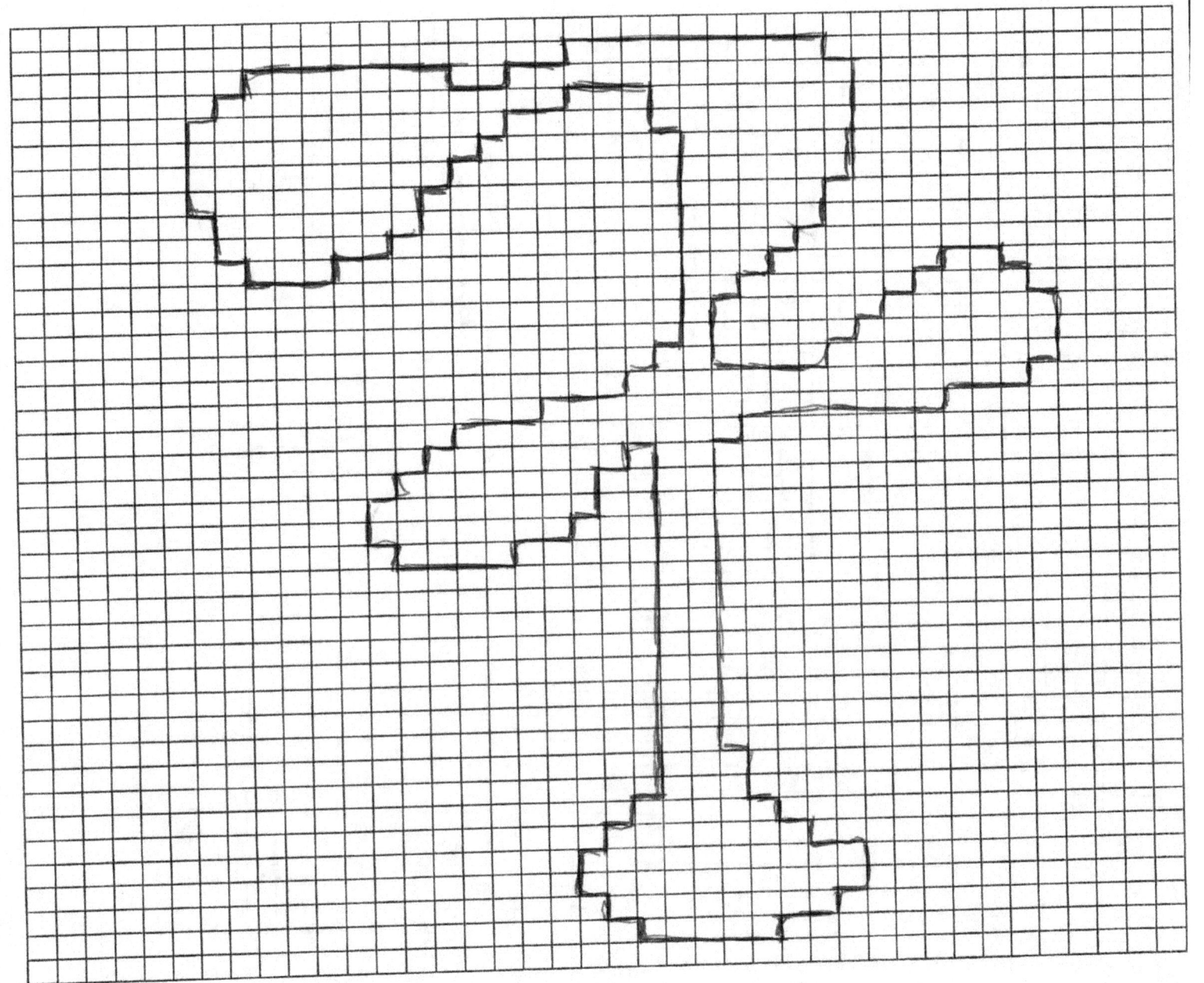

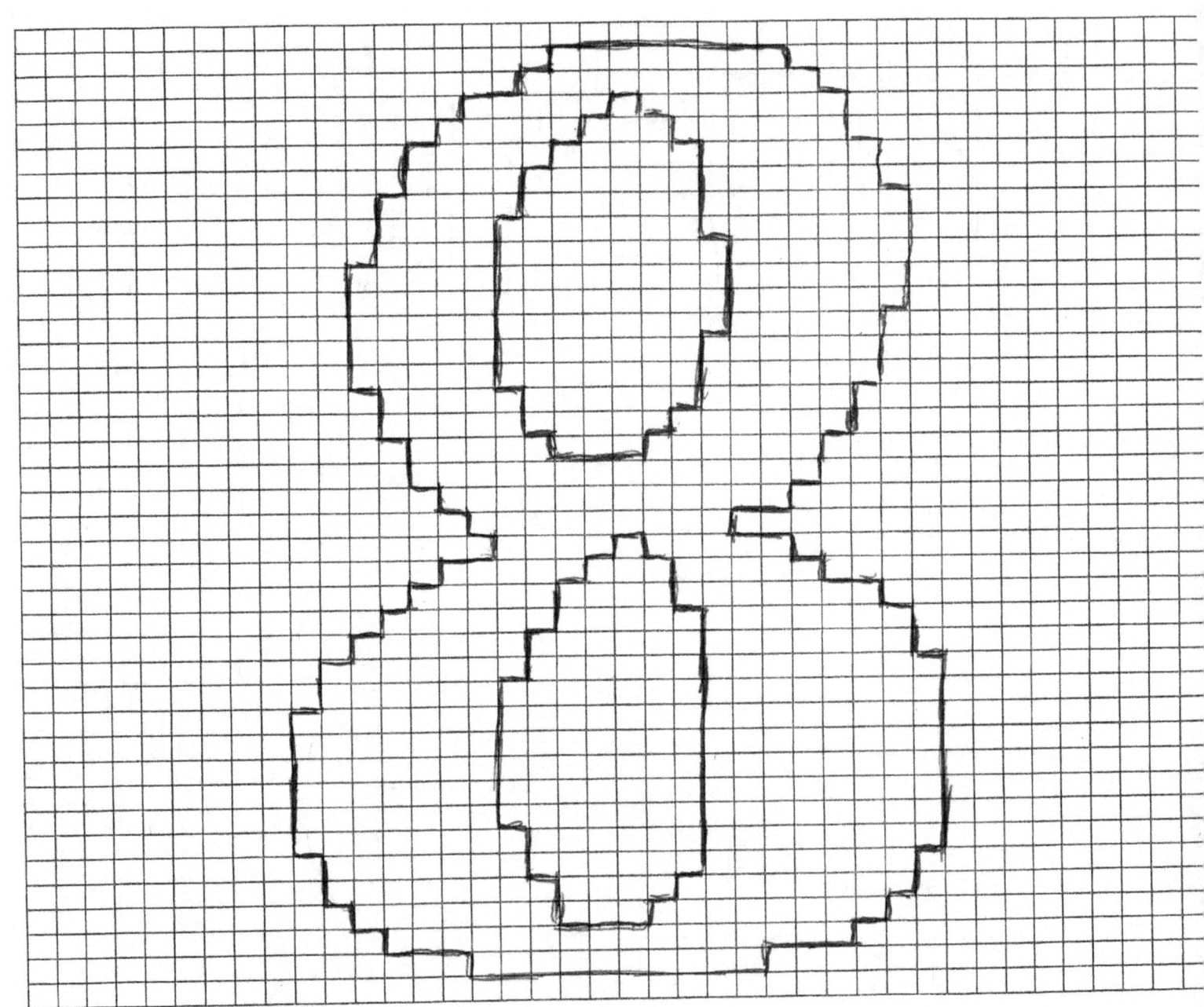

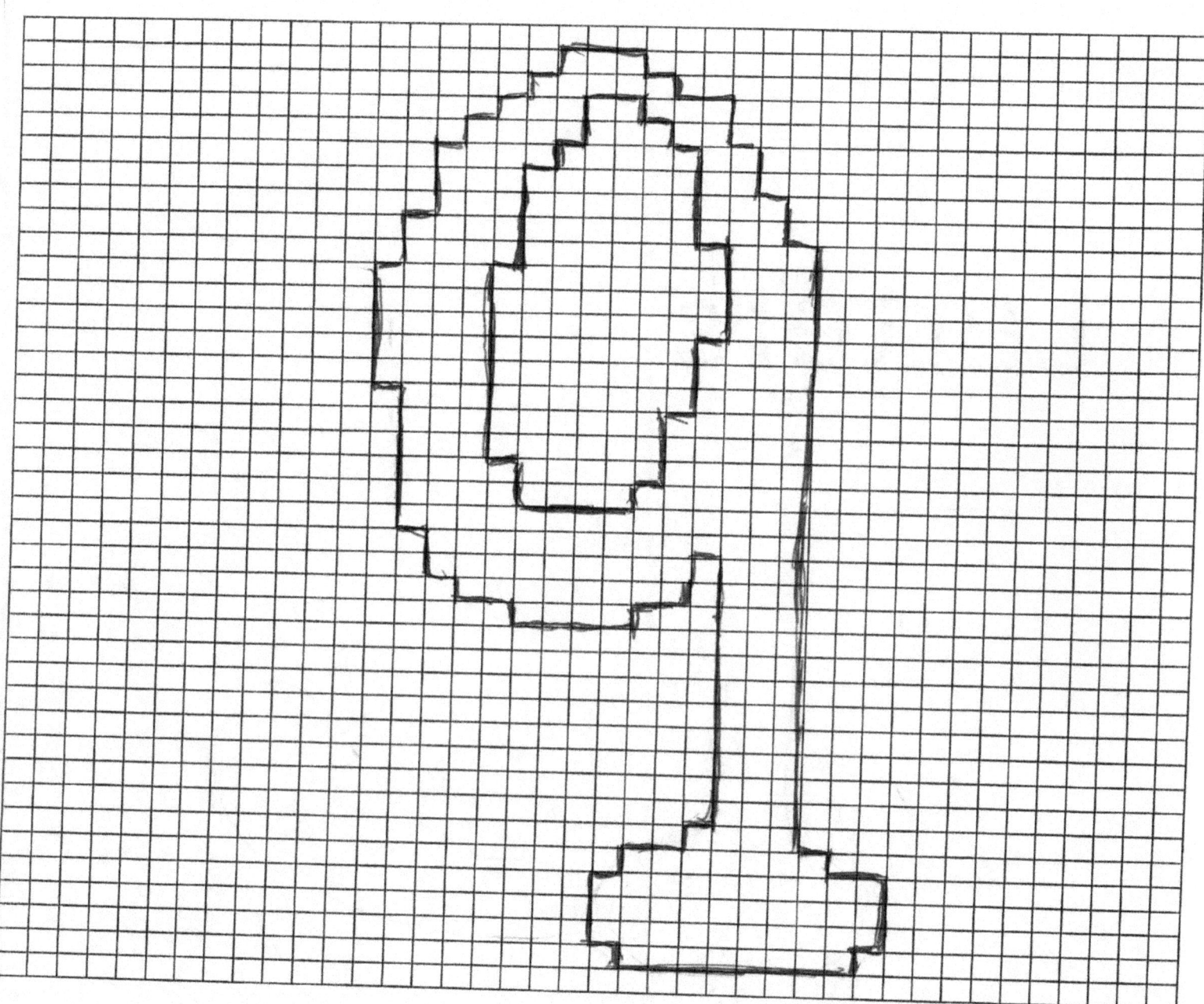

Letters

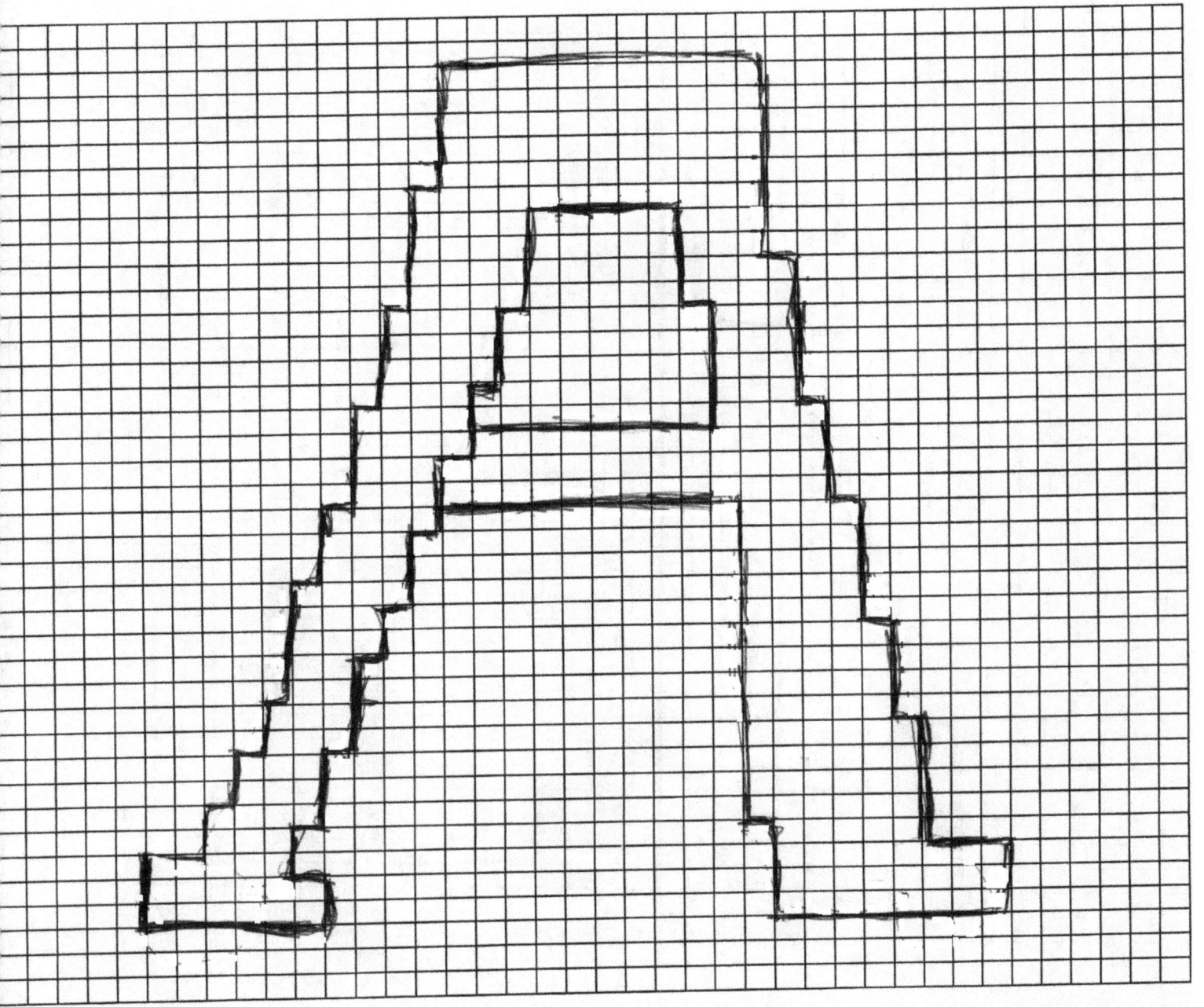

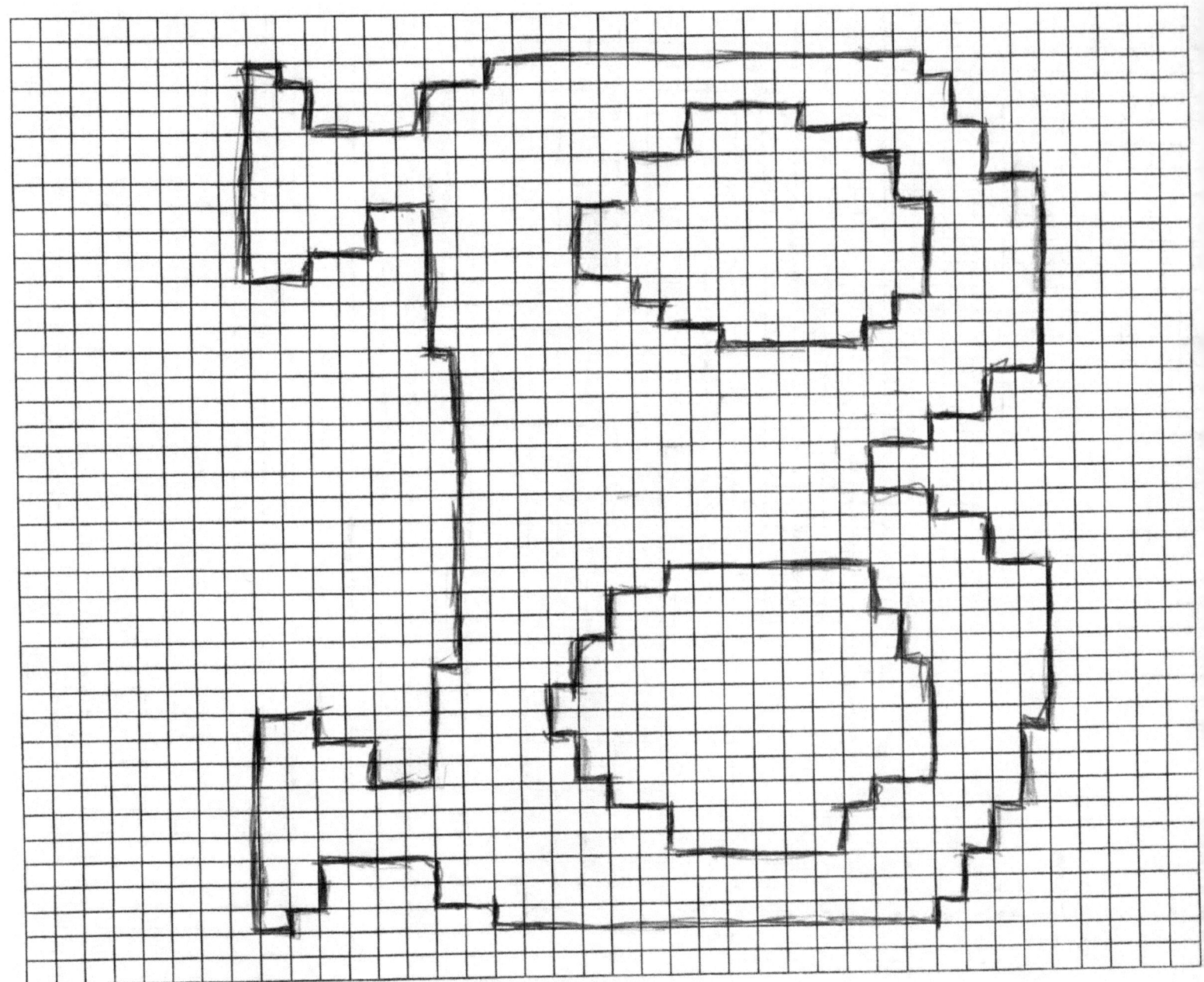

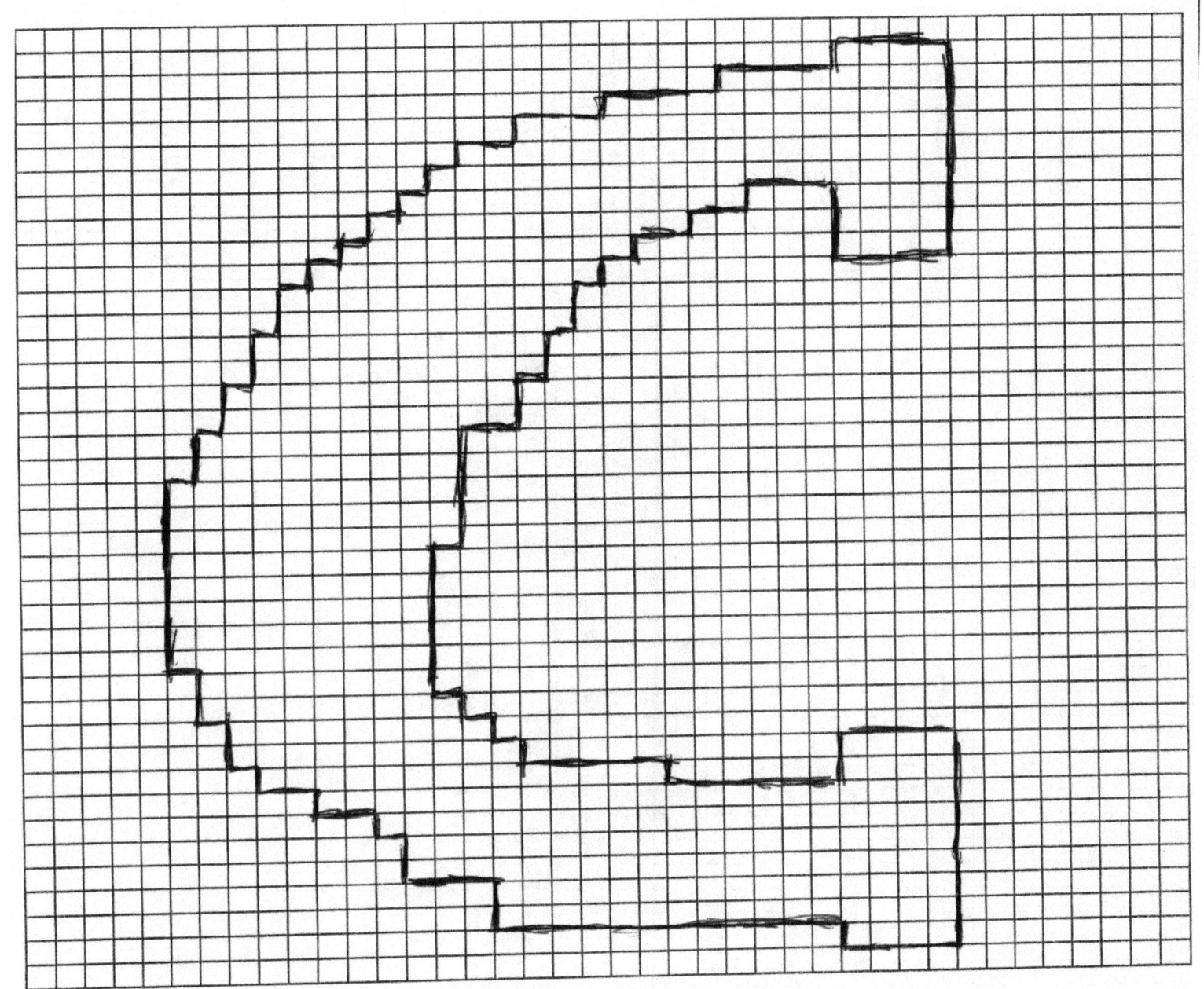

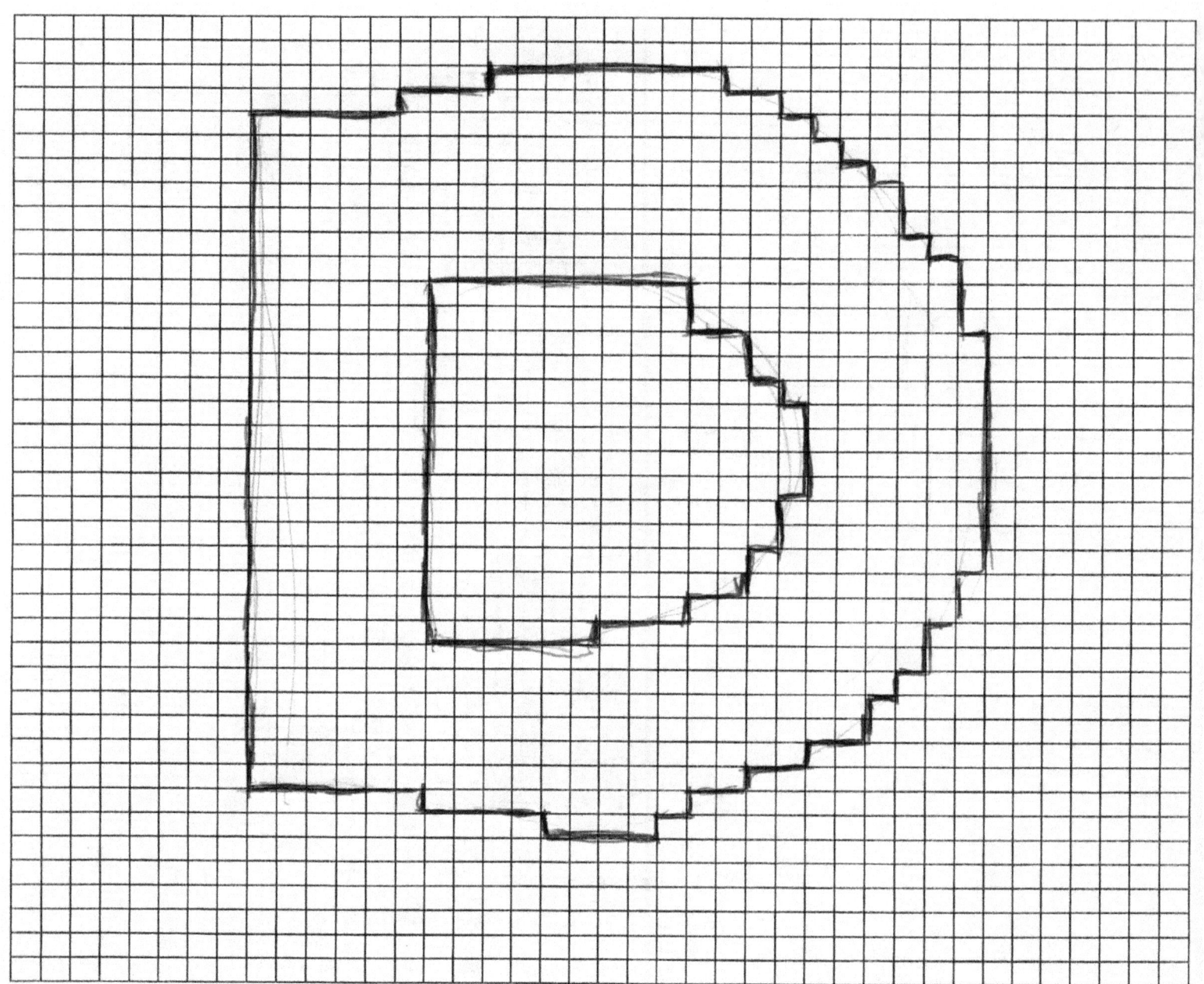

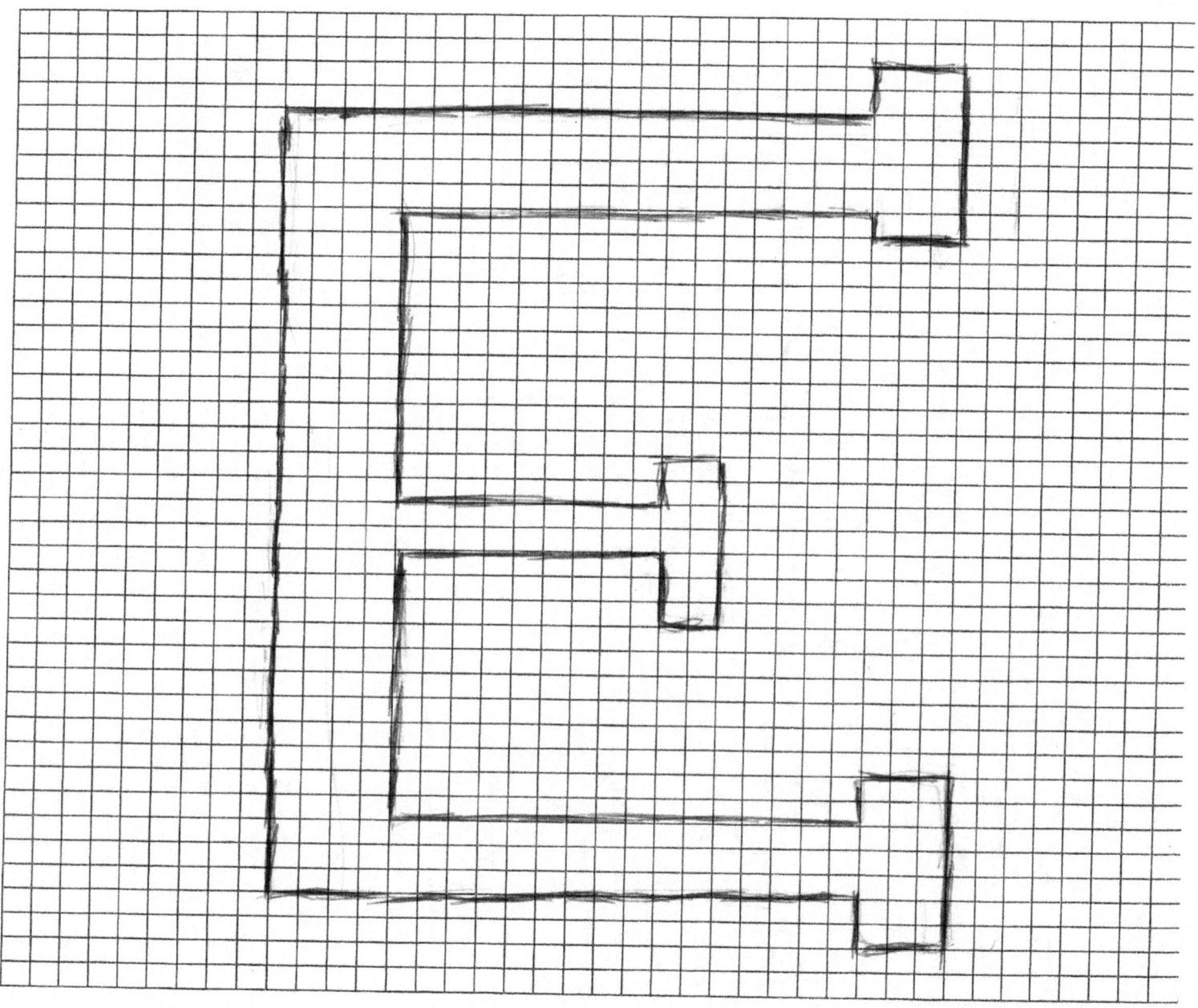

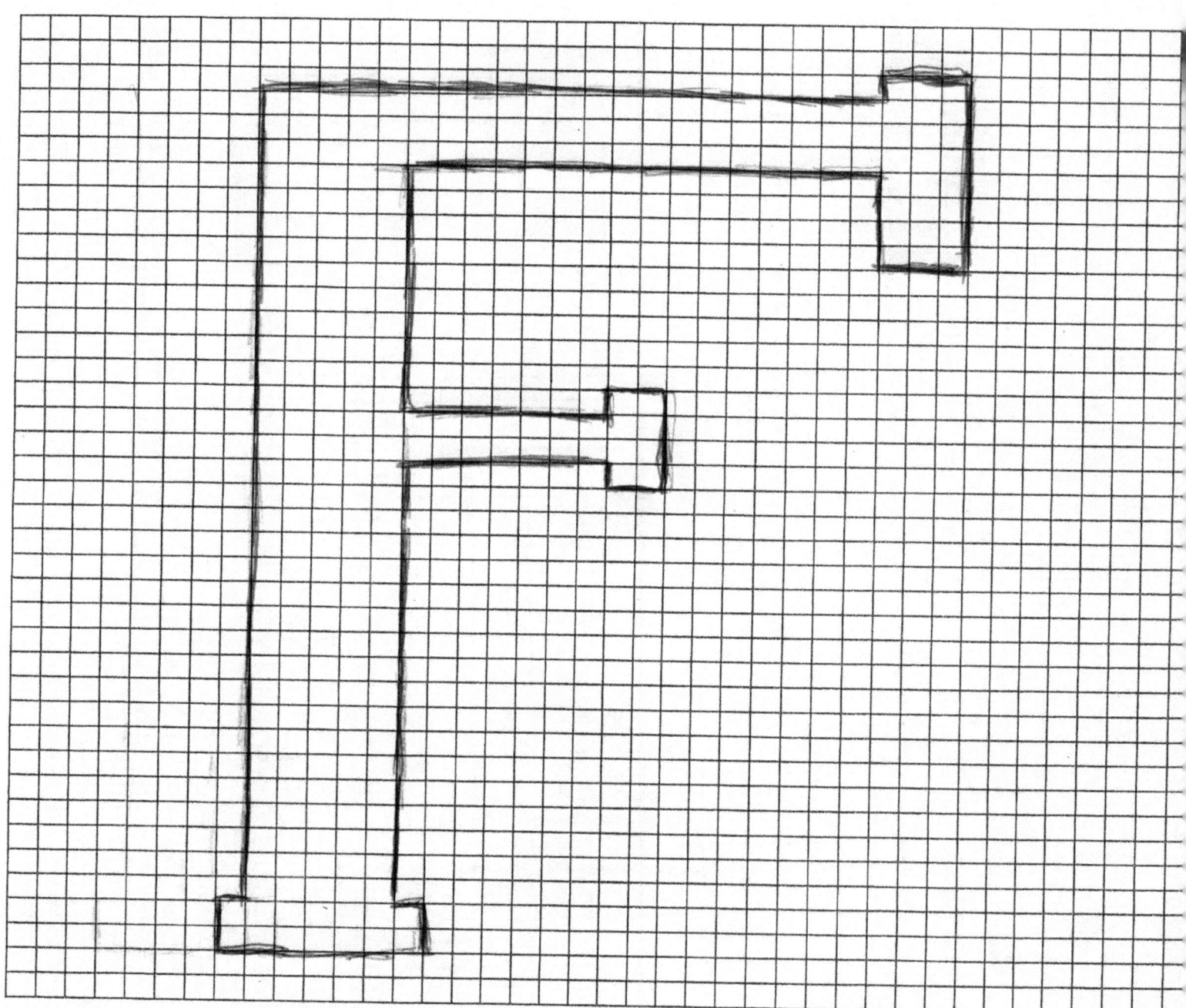

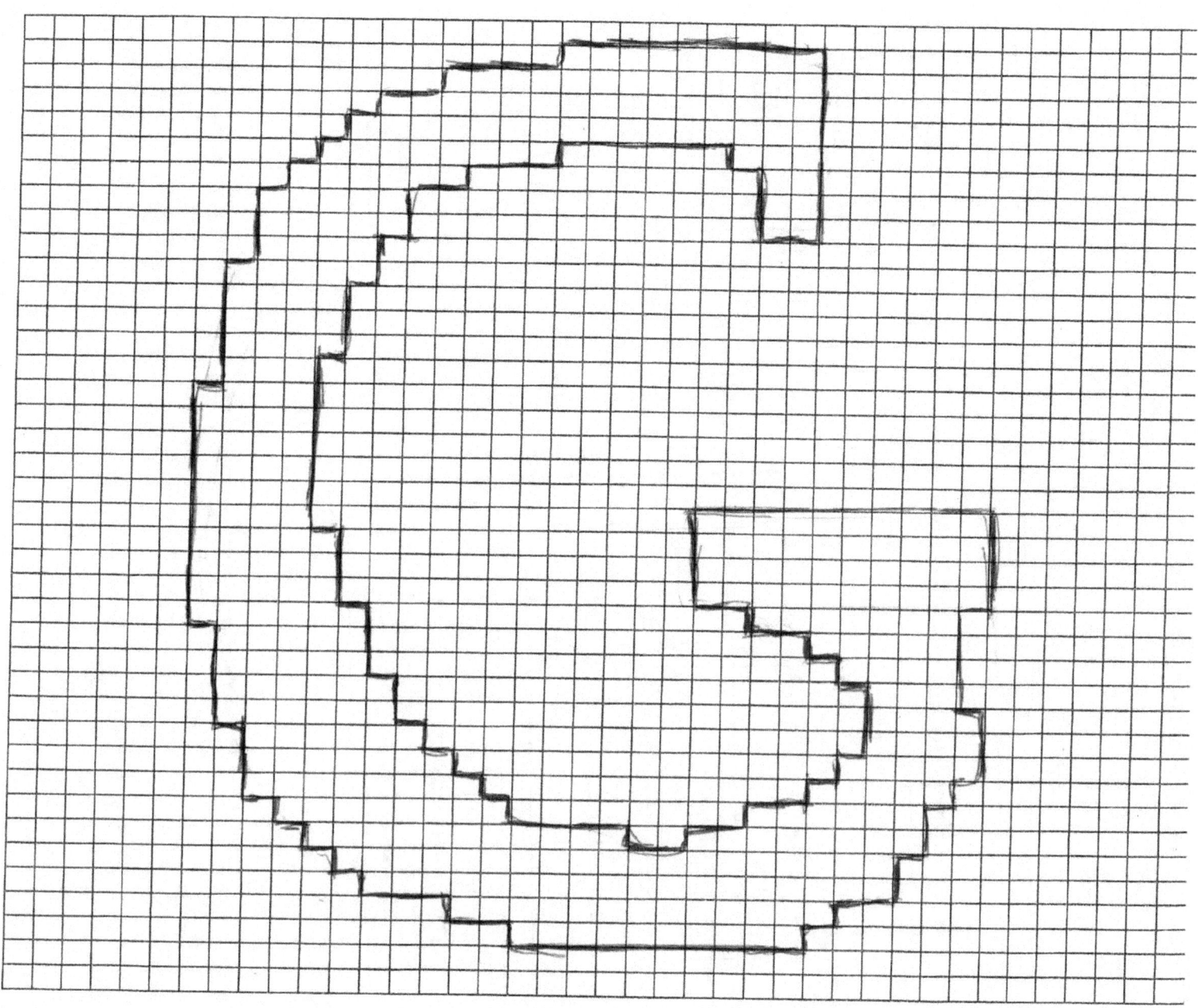

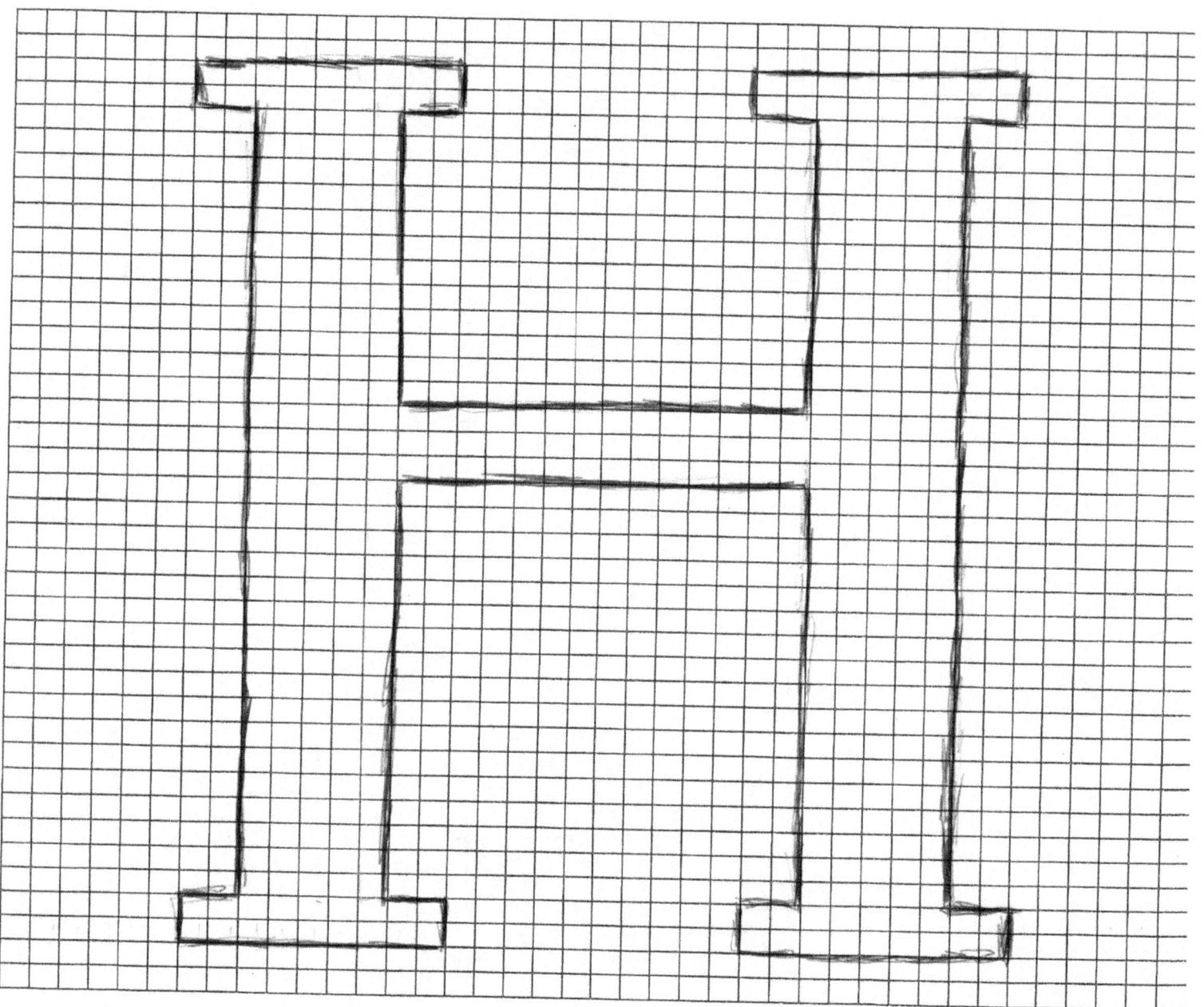

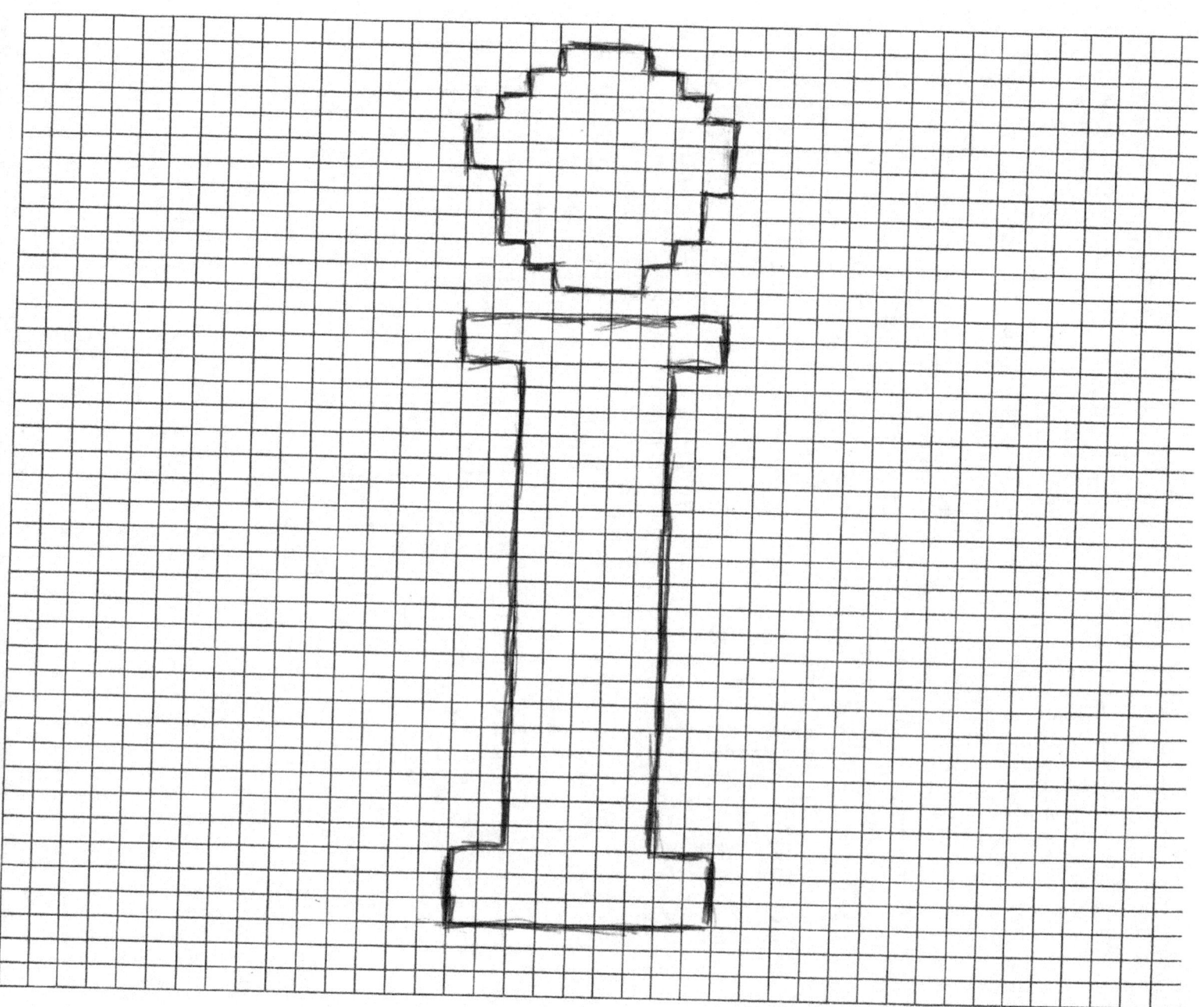

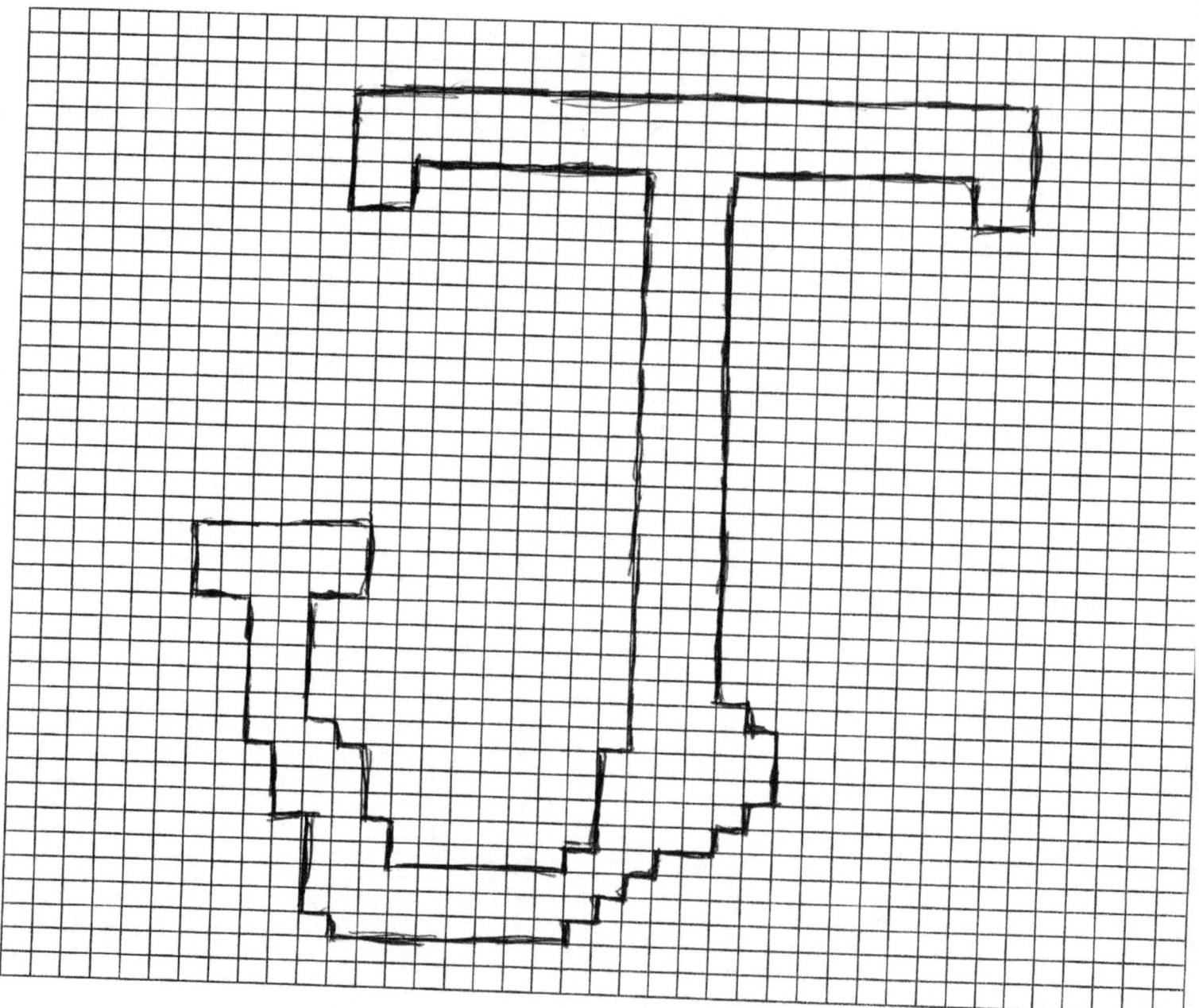

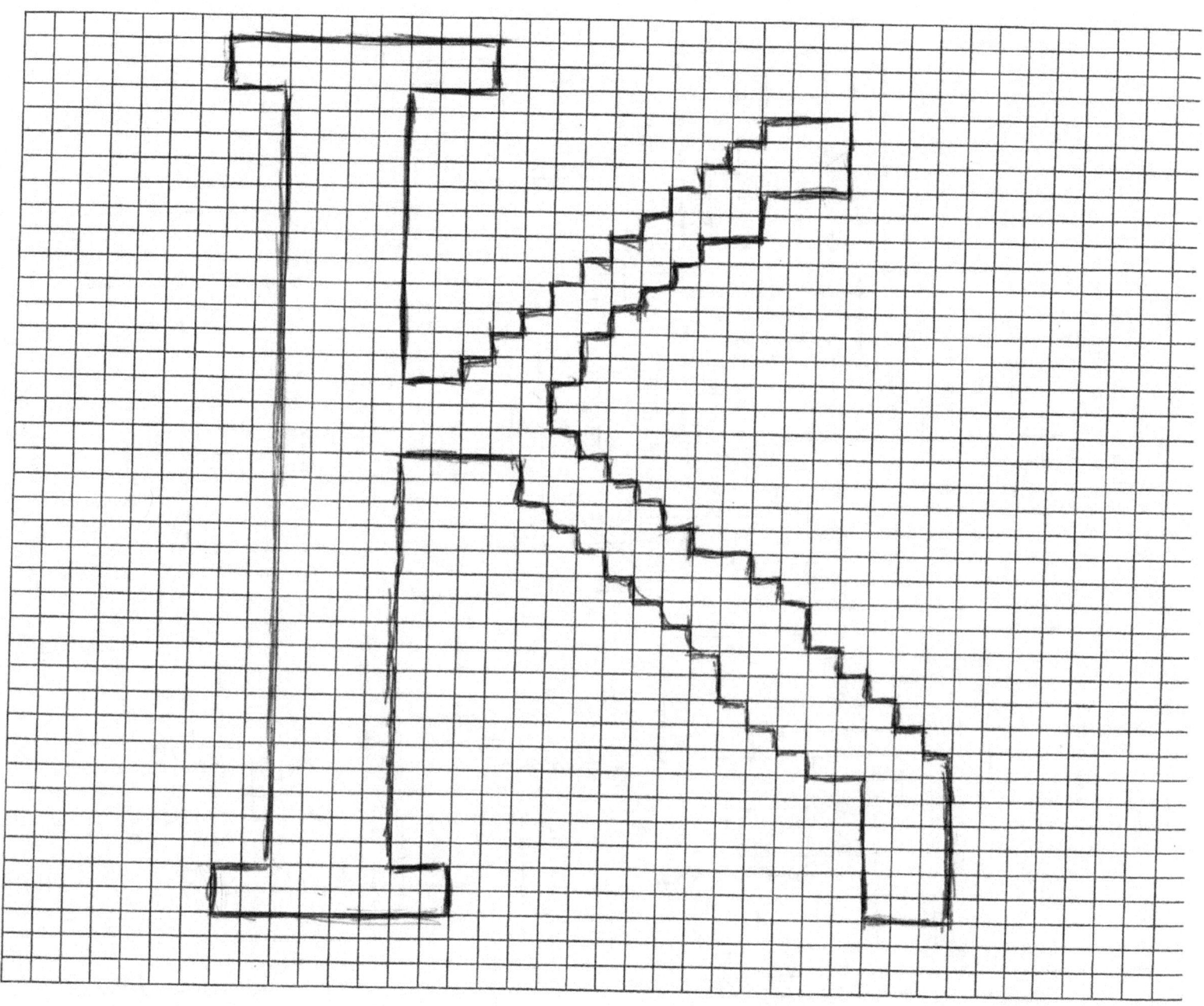

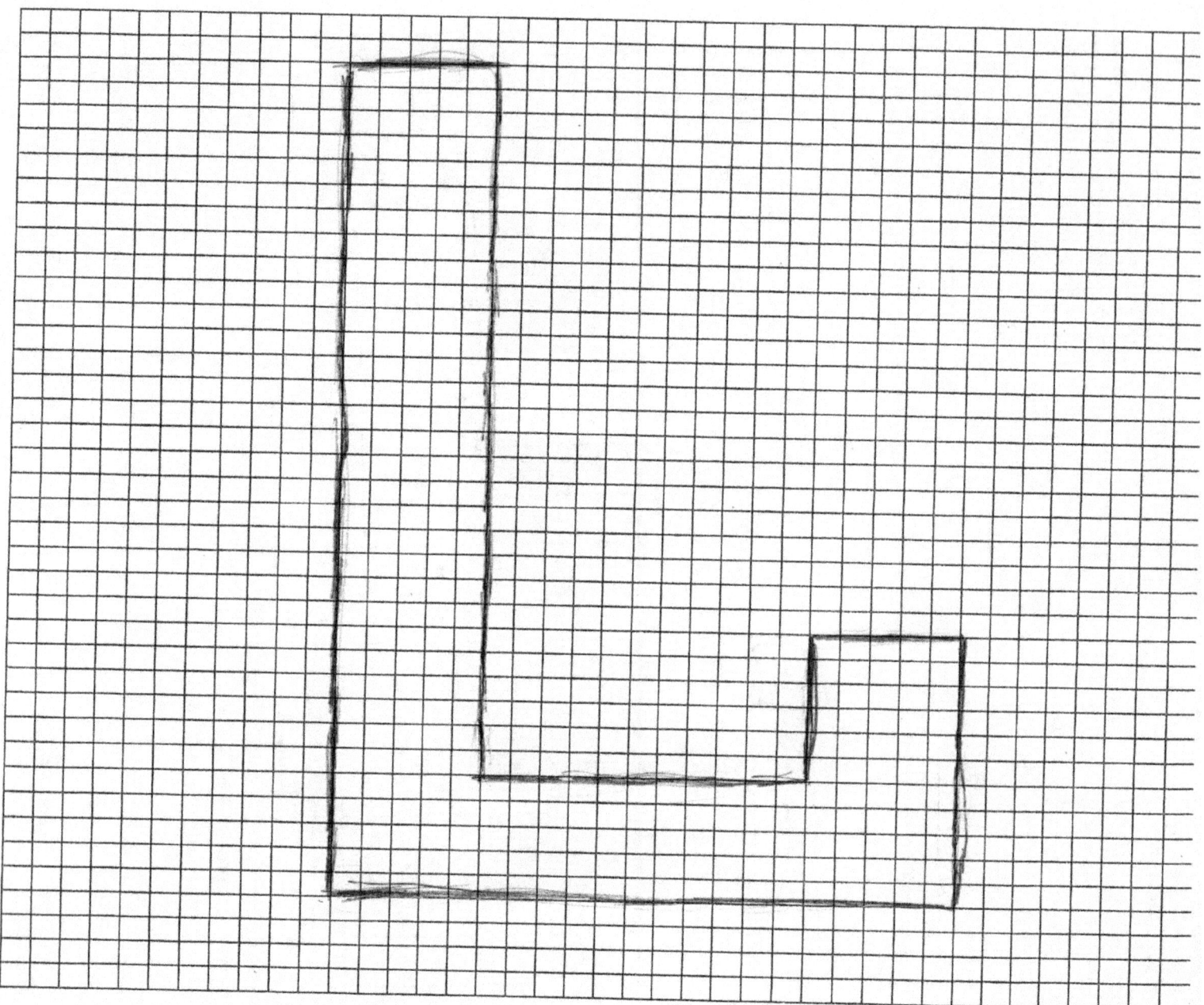

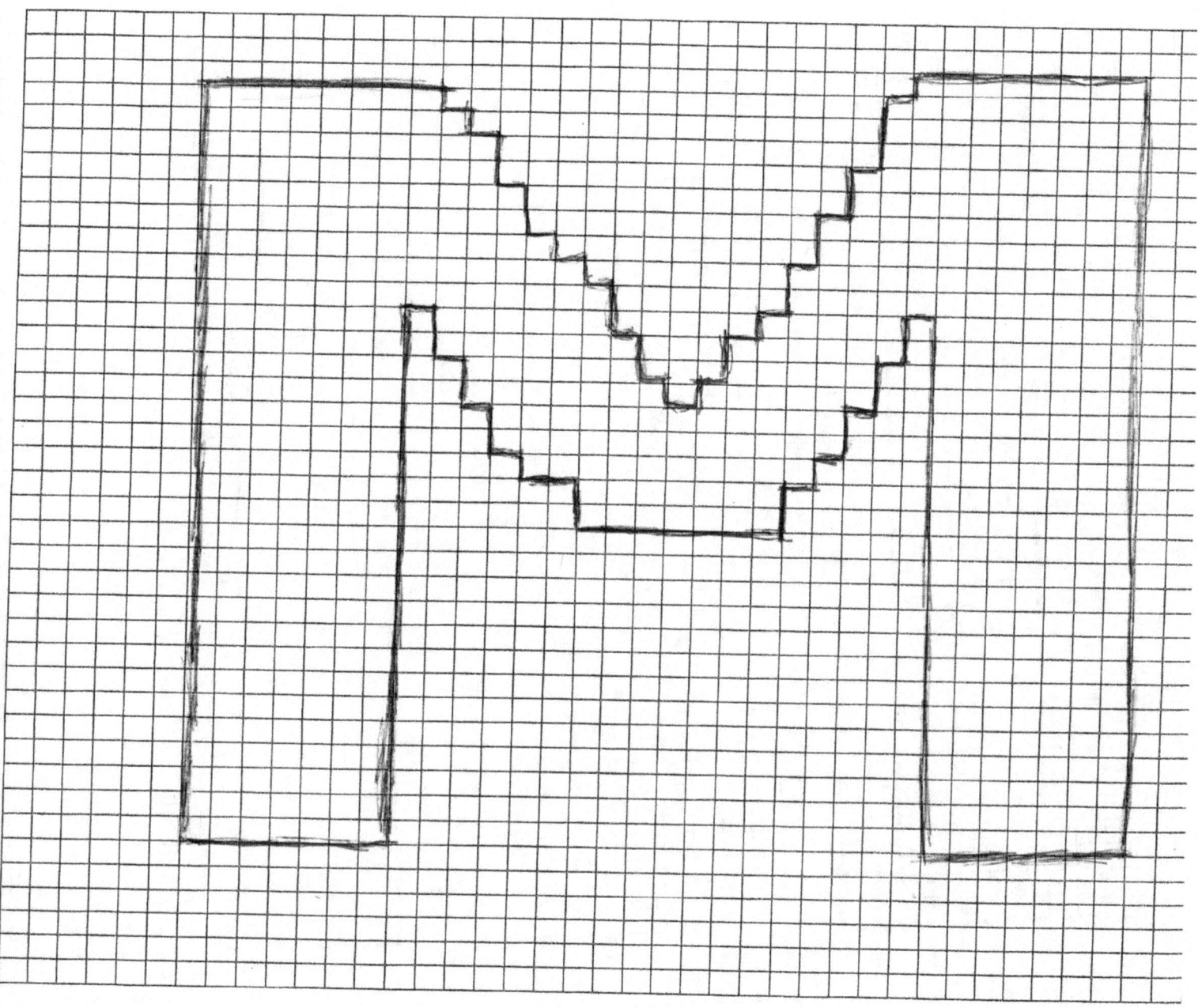

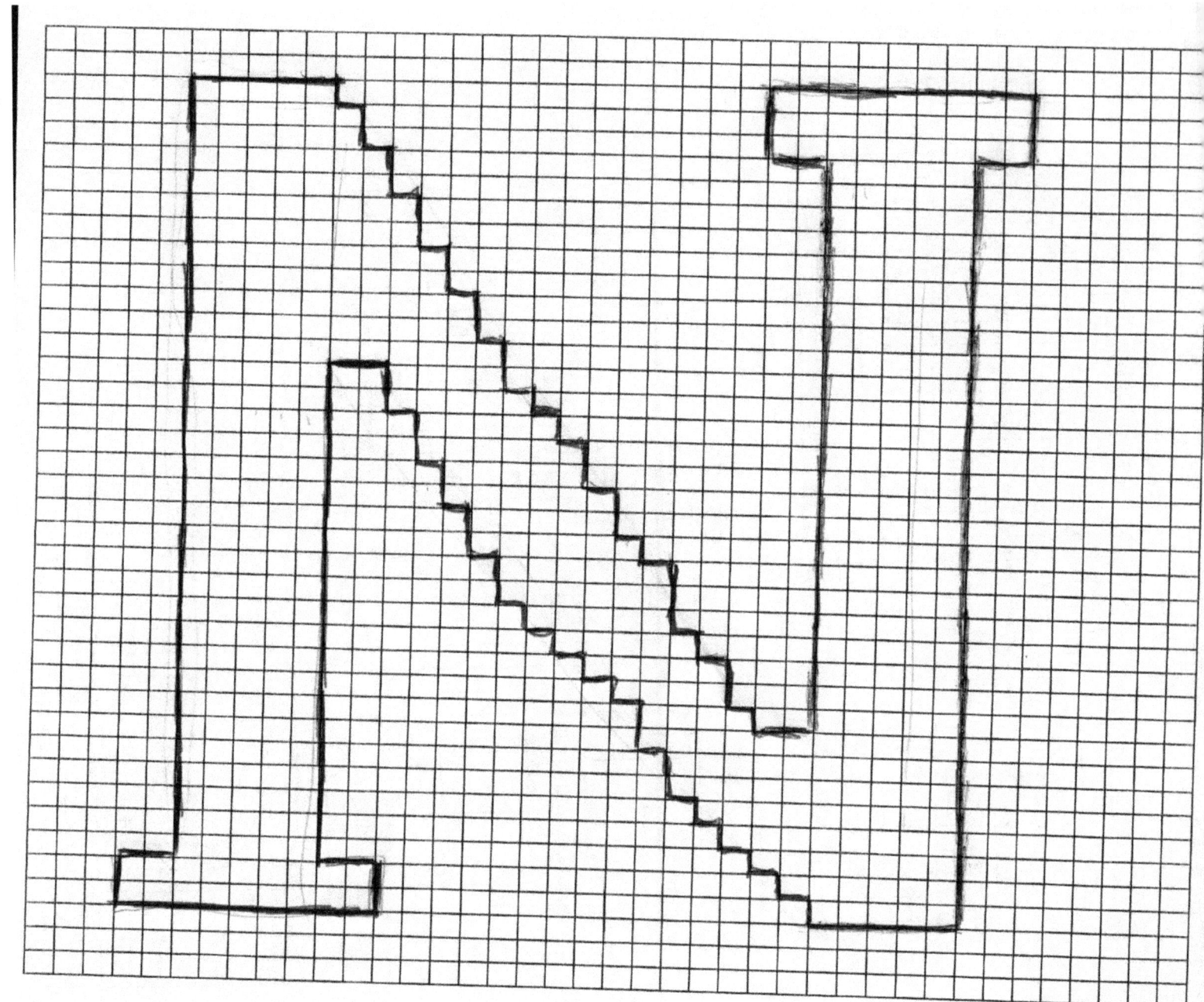

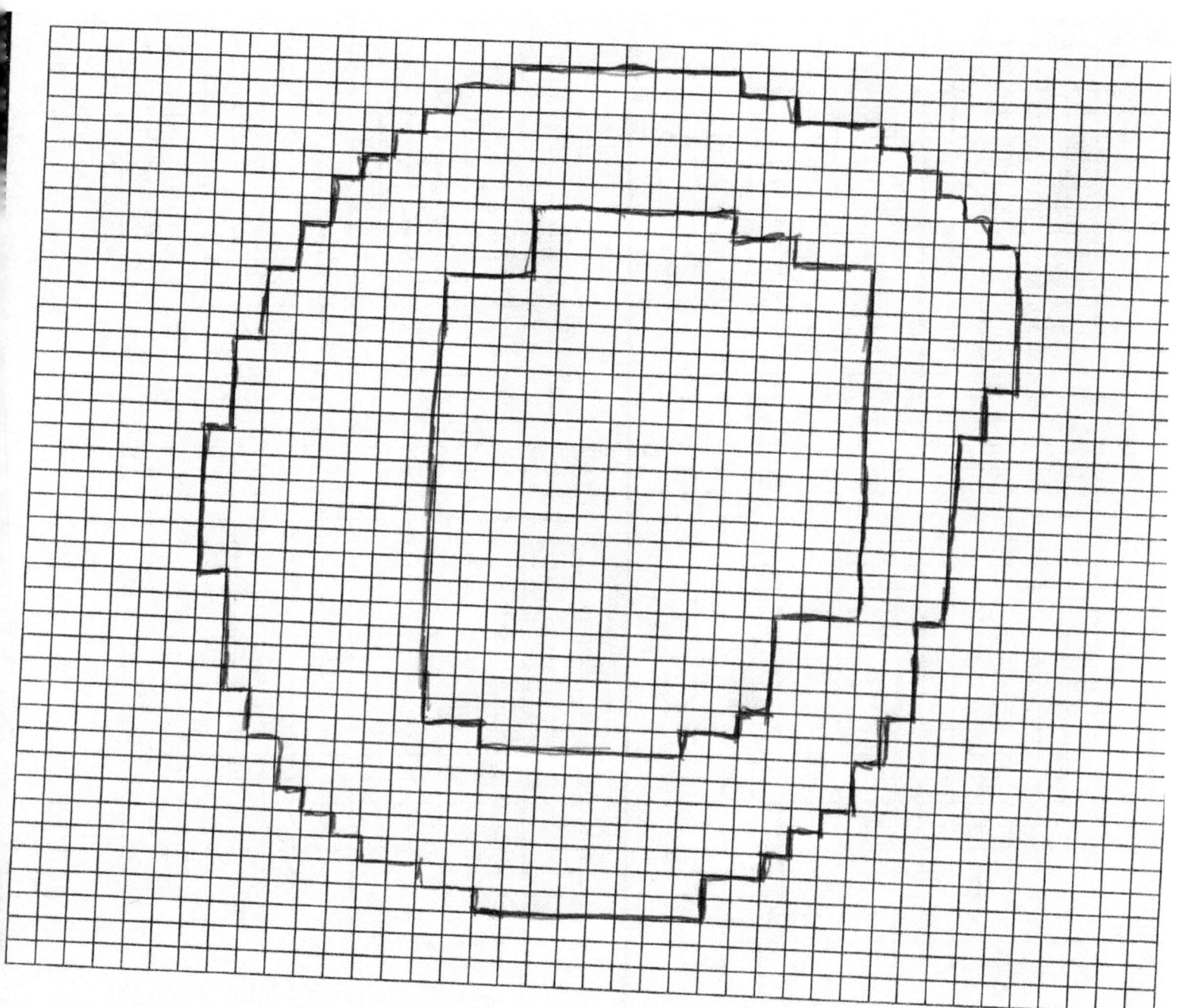

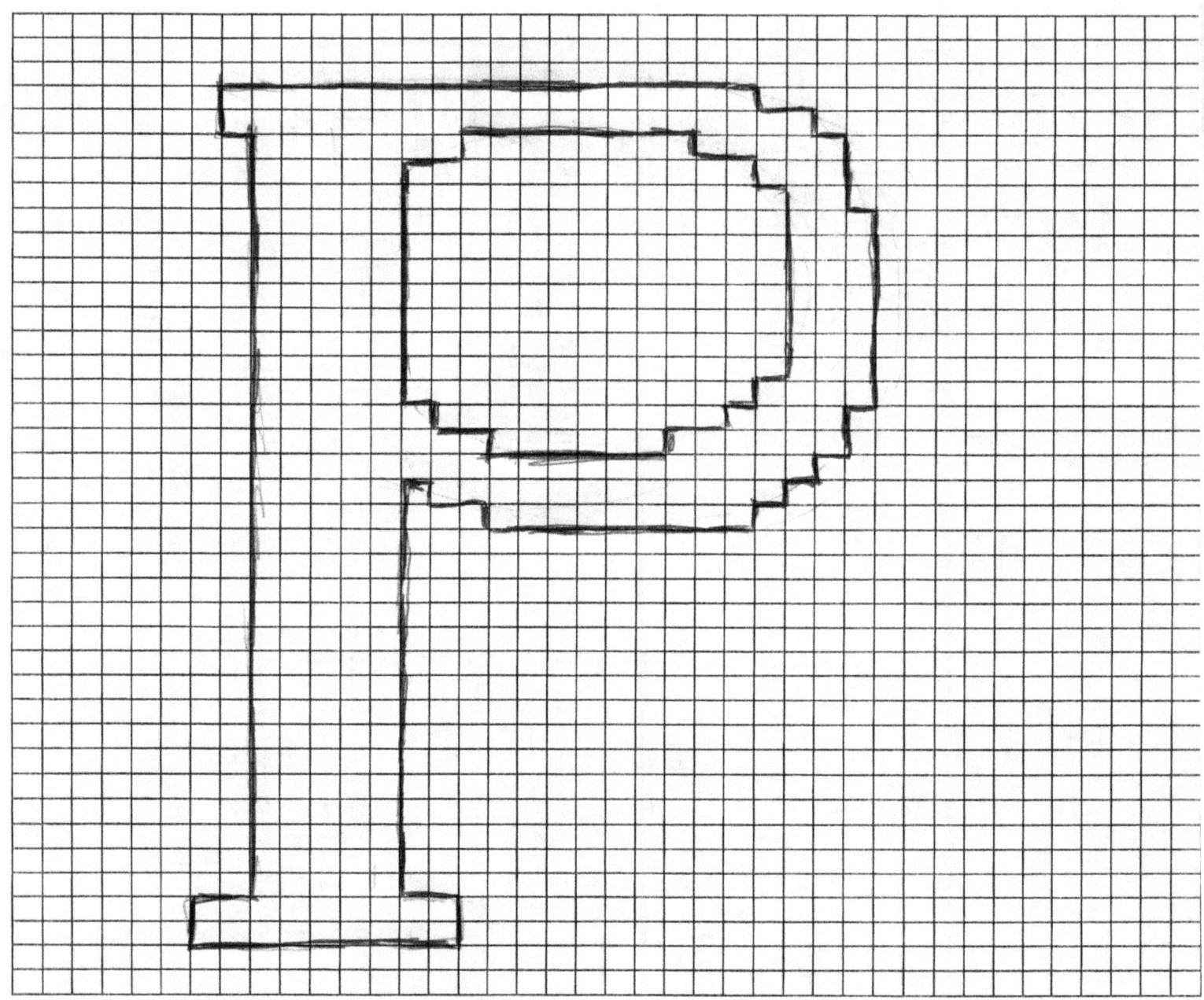

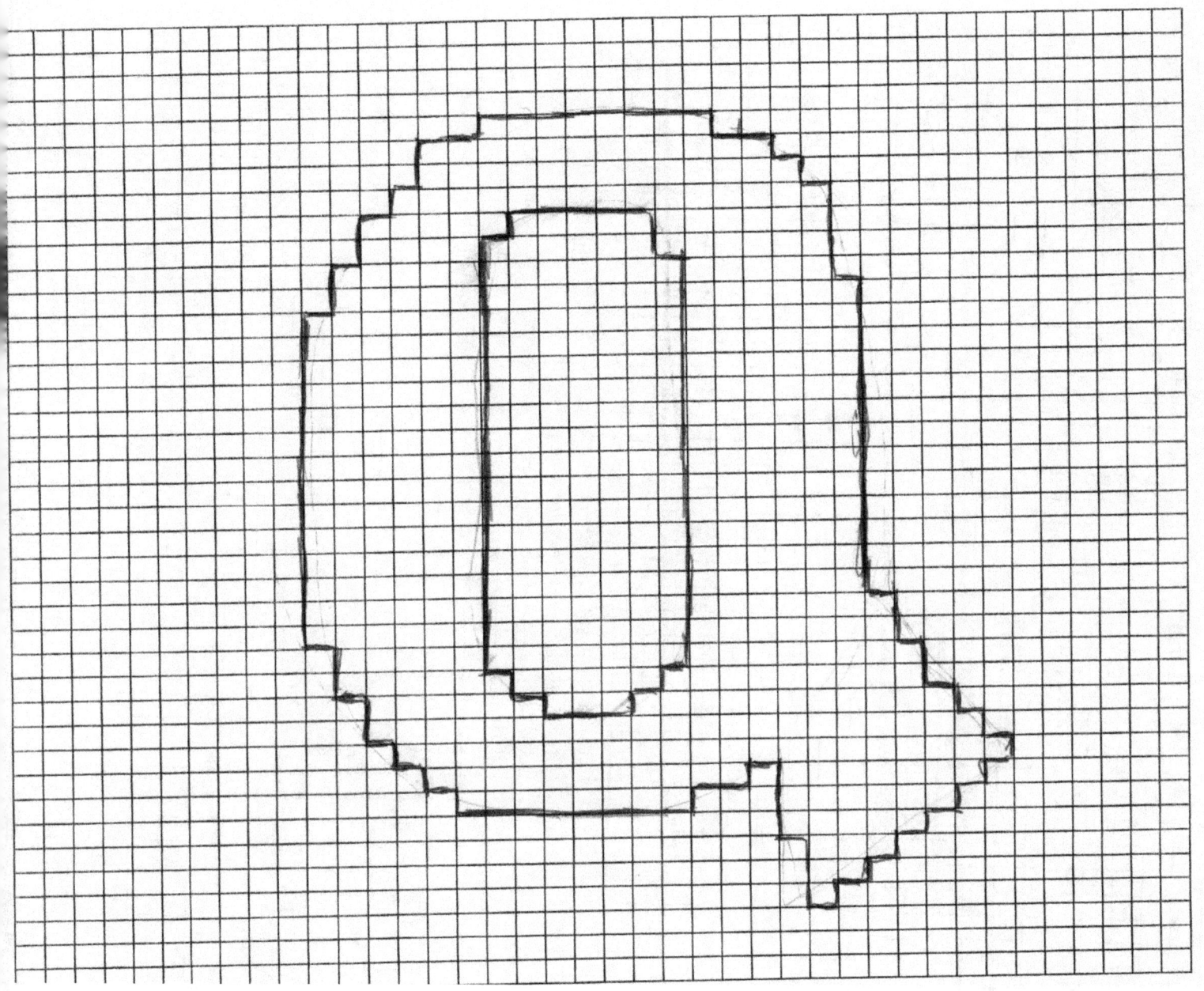

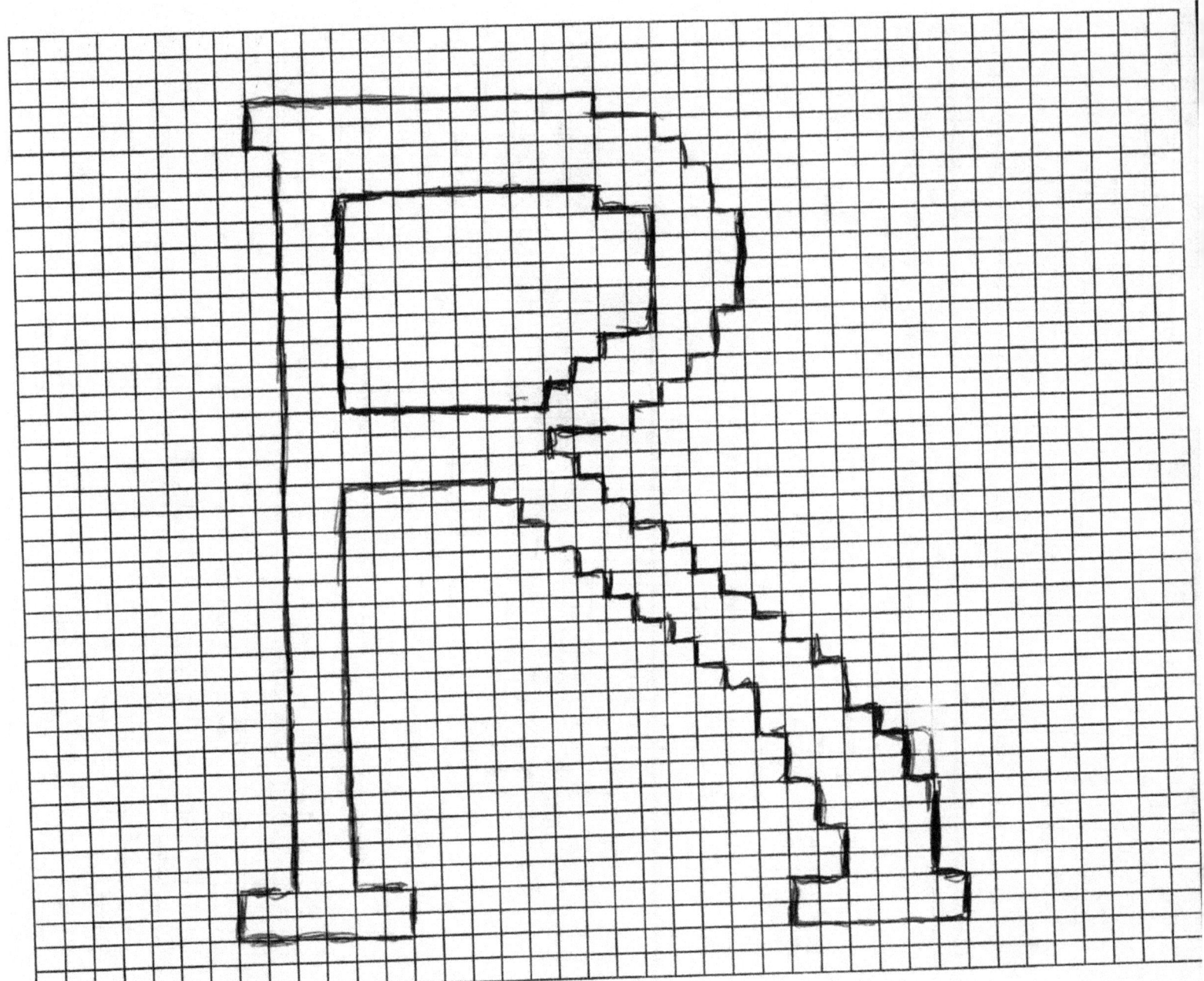

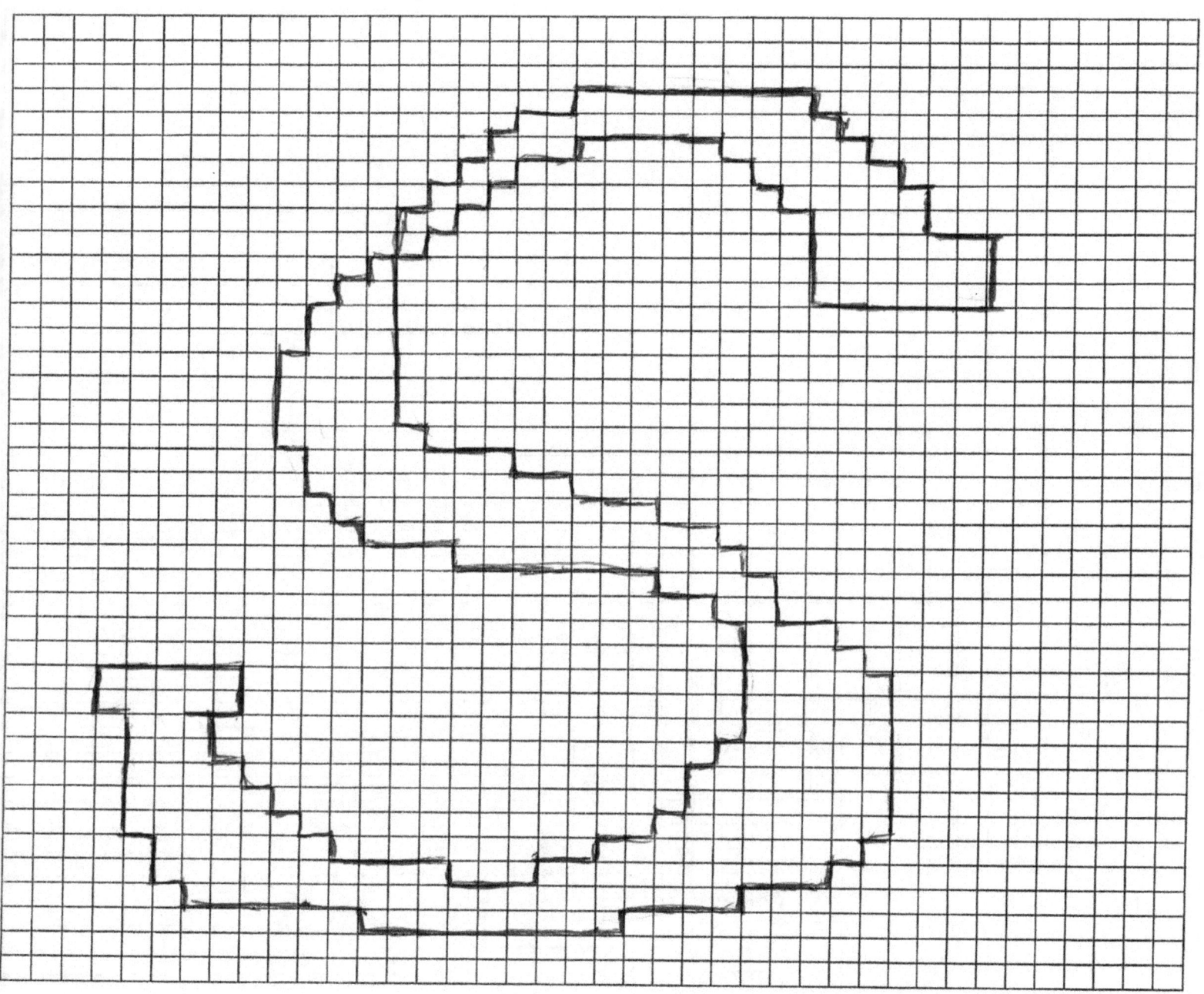

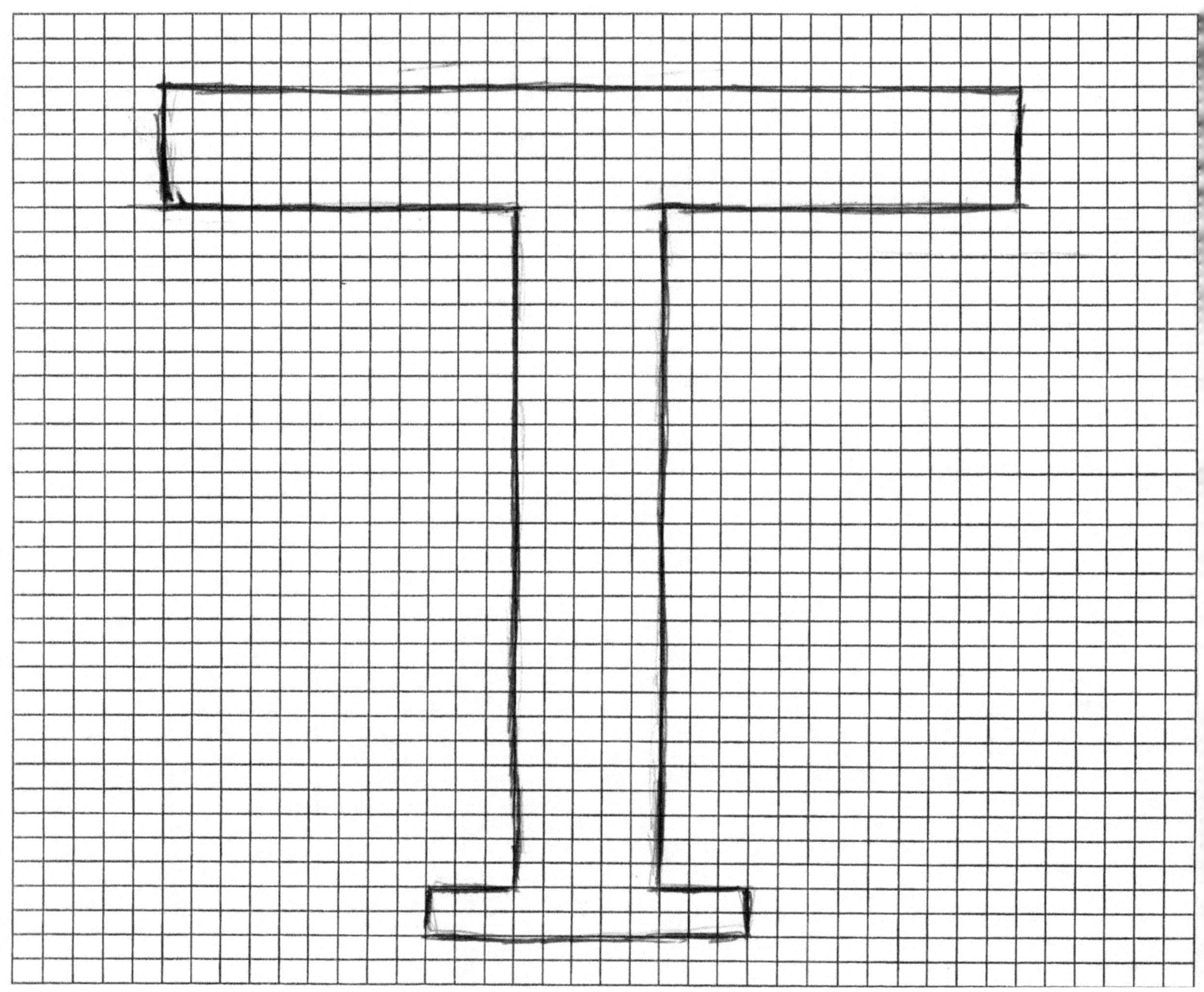

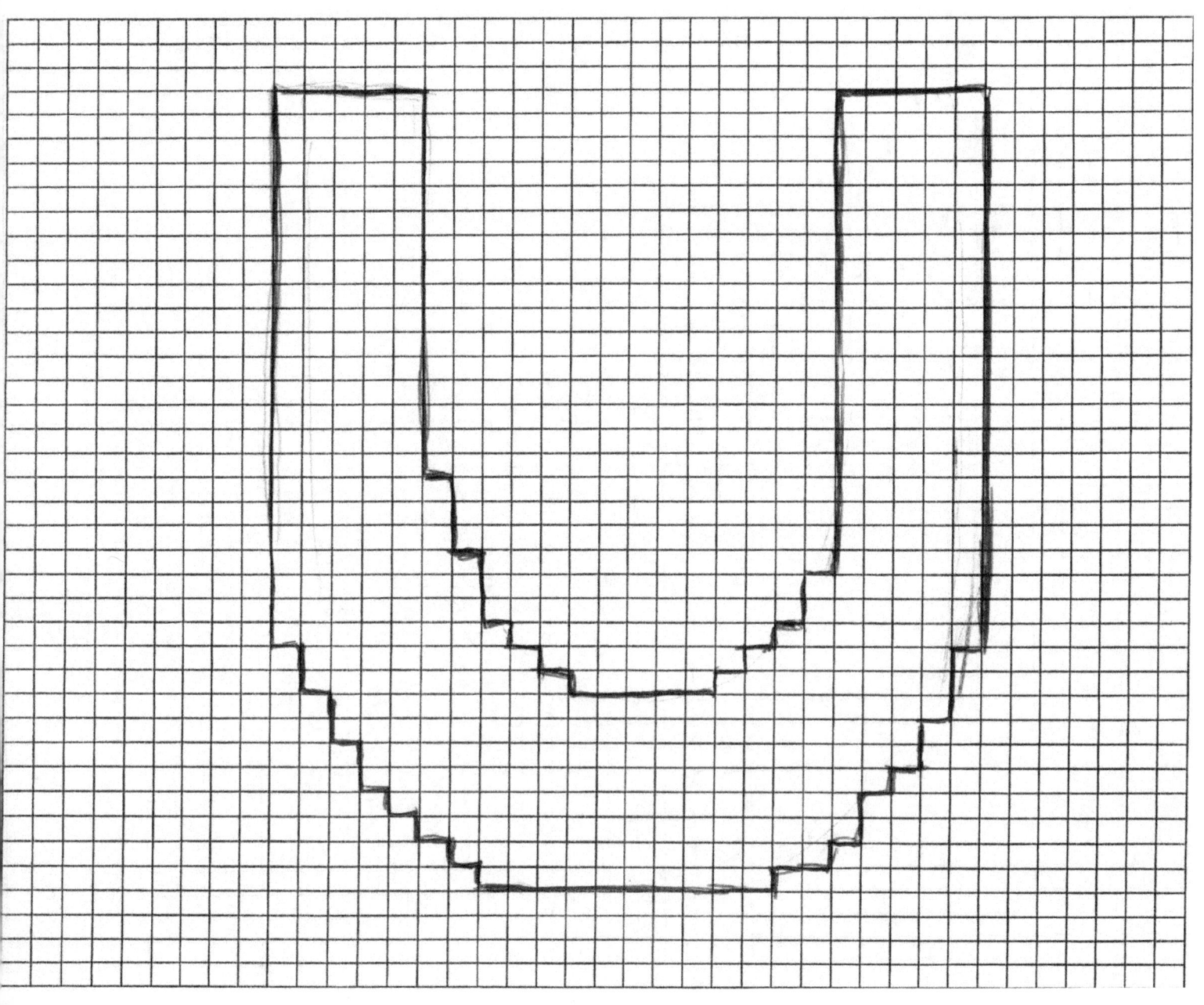

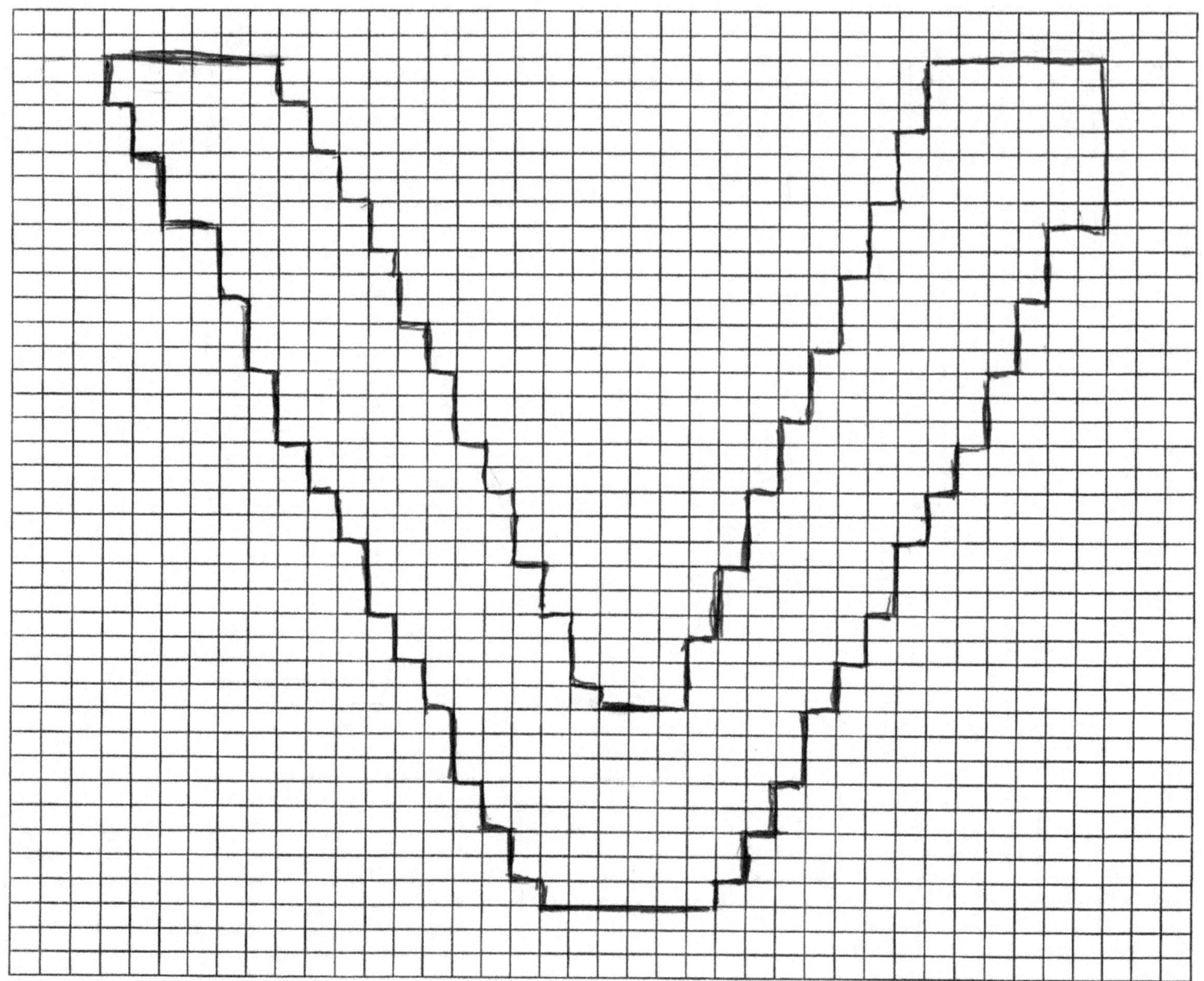

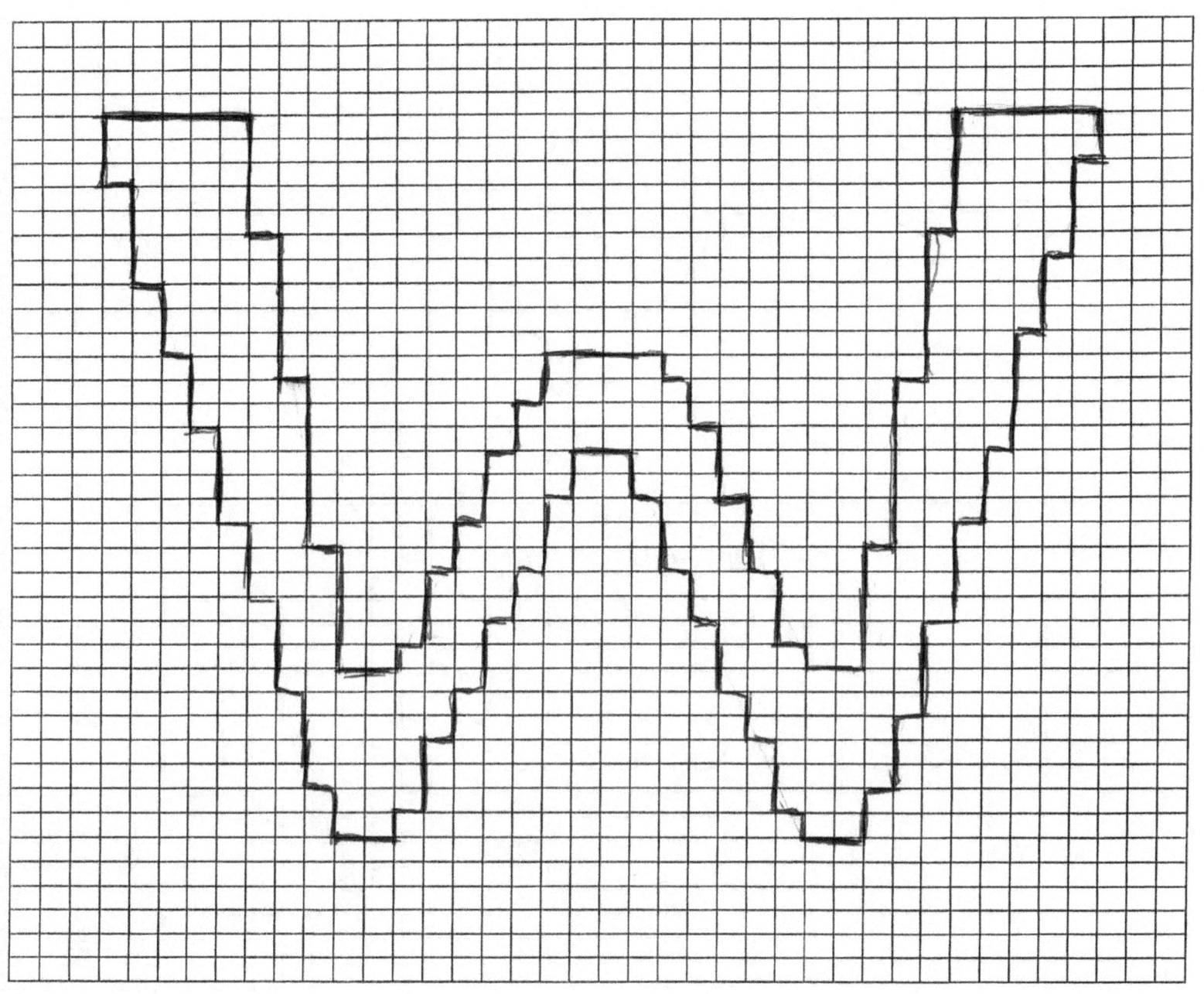

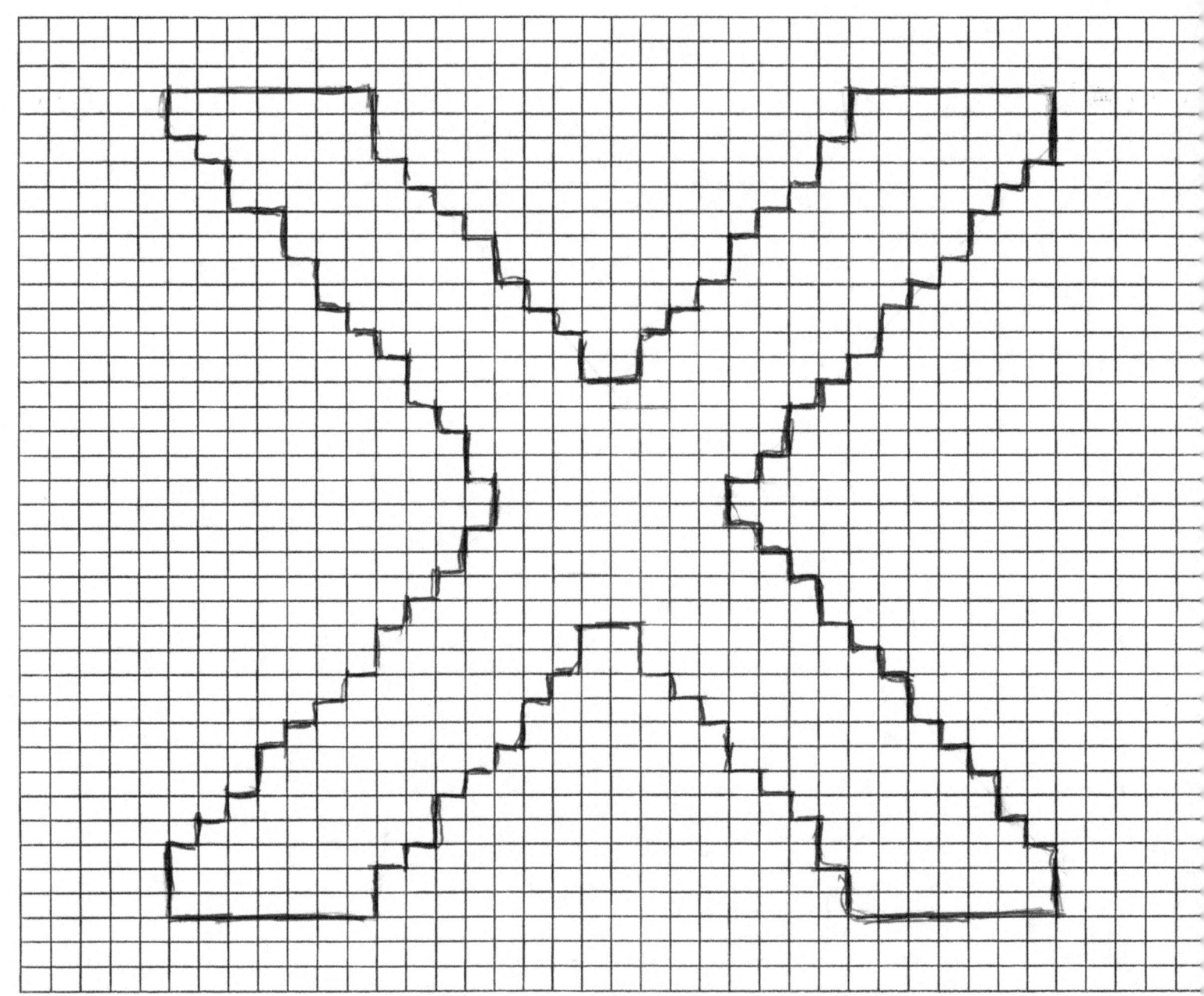

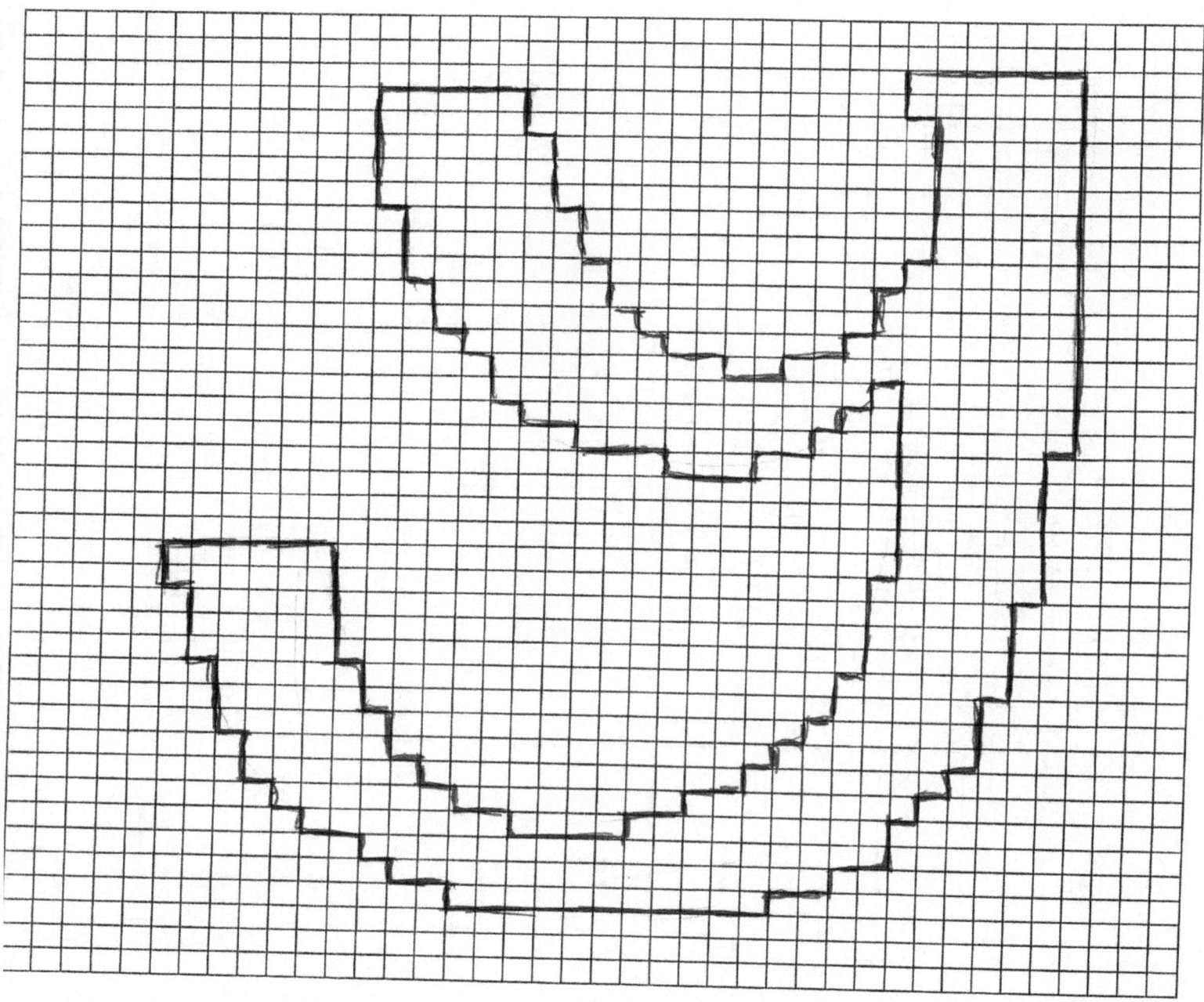

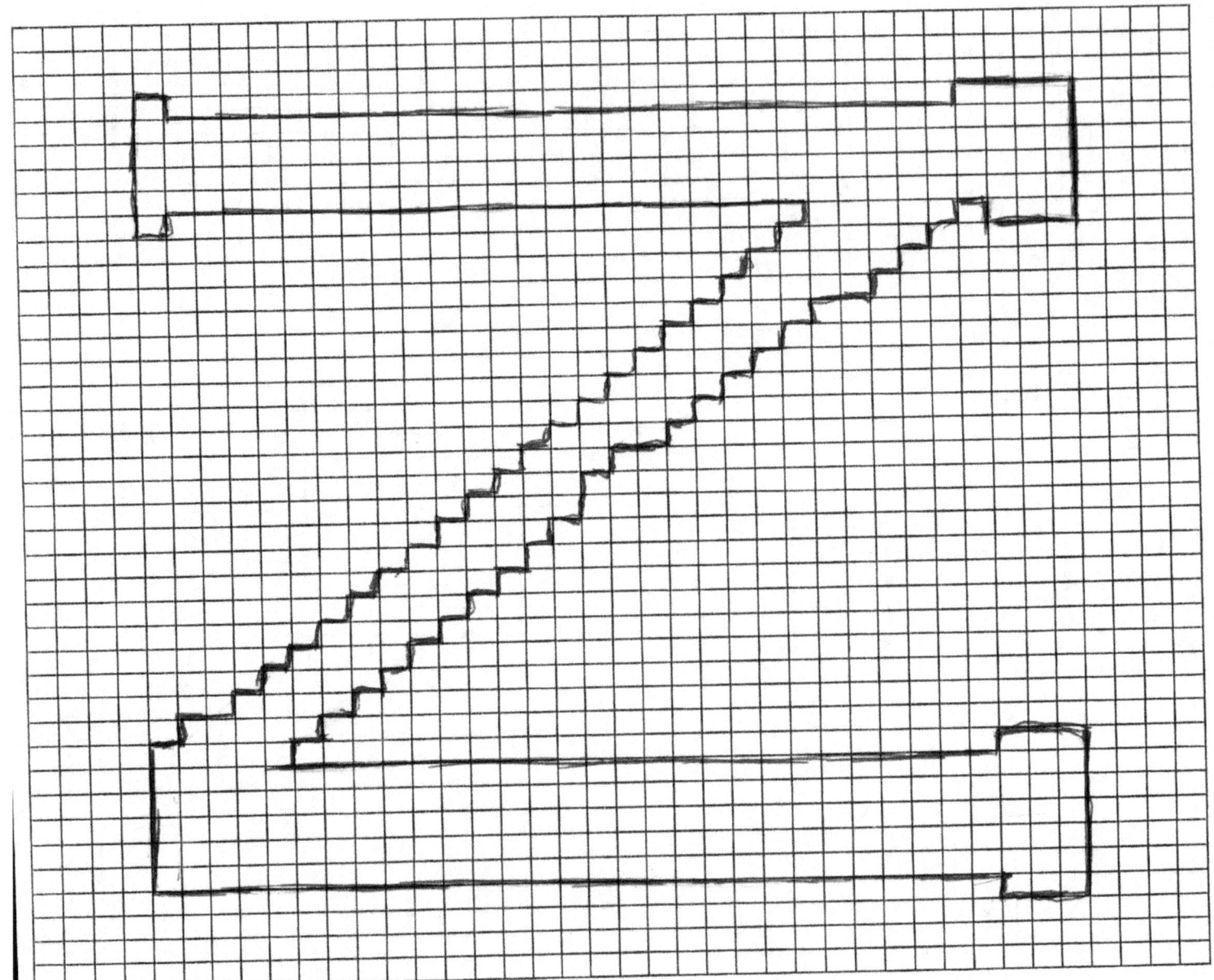

Dinosaurs

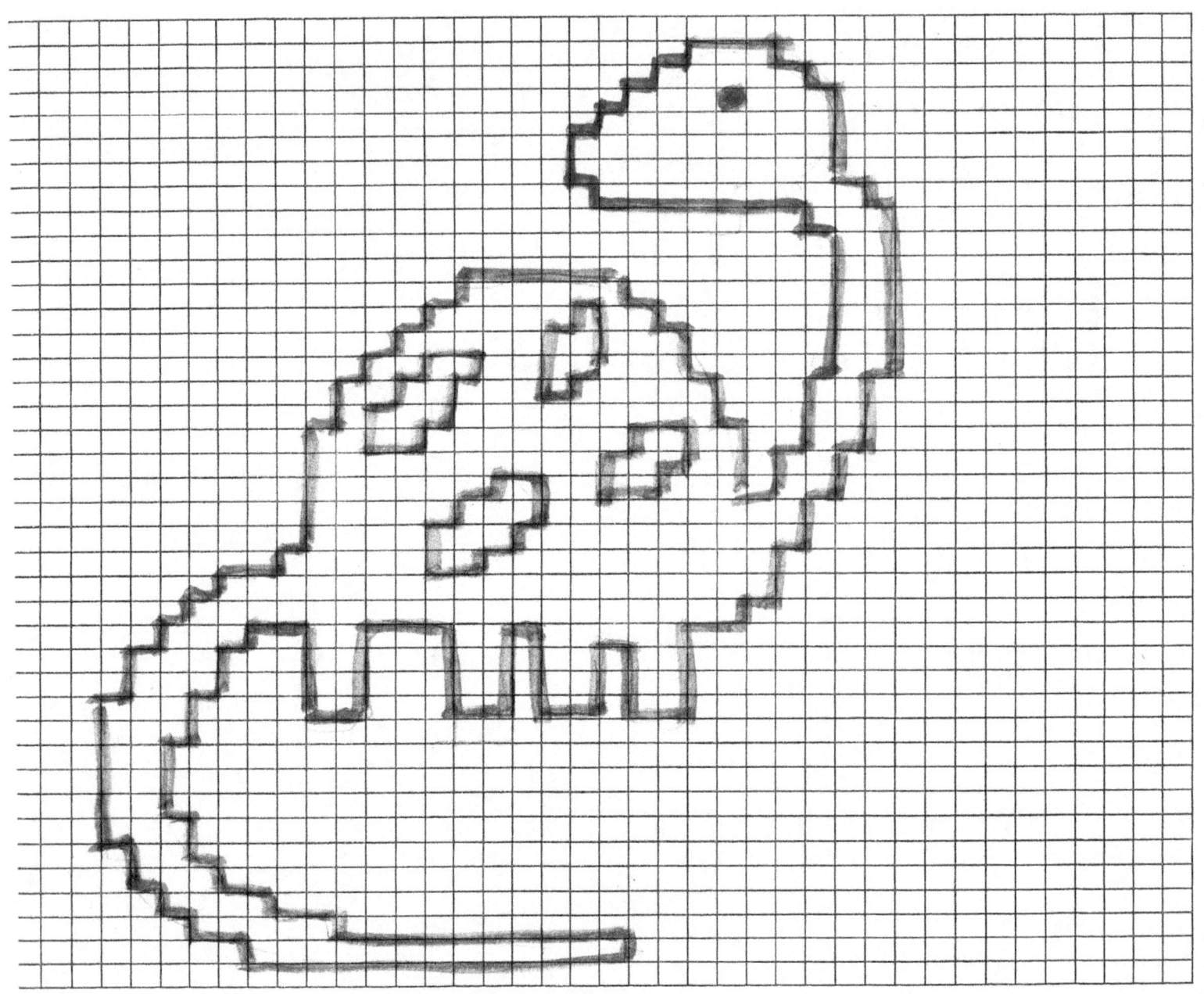

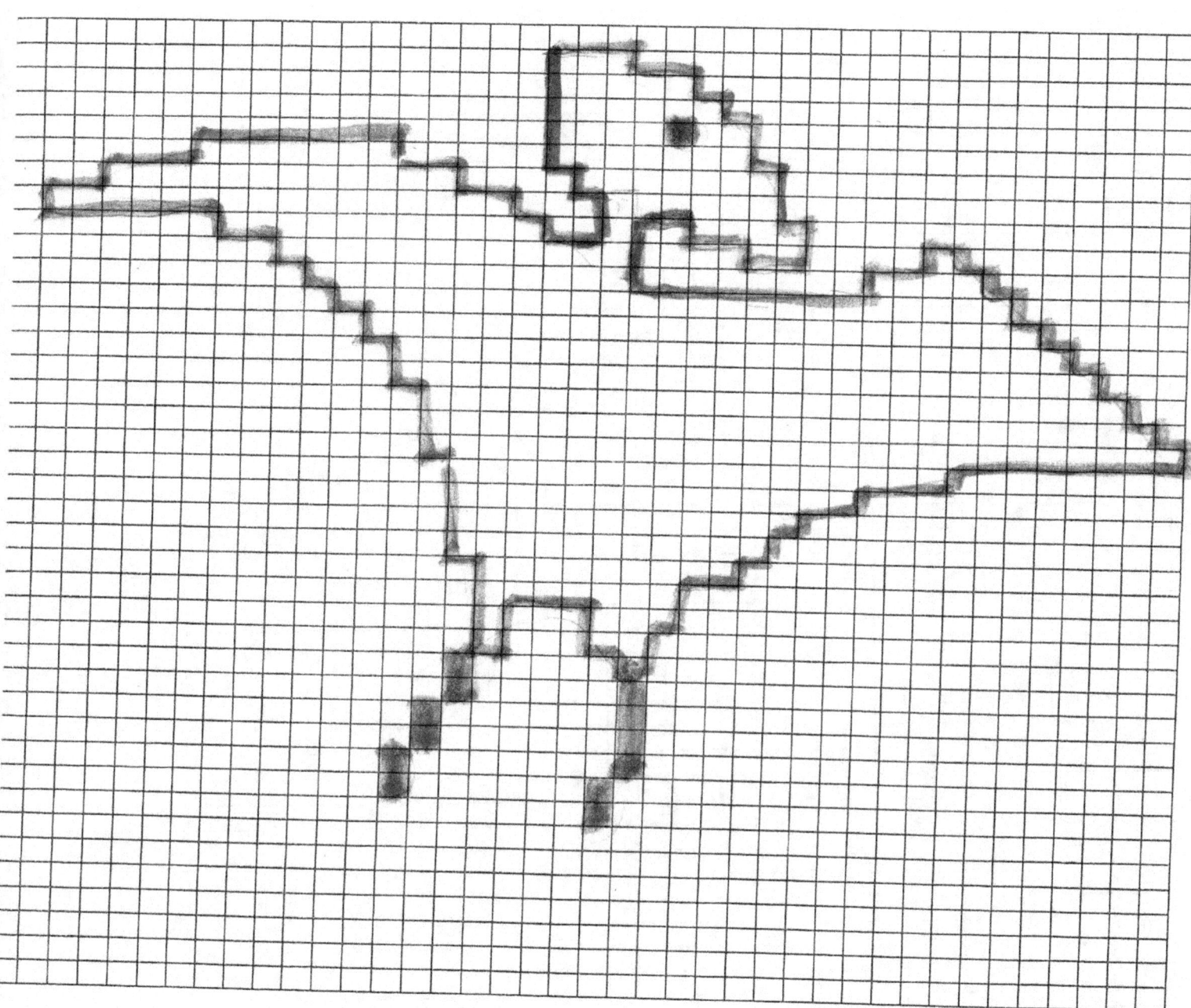

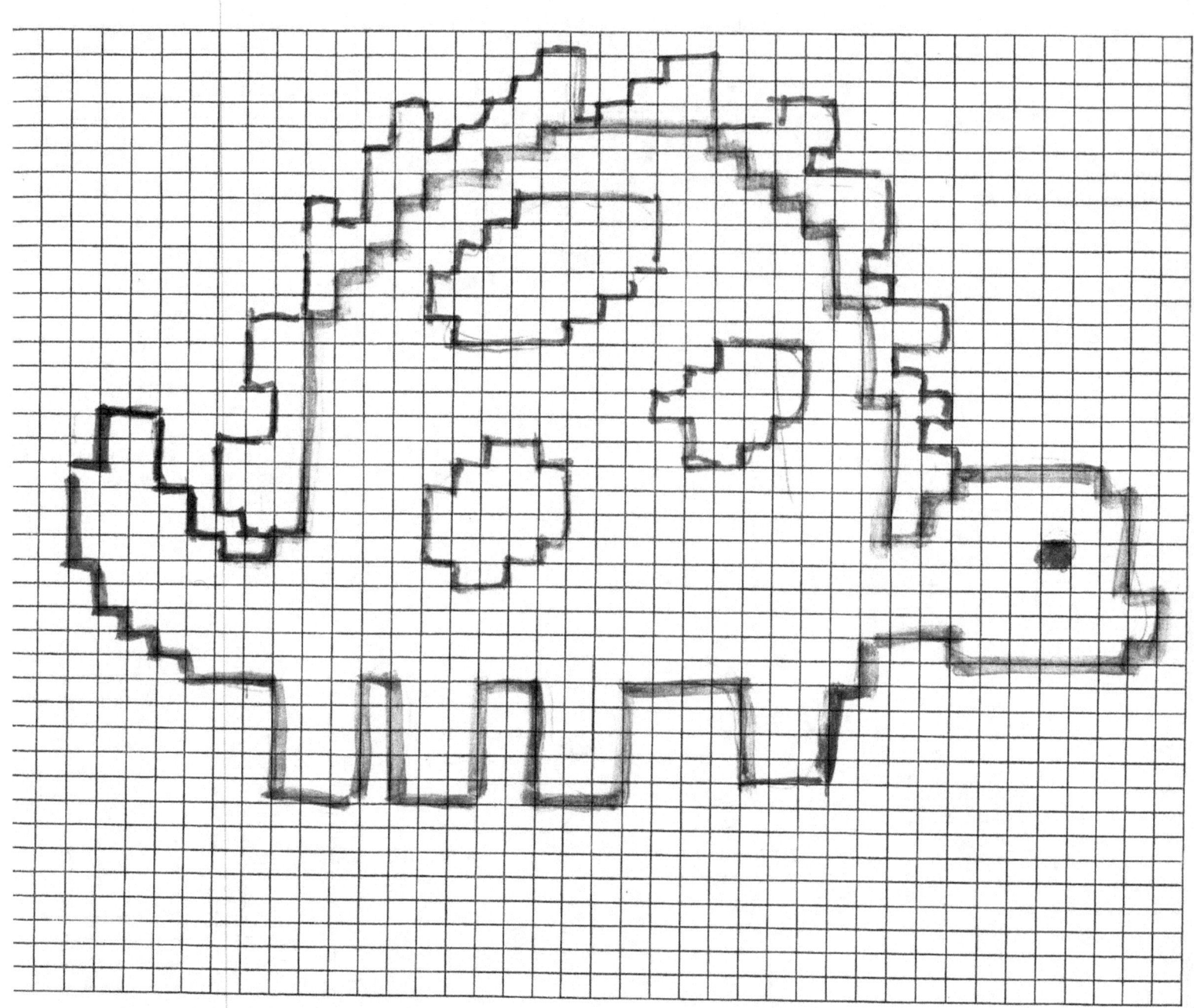

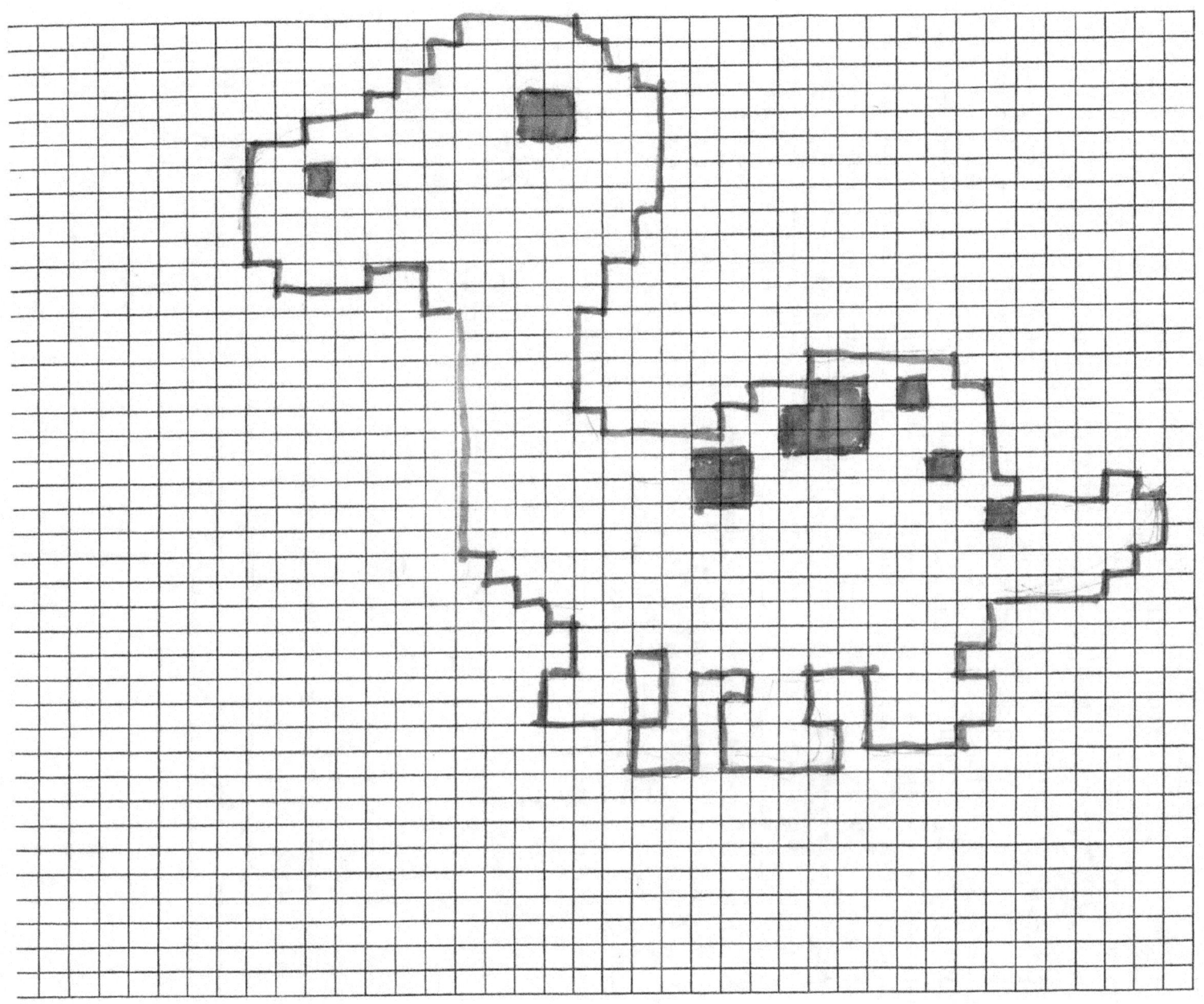

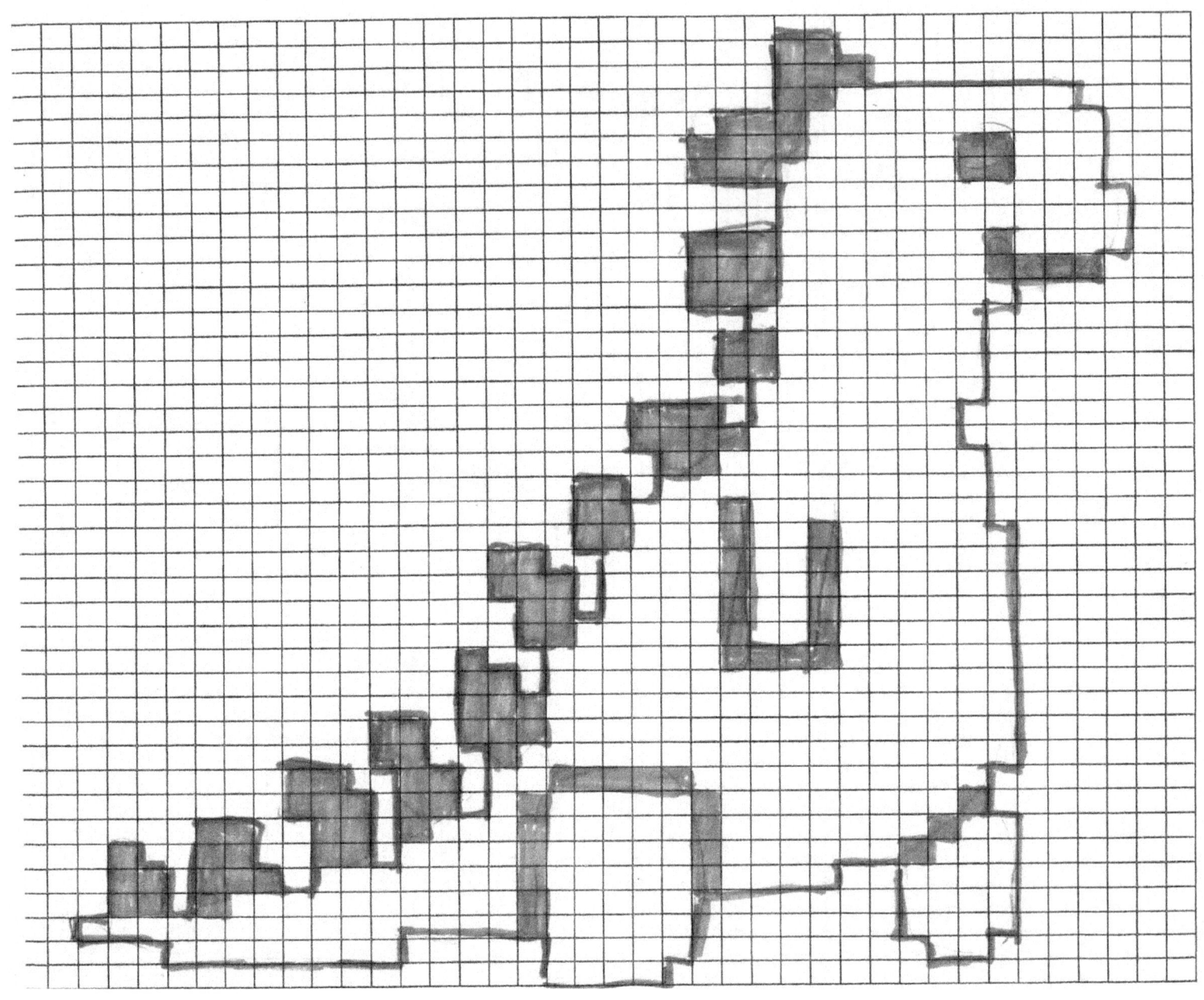

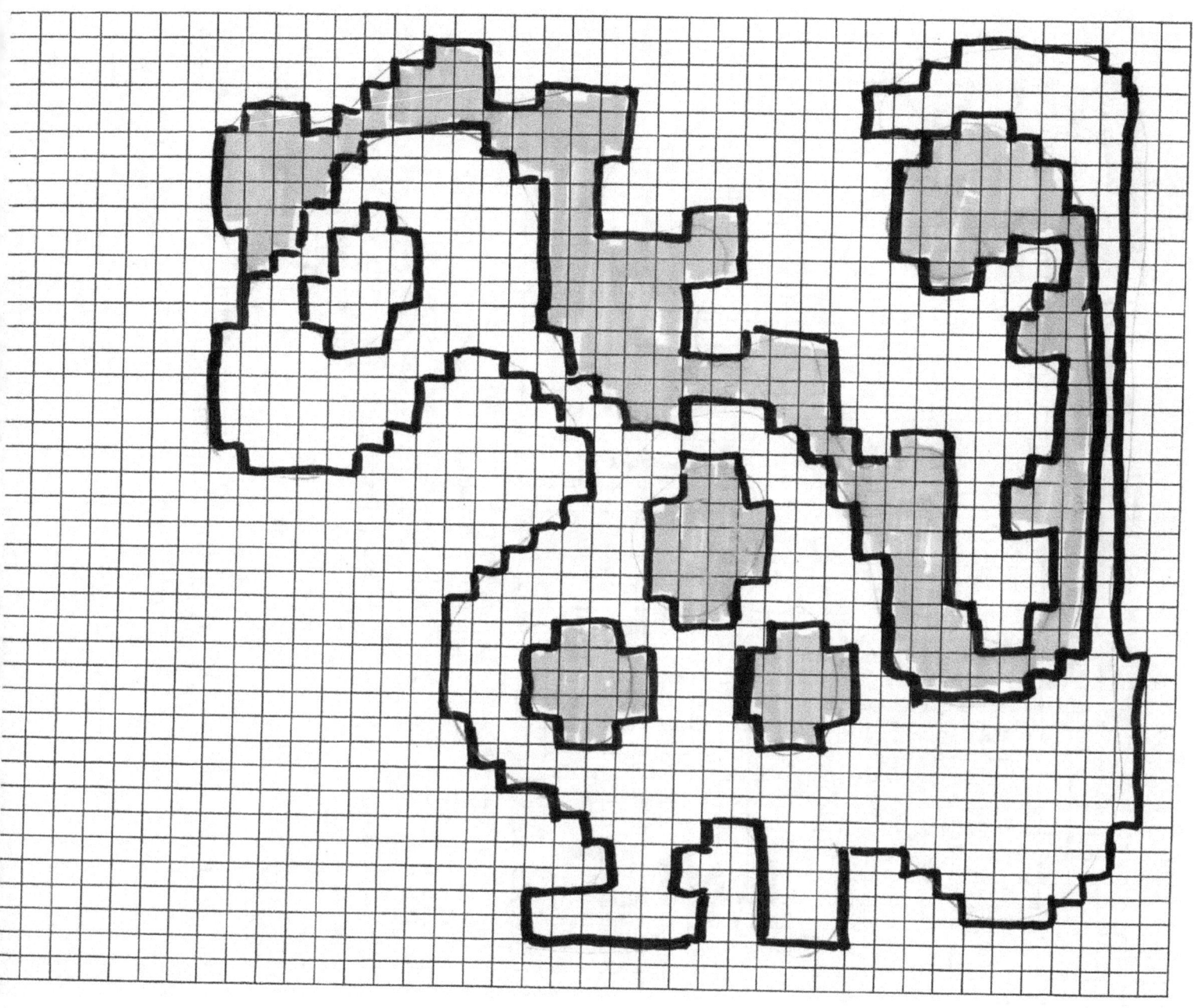

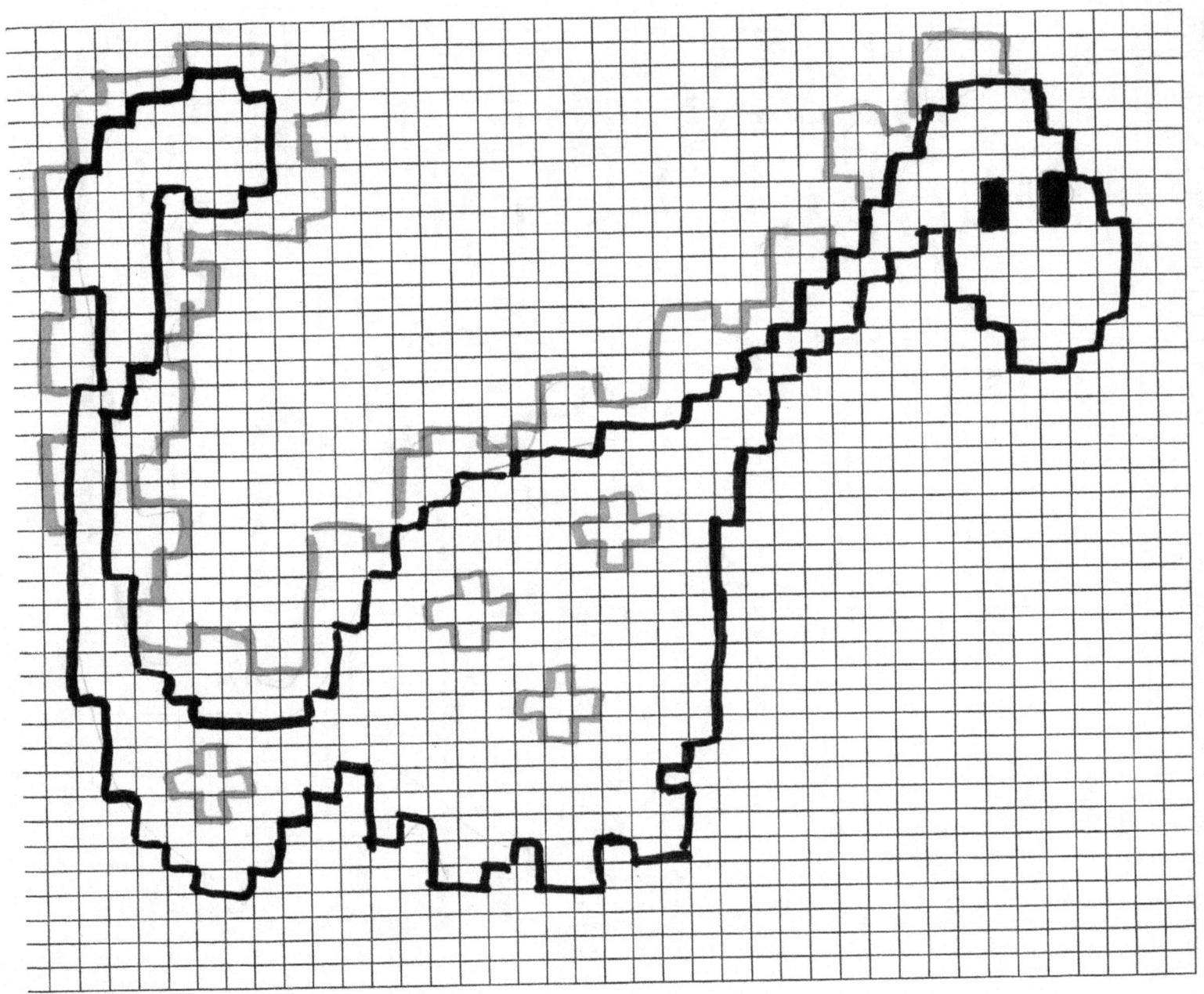

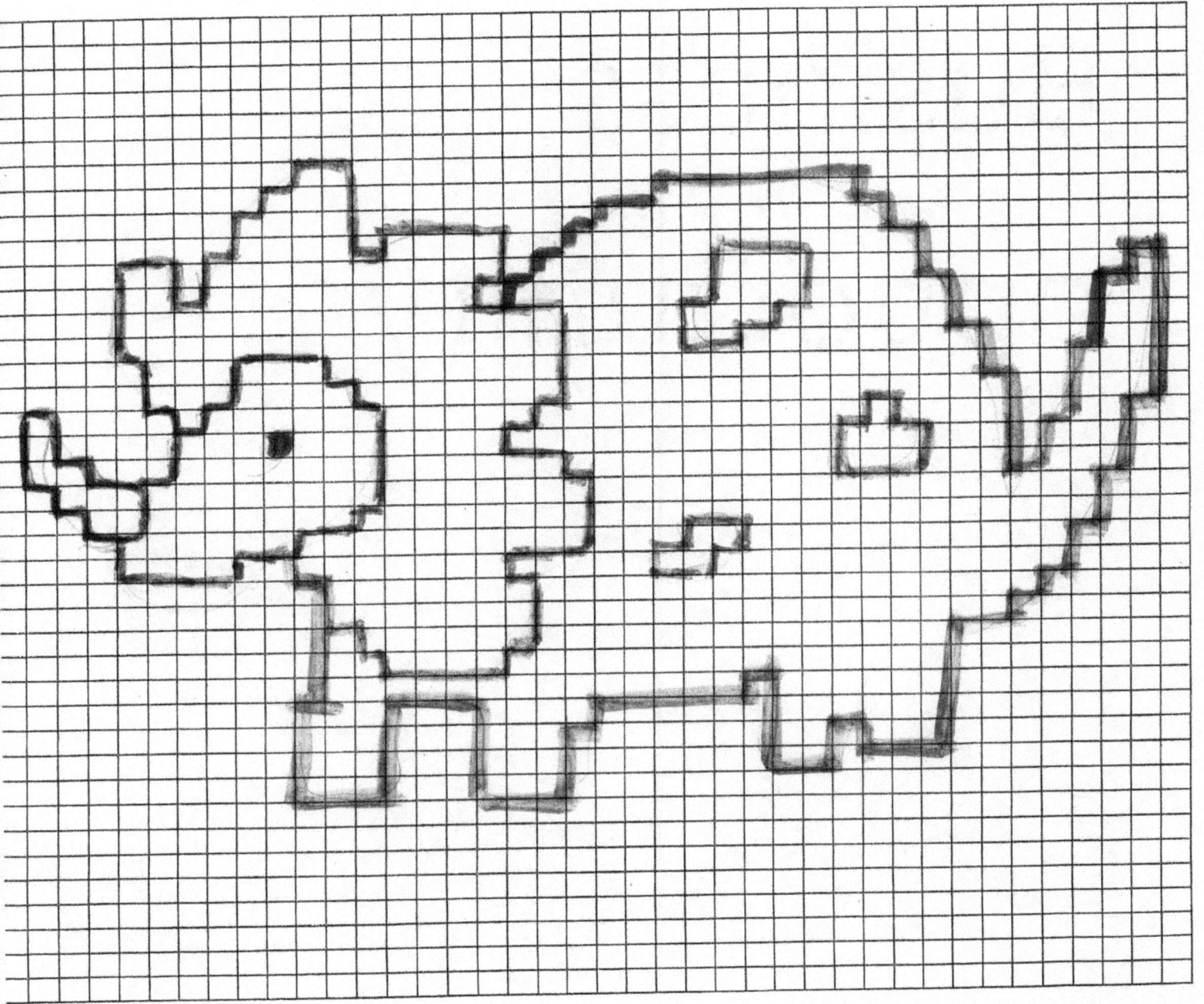

Business opportunity

If you like knitting, and would like to make money from it, you certainly can. There is a market for knitted blankets for :

- Newborns and children of any age
- Cats
- Dogs
- Special birthdays
- Special occasions

You can design your own patterns and sell them as exclusive one-of-a-kind. One-of-a-kind guarantees can be sold at a higher price. Of course, if you guarantee a one-of-a-kind, you must respect that and never do that pattern again. Do not offer this with these designs. If you cannot draw your own patterns, do not offer to clients until you are able to.

Tips on how to create and sell :

A knitted blanket with these squares normally has 2 layers (front and back) .

Have a price for regular one-color squares

Have a price for a square with a design

Have a higher price if someone asks for something specific

Have a price for one-of-a-kind designs, that you have drawn yourself, and are willing to never do again.

Explain to the clients that the designs look better with 3 colors maximum.

Give them an idea on how long it takes to knit.

When quoting a price make sure you are specific with taxes, delivery or mailing fees, or any other fees.

For a big project, keep the client informed. Never lie about delays.

Patterns do not always look good until knitted. Knit as many examples as you can to be able to show clients.

You should also knit the same pattern 2 times, with different colors, to show the diversity.

www.ingramcontent.com/pod-product-compliance
Lightning Source LLC
Chambersburg PA
CBHW080456240426
43673CB00005B/210